Supporting Inclusive Practice

The importance and understanding of inclusiveness in education has become an integral part of the education system. With emphasis on the well-being of families and children alike, the concept of an inclusive learning environment continues to focus on the interests of the child as a whole, not their condition, and this approach is at the forefront of supporting their emotional and educational well-being.

Now fully updated, this new edition of *Supporting Inclusive Practice* encourages the ongoing practice of inclusion with discussions, guidance and advice on how to build an inclusive environment.

This book encourages debate, reflection and discussion when relating to the teaching of:

- Children with English as an additional language.
- Gifted and talented children.
- Children with autism and physical and sensory disabilities.
- Children who have suffered loss, grief and bereavement.
- Children in Care or being 'looked after'.

Helping you to promote children's independence and emotional resilience, and with advice on working with families and professional agencies, this book is integral to all those at university training to work in the education sector, as well as teachers and teaching assistants who are truly looking to achieve inclusive practice in their classroom.

Gianna Knowles is a senior lecturer in Educational Studies at the University of Chichester, UK.

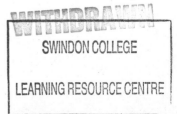

Supporting Inclusive Practice

Second Edition

Edited by Gianna Knowles

Routledge
Taylor & Francis Group

LONDON AND NEW YORK

First edition published in 2006 by David Fulton Publishers

This second edition published 2011
by Routledge
2 Park Square, Milton Park, Abingdon, Oxon, OX14 4RN

Simultaneously published in the USA and Canada
by Routledge
711 Third Avenue, New York, NY 10017 (8th Floor)

Routledge is an imprint of the Taylor & Francis Group, an informa business

Typeset in Bembo by
Keystroke, Tettenhall, Wolverhampton
Printed and bound in Great Britain by
TJ International Ltd, Padstow, Cornwall

British Library Cataloguing in Publication Data
A catalogue record for this book is available from the British Library

Library of Congress Cataloging-in-Publication Data
    Supporting inclusive practice / edited by Gianna Knowles. — 2nd ed.
       p. cm.
    1. Inclusive education. I. Knowles, Gianna.
    LC4015.S86 2011
    371.9'046—dc22   2010011185

ISBN10: 0–415–57900–7 (hbk)
ISBN10: 0–415–57899–X (pbk)
ISBN10: 0–203–84335–5 (ebk)

ISBN13: 978–0–415–57900–1 (hbk)
ISBN13: 978–0–415–57899–8 (pbk)
ISBN13: 978–0–203–84335–2 (ebk)

Contents

List of contributors

Karen Bassett is a higher-level teaching assistant (HLTA) with a Foundation Degree in Teaching and Learning Support from the University of Chichester. She has nine years' experience of working in education, initially managing a nursery school in West Sussex and now working with children who need additional support in order to thrive in their primary education. Karen's current role involves acting as special support assistant to children with speech, language and communication difficulties and as an HLTA she teaches maths in Key Stage 3 to Year 7 pupils. Because of her own disrupted childhood, Karen has a special interest in attachment styles and the impact these have upon academic progress and the personal, social and emotional well-being of looked-after children.

Gillian Goddard lectures part time at Edge Hill University in the North West of England, where she leads the Personal and Social Education specialism for the primary teacher training programme. She has also designed and co-ordinated a Foundation Degree in Supporting Teaching and Learning at Edge Hill University, which has a particular focus on pastoral care. As well as lecturing, Gillian provides one-to-one support for children and families experiencing difficulties with grief and loss. She has co-written *Supporting Every Child* (Learning Matters 2009) and is currently working on a book about teaching personal and social education.

Gianna Knowles is currently a senior lecturer in Educational Studies at the University of Chichester. She has 12 years' experience of being a classroom teacher in North London and the Midlands. She has also been an advisory teacher and an Ofsted inspector. Gianna's area of research is inclusion, diversity and social justice. She is the editor of the first edition of *Supporting Inclusive Practice* (Fulton 2006) and sole author of *Ensuring Every Child Matters* (Sage 2009).

Victoria Leslie is currently acting headteacher of a Chichester primary school. She has nine years' experience as a class teacher, including five years' experience working as a special educational needs co-ordinator (SENCO). Victoria is committed to creating an inclusive culture within her school, which has been praised by Ofsted for 'effectively nurturing and valuing each child'. In her roles within the school, Victoria has worked closely with a range of agencies and created the local base for an inclusivity project, which includes organising training for those working with children who have learning difficulties and/or disabilities. She is an associate lecturer at the University of Chichester and a regular reviewer for the National Association for the Teaching of English. She has collaborated in three cross-curricular learning packages published by West Sussex County Council. She has also spent time researching learning and teaching strategies in Mumbai, India, as part of a British Council programme.

Kathy MacLean is the head of the Ethnic Minority Achievement Service for the London Borough of Wandsworth. She had 15 years' experience of teaching in Lambeth and Wandsworth infant and primary schools before joining the Wandsworth Standards and Schools Division. Kathy gained her MA in English, Language and Literacy in Education from Surrey University in 2002. She is a trained EAL (English as an additional language) specialist and team leader, and gives advice and support to schools on EAL pedagogy and practice. Kathy provides professional development for the school workforce on the needs of children learning English as an additional language and about meeting the needs of newly arrived pupils from overseas.

Diana Seach is currently a senior lecturer in Early Years and Special Educational Needs at the University of Chichester. She also runs an international education and family consultancy in interactive play for children with autism. Diana's area of research is play and creativity with children who have special educational needs and developing culturally specific training programmes for the families of children with disabilities. She is co-author of *Supporting Children with Autism in Mainstream Schools* (Questions Publishing 2002) and author of *Interactive Play for Children with Autism* (Routledge 2007).

Barbara Thompson is currently a principal lecturer and subject leader for the MA Education Programme at the University of Chichester, having previously led Chichester's PGCE (postgraduate certificate in education) Primary Programme. Before moving into higher education she spent 17 years teaching in primary schools in the Midlands and the North of England. Barbara has a long-term interest in gender issues and before working at Chichester was an Open University tutor for the MA module on Gender and Education. Barbara has a PhD in Gender, Management and Leadership and publishes in the gender field.

Introduction

What this book is about

Gianna Knowles

In 1999 the then Department for Education and Skills (DfES), now the Department for Education (DfE), defined what it meant by inclusion by stating that it was about every child's entitlement to learning that would 'ensure that all pupils have the chance to succeed, whatever their individual needs and the potential barriers to learning might be' (DfES/QCA 1999: 3). Since 1999 and since the publication of the first edition of *Supporting Inclusive Practice* in 2006, all those who work in children's services – particularly schools, in this instance – have come a long way in their understanding of what meeting *individual needs* is about. Similarly, schools have a much greater understanding of what *barriers to learning* means for many children – not only those with specific learning challenges. That the inclusion agenda has been positively supported by schools, and that children are benefiting from having barriers to learning removed, was reported on by Ofsted in 2006. Their findings state:

> The most important factor in determining the best outcomes for pupils with learning difficulties and disabilities (LDD) is not the type but the quality of the provision. Effective provision was distributed equally in the mainstream and special schools visited, but there was more good and outstanding provision in resourced mainstream schools than elsewhere.
>
> (Ofsted 2006: 2)

However, as well as acknowledging the good work schools have put in to making inclusion work for children, they also noted that there was still further progress to be made in understanding fully that resources are only part of successful inclusion. Their findings showed that the greatest progress children make in their learning and the most successful examples of overcoming barriers to learning happen when those designing the learning activities fully understand the needs of the child, and when they provide learning activities that challenge and motivate that child. For example, those who work with children may be far better informed about autism than they were over a decade ago and have many resources in school to support children with autism. However, educators now have a better understanding that children who have autism are nevertheless children first and foremost; they are not characterized by the condition. That is to say, educators now understand that no two children who have been labelled as autistic will present in the same way. Resources that 'work' for one child may not be at all suitable for another child. What is needed is an understanding of how autism might present in any child, plus the skills, knowledge and understanding of how to meet the needs of the child on an individual basis.

In this way the first edition of *Supporting Inclusive Practice* reflects the knowledge and understanding of what was seen as good inclusive practice at the time of publishing. Much of what the first edition contains still holds true and those who work with children will still derive a lot of relevant knowledge, ideas and support from the book. However, this second edition of *Supporting Inclusive Practice* has provided the opportunity to review new knowledge and understanding about inclusion that has been developed and published since 2006 and to offer the reader the most up-to-date examples of good practice in the areas under discussion. Not only this, but the Every Child Matters (ECM) agenda, which was only just being introduced in 2005 when the first edition was being written, is now more embedded in schools and needs to be more thoroughly explored in terms of how it relates to the areas of inclusion being discussed. In particular, the introduction of the ECM agenda has added to educators' understanding that it is necessary to consider a child's overall well-being, rather than just seeing the child as a learning need that must be met.

In reviewing the content of the first edition of *Supporting Inclusive Practice*, with a view to preparing a second edition, another factor that became apparent is the considerable ways in which knowledge and understanding about inclusion as regards diversity and equality have moved on, particularly in relation to race, ethnicity and achievement. For this reason, this edition of *Supporting Inclusive Practice* no longer includes a chapter on race and ethnicity. The depth of treatment this area of practice now requires, the range of concepts and aspects of practice the reader needs to consider, is broader than can be covered in one chapter – particularly in a book that has as its main focus developing classroom practice to support inclusion. The chapter on working with children for whom English is an additional language remains. While it does highlight some key aspects of learning relating to race and ethnicity, it is congruent with the other aspects of inclusion discussed in the book in that it is focused on developing skills, knowledge and understanding that support good classroom practice for children for whom English is an additional language.

Further aspects of inclusion have become more apparent over the past few years. Among these is the need to understand, support and include children who have suffered loss, including bereavement, and children in care (CiC), or looked-after children. Recent DCSF reports have shown that children who have these needs are still failing to enjoy school and failing to achieve (DCSF 2009). In particular the DCSF's report *Improving the Educational Attainment of Children in Care (Looked After Children)* states: 'every child in care is capable of success in learning and in life. Yet too many are let down educationally by the system that is supposed to look after them' (DCSF 2009a: 2). Therefore, new to this edition are chapters to help the reader develop skills, knowledge and understanding in supporting and including children with these needs.

In terms of inclusive practice, the curriculum established its principles of inclusion in 1999. That is:

> The National Curriculum secures for all pupils, irrespective of social background, culture, race, gender, differences in ability and disabilities, an entitlement to a number of areas of learning and to develop knowledge, understanding, skills and attitudes necessary for their self-fulfilment and development as active and responsible citizens.
>
> (DfES/QCA 1999: 12)

The inclusion aspect of the primary curriculum is supported by the introduction of the Every Child Matters (ECM) agenda, which was an outcome of the Children Act 2004 (Knowles 2009). The inclusive aims of the revised National Curriculum introduced in 2000 and the subsequent ECM agenda are evident in the aims of the proposed primary curriculum, which has as its first aim that 'all young people become: successful learners who enjoy learning, make progress and achieve . . .' (DCSF 2009b: 3).

Prior to the National Curriculum being first introduced, as a result of the Education Act 1988, it was felt by many who worked in education and formulated educational policy that the system then in place was not enabling children to reach the standards of achievement expected of them by the end of their primary school years. At that time too many children were underachieving. In order to combat what was sometimes referred to as 'the long tail of underachievement' (Slee *et al.* 1998), the National Curriculum was brought in, so all children would by law have entitlement to the same knowledge and understanding as everyone else. The idea was that this would provide some level of guarantee that all children would have an equal chance of achieving the same learning outcomes; particularly since an integral part of the National Curriculum is to ensure that learning is personalized, and at the same time that all children are included in any learning taking place. A National Curriculum ensures the possibility of an equal opportunity, in terms of learning achievement, for all.

When the National Curriculum was first introduced there were concerns that it would be very prescriptive in terms of what schools could teach. In effect, while the National Curriculum provides for a minimum of skills, knowledge and understanding that must be taught to children, it still leaves schools with plenty of autonomy in terms of choosing the methods by which those skills, knowledge and understanding must be taught. As long as schools can demonstrate that they are covering the content of the National Curriculum and are enabling children to reach the appropriate standards, schools can teach over and above the stipulated content of the curriculum and deliver it through the teaching methods they prefer.

Following the Education Act 1988, the first National Curriculum documents began to arrive in schools in the late 1980s and early 1990s. Testing children's achievement in relation to age-related expected levels of National Curriculum attainment began soon after. By 1997 the government felt it had enough evidence to claim that while many children were reaching the levels of attainment that might be expected from children of 7, 11 and 14, there were still too many children who were failing to meet their expected targets. It was from these findings that the inclusion agenda began to develop. It became better understood that to enable all children to enjoy and achieve at school it is necessary to provide accessible learning. A 'one size fits all' approach, where learning was delivered to all children in the same way irrespective of whether they had the skills, knowledge, understanding and capacity to access it, was placing barriers in the way of many children's enjoyment of and achievement in learning. As the research of MacBeath and Mortimore shows:

> children experience schools differently . . . achievement is not a simple linear progression but subject to ebbs and flows over time and in response to the influence of the peer group and pupils' own expectations on the basis of gender, race and social class.
>
> (MacBeath and Mortimore 2001: 2)

The first edition of *Supporting Inclusive Practice* began with the quote: 'We have discovered how to engineer the blueprint of living beings but we are still searching for an environment in which children can learn with enjoyment and effect' (MacBeath and Mortimore 2001: 1). While there is evidence of some progress towards finding that 'environment in which children can learn with enjoyment and effect', the research also shows that we are not there yet. As we have seen from the brief summary of the history and revisions of the National Curriculum that schools have been working with over the past 20 years, every now and again it is helpful to review the progress that has been made, make any necessary adjustments in light of those findings and move to the next stage in the journey towards enabling all children to *learn with enjoyment and effect*. In the same way, for this second edition of *Supporting Inclusive Practice* we have reviewed the first in light of what has been learnt about inclusion since 2006. We have made adjustments based on that new knowledge and understanding so the material we present in this edition, we believe, will reflect the best practice available to those who work with children, or who intend to work with children, helping readers to develop their skills, knowledge and understanding of how to provide the best inclusive practice.

Chapter 1 of this book asks the question, *what do we mean when we talk about inclusion and that Every Child Matters?* In exploring the answer to this question the author revisits the principles that underpin the concept of inclusion and the Every Child Matters (ECM) agenda, and looks at what inclusive practice might be with particular reference to the detail of the ECM agenda. The chapter also sets the context for the following chapters and aspects of inclusion discussed in them. It reminds the reader why it is important to have inclusive schools and an inclusive society where all can achieve well-being.

Chapter 2 explores how to support and include *children for whom English is an additional language* (EAL). It provides practical advice, enabling readers to develop an inclusive and collaborative approach that supports the learning of these children. It explores the importance of understanding the diversity of children's linguistic needs and experiences, and how these can be reflected in planning so as to ensure an appropriate level of challenge in learning. The chapter also helps the reader to select and prepare suitable teaching resources and learning activities for the provision of contextual and linguistic support across the curriculum.

Chapter 3 explores with the reader *gender issues in the primary classroom*. It provides an overview of some of the key issues related to gender and education and places current theories and concerns about gender inequalities within a historical framework by asking the question 'How did we get where we are today?' It examines key theories and debates that may underpin how we think boys and girls, men and women, 'do gender', and considers current gender concerns – particularly the concern that boys underachieve – and critically analyses some of the strategies that are being used in classrooms to address these concerns. The chapter considers the possibility that, amidst the current furore about boys' underachievement, girls are once more in danger of becoming 'invisible' in classrooms.

Chapter 4 discusses how to support and include *children who are gifted and talented*. It explores what is meant by the term, and provides a guide for what behaviours gifted and talented children might display. It discusses the current government definition of gifted and talented, and examines potential barriers to learning for these children. Finally the chapter asks the reader to reflect on how gifted and talented children who are not recognized as such may fail to reach their potential, or become bored and disaffected with learning.

Chapter 5 focuses on *children with autism and Asperger's syndrome*. It provides an overview of the latest research and understanding about the autism spectrum and describes in positive terms how each child with a diagnosis of autism or Asperger's syndrome will have individual personal, social and learning needs. It challenges some of the assumptions made about these children's communication, social understanding and behaviour, and explores the need to understand children in relation to their developmental profile rather than in terms of deficits in development. The chapter emphasizes the need to identify the pupil's skills, strengths and abilities and how these can be used to motivate the child's learning and interactions with others. It also highlights some of the key interventions and strategies for supporting children with autism and Asperger's syndrome in the classroom, and encourages the reader to consider the appropriateness of the intervention for the individual and to focus on strategies that promote inclusion.

Chapter 6 discusses how to support and include *children with physical and sensory disabilities*. It explores the legislation that is in place to support these children and discusses what constitutes good provision for children with a physical or sensory learning difficulty – noting in particular that children who have a disability are first and foremost children, and should not be defined by their disability. It discusses what is regarded as good practice in schools in terms of supporting disabled children, exploring the importance of listening to children and their families in developing provision, since they are experienced and expert in terms of knowing how to manage the condition. The chapter also discusses the importance of multi-agency working to support and include disabled children in schools, and explores how key partnerships between children, young people, the voluntary sector and statutory agencies, including the Department for Children, Families and Schools' Early Support Programme, can facilitate effective partnerships in supporting children.

The aspect of inclusion forming the focus of Chapter 7 is that of *children who have suffered loss and grief, including bereavement.* As our understanding of inclusion has developed, so too has our recognition of the breadth of the range of need that can impact on a child's enjoyment and achievement of learning. This chapter concerns an aspect of need that may affect any child at some point during their school life. In discussing this, the chapter seeks to develop understanding of grief and loss reactions in children and reflects on the impact of loss and bereavement on children and families and how these can become barriers to inclusion. The chapter helps readers to develop ways that children and families experiencing loss and bereavement can be supported in an education setting. It enables readers to be aware of their own professional boundaries in respect to loss and bereavement in children, and helps them to be confident in seeking help and support from other professionals when needed.

In the same way, Chapter 8 addresses an aspect of inclusion that those who work with children have become increasingly aware of: how to support and include *looked-after children*. The chapter begins by exploring what is meant by this term and discusses the relevant legislation. It discusses the particular needs of looked-after children, the potential barriers to enjoyment and achievement at school for these children, and the role of education in supporting them. The chapter explores the impact of trauma and loss on looked-after children and how understanding attachment theory can help in supporting them.

Chapter 9, 'Planning your teaching to ensure Every Child Matters', demonstrates that, while the book has explored a range of different needs that children bring to the classroom, well-designed activities that are accessible in a range of ways can be developed to meet many different learning needs and learning styles. The chapter explores what unites children in terms of learning (that is, learning styles), what motivates them to learn, what interests them about learning and how the enjoyment they get from learning can be used to motivate them further. It discusses how children can be given a voice and be involved in planning their own learning, particularly through the practice of personalized learning and Assessment for Learning.

Bibliography

Department for Children, Schools and Families (2009a) *Improving the Educational Attainment of Children in Care (Looked-After Children).* London: DCSF.

—— (2009b) *Public Consultation on Curriculum Reform: Consultation Overview.* London: DCSF.

DfES/QCA (1999) *The National Curriculum: Handbook for Primary Teachers in England KS1 and KS2.* London: DCSF.

Knowles, G. (2009) *Ensuring Every Child Matters.* London: Sage.

MacBeath, J. and Mortimore, P. (2001) *Improving School Effectiveness.* Buckingham: Open University Press.

Office for Standards in Education (2006) *Inclusion: Does It Matter Where Pupils Are Taught?* London: HMSO.

Slee, R., Weiner, G. and Tomlinson, S. (1998) *School Effectiveness for Whom?* London: Falmer Press.

Chapter I

What do we mean when we talk about inclusion and that Every Child Matters?

Gianna Knowles

Inclusivity: how far all pupils benefit, according to need, from what the school provides.

(Ofsted 2003: 77)

Introduction

This chapter aims to explore the principles that underpin the concept of inclusion and the Every Child Matters (ECM) agenda, and to discuss what inclusive practice might look like in schools. Its purpose is to provide readers with knowledge and understanding which will help them to approach, in an informed way, the issues raised throughout the rest of the book. The chapter explores why it is important to have inclusive schools that enable children to work towards realizing the outcomes of the ECM agenda, and it discusses why educators need to be aware of the range of needs children bring to their learning, so as to provide appropriate learning activities and to ensure that their needs do not become barriers to their learning.

Inclusion and the National Curriculum

The revised National Curriculum, published in 1999, came into effect in schools in 2000 (DfES/QCA 1999). The principles that underpin the National Curriculum 2000 clearly define what is meant by inclusion; namely that all children, whatever their needs, have an entitlement to 'effective learning opportunities' (ibid.: 30). The National Curriculum 2000 sets out three principles that are essential for schools to consider if they are to develop an inclusive approach to education. They state that schools should be:

1 setting suitable learning challenges;
2 responding to pupils' diverse learning needs; and
3 overcoming potential barriers to learning and assessment for individuals and groups of pupils.

(ibid.)

Setting suitable learning challenges

> Teachers should aim to give every pupil the opportunity to experience success in learning and to achieve as high a standard as possible.
>
> (ibid.)

The National Curriculum, in all its forms, is a statutory entitlement for all children; that is to say, all children are legally entitled to be taught the skills, knowledge and understanding that the National Curriculum embodies. This is significant for two reasons. Firstly, it means that all schools have a duty to teach all children the skills, knowledge and understanding outlined in the National Curriculum – therefore, all children can expect to have an education that develops the same skills, knowledge and understanding as any other child is learning. Secondly, not only can a child expect a certain minimum entitlement as to what constitutes their education, but also those working with children in mainstream schools have a legal duty to ensure that all children are taught the knowledge, skills and understanding covered by the National Curriculum in ways that suit the children's abilities.

Activity

Below is a set of indicators that **inclusive learning activities** should demonstrate. Reading through the list below, reflect on how many of these indicators are present in the learning activities you are part of. Learning activities must be responsive to the diversity of the children's learning needs in all classrooms.

- All children are able to access the learning activities.
- Children are actively involved in their own learning; they are engaged with the learning activity, they understand what is required of them and know what the success criteria for the activity are.
- Where the activity is a collaborative activity, all children have the opportunity to be part of that collaborative learning.
- The learning outcomes for the activity have been based on the assessment of the children's prior learning to ensure that the activity has the appropriate learning expectations for the children, and constitutes the next step in their learning progress.
- Classroom discipline emphasizes positive, wanted behaviours and is based on mutual respect, so that children and adults in the classroom understand that everyone is different and will, therefore, require different approaches to their learning.
- All children access all learning activities, wherever they take place, including outside learning environments and PE lessons.

Responding to pupils' diverse learning needs

Most children at some point in their education will have a particular need that, if not met, will constitute a barrier to their enjoyment and learning in school. For example, learning may be inhibited because of a child's gender; a particular special need such as dyslexia or autism might impact on a child's learning, as can a sensory or physical disability such as visual impairment or cerebral palsy. The school may unwittingly set up barriers to a child's learning because of a lack of appropriate insight into that child's social or cultural background. Children from white working-class families and various ethnic groups, including Gypsy Travellers, refugees and asylum seekers and those from diverse linguistic backgrounds, are those most likely to 'slip through' the learning net. Therefore, when planning learning activities it is important to be aware of these different groups of children, because one's own background and experience are apt to influence how we approach planning and delivering learning experiences. Just as we need to keep updating our subject knowledge to ensure that we have a good understanding from which to plan and teach, we also need to keep checking that we have done the necessary research in order to teach children in a group of which we have little experience – or a group which we had not previously considered to have particular needs which may impact on learning.

This chapter outlines the main principles of inclusion; the remainder of the book will seek to look at these different groups in more detail and explore how schools can ensure that they are meeting the needs of this diverse range of children when planning for learning.

Overcoming potential barriers to learning

Activity: building an inclusive environment

Below is a set of indicators that any truly inclusive school will demonstrate. How many of the indicators apply to your school?

- Children help each other.
- All adults support each other and work together.
- All adults and children treat each other with respect.
- Parents are welcome and there is evidence of a strong, mutually supportive partnership between the school and parents.
- The school has close links with the community, is involved in the work and activities of the local community, and the community has strong links with the school.

Schools that are able to demonstrate they are meeting the above criteria are well on their way to establishing an inclusive environment for children. The next phase in development is to continue to develop this inclusive practice, but within the school as part of the broader setting of a children's service, as required by the new legislation. For ECM to realize the ambition of improving the lives of all children, and to ensure that all five outcomes listed are met for each child, the following measures have been agreed (DfES 2001):

- More specialized help to promote opportunity, prevent problems and act early and effectively, if and when problems arise.
- The reconfiguration of services around the child and family in one place – for example, where extended schools are bringing together professionals in multi-disciplinary teams.
- The development of a shared sense of responsibility across agencies for safeguarding children and protecting them from harm.
- Listening to children, young people and their families when assessing and planning service provision, as well as in face-to-face delivery.
- Developing strategies to improve children's self-esteem.
- Development for both teaching and support staff in how to ensure that learning activities are accessible to all children.
- Considering how support staff are managed and deployed to better ensure inclusion.
- Improving the school environment for all children and adults with a disability.
- Improving the induction process for children new to the school.
- Reviewing the way in which children have a 'say' in school issues and evidence that the children's ideas and concerns are implemented or resolved.
- Improving the partnership with parents.

In 2001 the Special Educational Needs and Disability Act provided a new legal frame-work for the inclusion of children with SEN in mainstream schools. It significantly:

> strengthens the right of children with SEN to attend a mainstream school, unless their parents choose otherwise or if this is incompatible with 'efficient education for other children' and there are no 'reasonable steps' which the school and LEA can take to prevent that incompatibility.
>
> (Ofsted 2004: 3)

In the same year, the Disability Discrimination Act placed new duties on schools not to treat disabled pupils less favourably than others and to make 'reasonable adjustments' to ensure that they are not disadvantaged (ibid.).

From these most recent pieces of legislation we can see the government firmly signalling the principles of what is to be seen as an inclusive education. The new legislation requires that mainstream schools include all pupils fully, making appropriate changes to organization, curriculum, accommodation and teaching methods. It places duties on schools and LAs to ensure that this happens.

The Every Child Matters agenda

In 2004 the work on inclusion that had been undertaken in schools was further strengthened and developed by the introduction of the Every Child Matters agenda (DfES 2004a). ECM was in part a response to the tragic death of Victoria Climbié in 2000; the subsequent inquiry into the failure of the services involved in her care has led to the development of the ECM agenda.

Case study

Victoria Climbié died on 25 February 2000. She had 128 separate injuries on her body, including cigarette burns, scars where she had been hit by a bike chain and hammer blows to her toes. The eight-year-old died from abuse and neglect while living with her aunt, Marie-Thérèse Kouao, and her aunt's boyfriend Carl Manning. Both were jailed for life for her murder in January 2001.

A public inquiry into her death in 2001 called for radical reforms of child protection services in England. The inquiry found that Victoria was seen by dozens of social workers, nurses, doctors and police officers before she died, but all failed to spot and stop the abuse. Lord Laming, who described Victoria's death as the worst case of neglect he had ever heard of, headed the inquiry. He stated: 'I remain amazed that nobody in any of the key agencies had the presence of mind to follow what are relatively straightforward procedures'.

In response to the findings of the inquiry, the then Health Secretary, Alan Milburn, said that the relevant agencies had had more than a dozen opportunities within 10 months to act to save Victoria but had failed to do so. In a special statement to the House of Commons he stated: 'This was not a failing on the part of one service, it was a failing on the part of every service' (http://news.bbc.co.uk/1/hi/uk/2698295.stm).

The inquiry found that one of the factors that contributed to the death of Victoria was the failure of the range of agencies involved in her care to work with one another. At the time, separate agencies had responsibility for particular aspects of children's and young people's welfare. That is, traditionally schools were concerned with a child's education, and social services with the child's home background. While the two agencies did have some contact with one another there was no requirement or understanding of the need to work together to support children and families. As a result of the inquiry into Victoria's death, the Children Act 2004 and subsequent ECM agenda, all local authorities have restructured to ensure that those services that are responsible for the education and welfare of children are brought together under one umbrella. Further to this, all services that provide for the needs of children are united in their requirement to enable children to meet the five outcomes of the ECM agenda. These outcomes are that all children should: be healthy; be safe; enjoy and achieve; make a positive contribution; and enjoy economic well-being (DCSF 2008).

The five ECM outcomes are broad because they recognize that for children to achieve well-being they need a range of factors in their life to be working well. For example, schools are primarily concerned with children in terms of education and learning; however, the ECM agenda recognizes that in order to enjoy and achieve children need to be healthy and safe as well. Similarly they need to be living in a home that has achieved economic well-being – that is, not living in poverty – and they need to feel part of the community both at school and in a wider sense, to enable them to learn how to make a positive contribution to the community (Knowles 2009).

The Every Child Matters outcomes

Be healthy

Since the inception of the ECM agenda most schools have already put in place many measures to support this outcome, including being part of the government's National Healthy Schools Programme (www.healthyschools.gov.uk 2009).

National Healthy Schools status

For a school to achieve National Healthy Schools status (www.healthyschools.gov.uk 2009), the school has to demonstrate that it meets certain criteria in the four themes outlined below.

1   Personal, social and health education: including sex and relationship education (SRE) and drug education (including alcohol, tobacco and volatile substance abuse). To achieve in this theme the school needs to be able to demonstrate how its teaching of the personal, social and health education (PSHE) aspect of the curriculum contributes towards children achieving all five of the ECM outcomes. It also needs to show how it uses this aspect of the curriculum to enable children to develop the 'knowledge, understanding, skills and attitudes to make informed decisions about their lives' (ibid.), particularly in relation to sex and relationship education (SRE) and drug education – including alcohol, tobacco and volatile substance abuse, as appropriate to the age of the children being taught.

2   Healthy eating: to achieve in this theme the school needs to show that it enables children to understand the importance of eating a healthy diet; not just at school, but as a long-term lifestyle choice. Not only does the school have a role in educating children about healthy eating, but it also needs to actively support healthy eating by ensuring that 'healthy and nutritious food and drink is available across the school day' (ibid.).

3   Physical activity: schools meet the criteria of this theme by enabling children to understand that physical activity is important in everyday life and a large component of being healthy. The school must actively encourage children to engage in physical exercise and provide children with opportunities to be involved in physical and outdoor activities.

4   Emotional health and well-being, including bullying: as indicated by this final theme, in order to achieve NHSS (National Healthy Schools status) schools have to demonstrate that they understand that being healthy is about mental health as well as physical health. Both these aspects of health are important to the ECM agenda. The 'be healthy' outcome recognizes that for children to achieve well-

being and to enjoy and achieve at school, they need to be physically healthy, but also enjoy 'positive emotional health' (ibid.). A nationally healthy school is one that enables children to 'understand and express their feelings, build their confidence and emotional resilience, and therefore their capacity to learn' (ibid.).

Case study

Farhad is 10. He says:

> I like to be healthy. I know my mum always makes a healthy packed lunch for me and I like it when we have fruit at school. When I was in year 2 I don't think we had fruit then and we could eat crisps at break. When the school said we couldn't have crisps and they would give us fruit we thought 'oh no!', but actually it worked out OK. I like bananas best – but you have to be careful not to get the squished ones with black bits on the skin. Now I am in year 5 I know about carbohydrates and sugar and stuff and like, it doesn't mean I have stopped eating crisps and sweets and stuff completely, but I do think about it more.
>
> We do PE and things at school, I think I do more PE now than I did in year 3 or 4 but there are more things to do. Like, I do PE in school time and a football club after school. There is a street dance club which I would *really* like to do, but it's the same day as the football. I have a PC at home and a games console and now I do think, 'Well, I've been playing this for a while now, perhaps I should go out' and I text my friends and we play football or something.
>
> I would walk to school but my mum works and it works out better if she drops us off – me and my sister, who is in Mrs Sing's class. Also she says it means she knows we have got to school safe. When I go to my new school in year 7 I will walk then.

Stay safe

The aims for this outcome of the ECM agenda fall into two areas. The first aspect requires that schools should work with children and families to ensure that children are safe from: 'maltreatment, neglect, violence and sexual exploitation . . . accidental injury and death . . . have security, stability and are cared for' (DCSF 2008). These aims relate to the roles schools have in safeguarding children and if educators feel that there are any safeguarding issues that they need to pursue in relation to a particular child then there is very clear guidance about how to proceed.

Activity: safeguarding children and child protection

This is a very important area of keeping children safe, but the wealth of information can seem quite daunting. The Every Child Matters website has a section that deals specifically with these elements of children *being safe*:

www.dcsf.gov.uk/everychildmatters/safeguardingandsocialcare.

You may find it helpful to find and familiarize yourself with the content of the following documents in particular:

HM Government, 'Working together to safeguard children'. London 2006 (to be updated 2010).
HM Government, 'What to do if you are worried a child is being abused'. London 2006.

These are helpful documents to know about, as they provide information about what constitutes abuse and set out the procedures for reporting suspected abuse. They also explain what is likely to happen following a report, and who is responsible for acting on a disclosure or reported suspicion of abuse. They also explain how the different agencies that work with children – for example, schools, social services, the police and health workers – must work in a multi-agency way over safeguarding.

All schools will have a child protection policy and a named member of staff to whom any disclosed or suspected abuse must be reported. Ensure you have read the policy of all schools you may be involved with and ensure you know which member of staff deals with child protection.

What do I do if a child tells me that he or she is being abused?

If you have looked at the document 'What to do if you are worried a child is being abused', you will know that if a child tells you that he or she is being abused, it is known as a 'disclosure'. If a child discloses this information to you, you have a *legal* duty to pass that information on; you must tell the child this, you cannot tell the child you will 'keep it secret' or not tell anyone. Indeed, if you do not pass the information to the member of staff responsible for child protection then you are colluding with the abuser; supporting the abuser in continuing to abuse the child.

The NSPCC also advises that you (Knowles 2006: 86):

• Keep calm – if the child detects you are scared, upset or surprised he or she may not feel able to continue to talk to you, and may start to deny what he or she has already said.

- Listen very carefully to what the child tells you, but do not make any comments except to show that you are concerned and listening.
- Allow the child to tell you as much as he or she wishes; and do not force the child to disclose more.
- Reassure the child that he or she has done the right thing in telling you, explain that you believe what you have heard and that the abuse is not the child's fault.

It is also recommended that you keep notes abut what the child has told you, including date of disclosure, etc.

You may find these difficult issues to read about and talk about. This may be because you, too, suffered abuse as a child. However angry, upset or scared these issues make you feel, when you are working in a school your first duty is to the children you are working with. If you have unresolved worries and anxiety about these issues it may be useful for you to seek some support for yourself. While this prospect may make you feel upset and scared, it is part of your legal and professional responsibility, to ensure that you are best able to support the children you work with to *stay safe.*

The second aspect of 'be safe' aims that schools need to try to make sure that children are free from 'bullying and discrimination' (DCSF 2008). All schools have an anti-bullying policy and are used to working with children to explore what bullying is and how to prevent it. Indeed, the personal, social and health education programme of study provides considerable scope for exploring these issues with children.

However, when it comes to ensuring that children are not subject to discrimination and that they do not discriminate against others, there is mixed practice. Sometimes those who work with children will unwittingly hold attitudes, values and beliefs which lead them to discriminate against children – this is dealt with in more detail in the discussion of the next ECM outcome. Where discrimination is not addressed in schools it is often because educators themselves do not necessarily understand what it means, or believe it does not happen in their school and therefore does not need to be addressed. In terms of discrimination about race and ethnicity, this attitude is often found in schools that are 'mainly or all white schools' (DfES 2003a).

Modern Britain is often referred to as a multicultural or multi-ethnic society (Osler 2003: 9). Osler explores what this means, outlining how policies encouraged post-war immigration of Afro-Caribbean individuals and families to fuel the depleted workforce and to enable the rebuilding of Britain, and how this has led to the 'growth of visible minority communities' (ibid.: 10). The growing diversity of cultures and communities in Britain has brought with it the problems of racism and discrimination. The racist and discriminatory behaviour that occurs in schools can be complex and falls into a range of categories. The most observable form is overt racist behaviour, for example name-calling, intimidating behaviour by an individual or group towards other individuals or groups, deliberate exclusion from social activities and, more recently, the use of mobile phone text messaging to distribute racist texts and pictures.

However, racism is not always observable. The Macpherson Report, published in 1999, on the inquiry into the racist murder of the teenager Stephen Lawrence, identified a further type of racist behaviour – that of institutional racism. A central part of the report was concerned with a discussion about what constitutes racism:

> Racism in general terms consists of conduct or words or practices which disadvantage people because of their colour, culture or ethnic origin. In its more subtle form it is as damaging as in its overt form.
>
> (Macpherson 1999: para 6.4)

In exploring the 'subtle' forms that racism can take, the notion of institutional racism developed:

> the collective failure of an organisation to provide an appropriate and professional service to people because of their colour, culture or ethnic origin. It can be seen or detected in processes, attitudes and behaviour which amount to discrimination through unwitting prejudice, ignorance, thoughtlessness and racist stereotyping which disadvantage minority ethnic people.
>
> It persists because of the failure of the organisation openly and adequately to recognize and address its existence and causes by policy, example and leadership. Without recognition and action to eliminate such racism it can prevail as part of the ethos or culture of the organisation. It is a corrosive disease.
>
> (ibid.: para. 6.34)

All schools have an anti-racist policy, outlining procedures for dealing with racist behaviour when it is found to be occurring. These policies are a legal requirement as a result of the 2000 Race Relations (Amendment) Act. This Act was passed after the Macpherson Report and requires schools to work within the statutory Code of Practice produced by the Commission for Racial Equality (CRE). In the light of this legislation, and through the development of the concept of institutional racism, school policies now need to be proactive, not reactive, in tackling the issue of racism and equality of opportunity for all children, whatever their cultural background. That is, schools must seek to prevent racism occurring, not simply react when it does occur. In the light of the 2000 Race Relations (Amendment) Act, school policies must aim to:

- eliminate racial discrimination;
- promote equality of opportunity; and
- promote good race relations.

Schools are not being inclusive simply by dealing with racist incidents as they occur; they must actively put in place strategies and actions that ensure equality of opportunity and promote good race relations. To ensure that equal opportunities policies take effect, schools must:

- monitor pupils' achievement and behaviour, including attendance and exclusion, by ethnic group, and set targets for improving these areas of schooling, in part through deploying grant-aided support more effectively;

- keep curricular and pastoral strategies under review to ensure they benefit all ethnic groups;
- give clear priority to ensuring that pupils from ethnic groups make good progress; and counter harassment and stereotyping.

(DfES 2003a: 9)

Mainly white schools

This shift in emphasis, in terms of legislation, policies and actions with regard to ensuring the inclusion of minority ethnic cultures, is perhaps most challenging for those schools that have an entirely white, or mainly white, pupil intake. While all schools have policies to outline how to deal with racist behaviour when it is found to occur, mainly white schools have often felt this policy to be redundant, claiming that since they have no children from minority ethnic cultures, no racism occurs. However, this is the very institutional racism that the Macpherson Report highlights. There is a duty upon the school to promote race relations and to counter stereotyping. To believe that inclusion of children from minority ethnic cultures is irrelevant because there are few, or no, such children attending the school is 'unwitting racism' (Macpherson 1999: para. 6.17), in as much as it shows 'lack of understanding, ignorance and mistaken beliefs' (ibid.) about the cultural diversity of the Britain we now live in. If children in mainly white schools are not provided with the opportunity to explore and engage with the diverse cultural heritage of Britain they will continue to view children from cultures different to their own as 'other' and 'alien'. As the government document *Aiming High: Understanding the Educational Needs of Minority Ethnic Pupils in Mainly White Schools* states (DfES 2003a: 3):

- many teachers in mainly white schools minimize the significance and value of cultural diversity;
- many minority ethnic pupils, in consequence, are discouraged from appreciating and expressing important aspects of their identity and heritage;
- mainly white schools are frequently not sufficiently aware of racism in the school population and in the local neighbourhood;
- in general, mainly white schools do not adequately prepare their pupils for adult life in a society that is culturally and ethnically diverse.

That is to say, just because there may seem to be no incidents of racist behaviour in mainly white schools, it does not mean that racism does not exist, or that racist beliefs are not held. Indeed the challenge for such schools is to find ways of exploring the beliefs of their pupils and to find ways of helping them to prepare for 'adult life in a society that is culturally and ethnically diverse' (DfES 2004a: 3).

So far this section of the chapter has dealt with inclusion as it relates to the diversity of cultures within Britain in terms of white, non-white or black cultural groups. However, minority ethnic cultures also include white minority ethnic groups. Recent constitutional reform in the UK, including the establishment of a Scottish Parliament and Welsh Assembly, and the development of a new settlement between Britain and Northern Ireland, has led to increased interest in and debate on what it means to be British and how citizenship is related to national and regional identities. So, for example, what does it mean to be British and Scottish? Meanings of nationality and identity are being re-examined and re-defined (Osler 2003: 11). As Osler states: 'the diversity and range of identities within the white population is something that tends to be overlooked when we are thinking about minority ethnic cultures' (ibid.).

We need to acknowledge that racism and discrimination in British society are not confined to 'visible' and established minorities, but that other individuals and communities, including refugees and asylum seekers, Jewish and Irish people, and Gypsies and Travellers, may currently experience racism, prejudice, disadvantage, harassment and violence (ibid.: 13). Indeed, the government has identified children from Gypsy Traveller families as those being most at risk of being failed by the education system (DfES 2003b: 7). Schools with Gypsy Traveller children are most often located in rural areas that mainly serve village communities (ibid.: 6): it is often these very schools that claim to be all, or mainly, white schools with no minority ethnic diversity.

Enjoy and achieve

The aims for meeting this outcome are that: 'children should be ready for school, attend and enjoy school, achieve stretching national educational standards at primary school and achieve personal and social development and enjoy recreation' (DCSF 2008). These aims are not new to schools; indeed it could be said that achieving these aims has always been the business of schools. However, as discussed at the beginning of this chapter, one of the reasons for the instigation of the inclusion agenda is that an unacceptably low number of children were reaching their potential in school or enjoying their schooling. We have already explored that one of the reasons children fail to achieve or 'enjoy and achieve' at school is because of barriers to learning which may be occasioned by their specific needs. However, barriers are not always there as a result of the child's needs; sometimes barriers are formed by the values, attitudes and beliefs held by those working with the children. Sometimes, these values, attitudes and beliefs, developed over years and often shared with those around us, can cause us to discriminate unwittingly against children by failing to provide learning activities that enable them to achieve. For example, it used to be very common for children for whom English is a second language to be put in groups with children who had an SEN arising from a learning difficulty. It was some time before educators could be persuaded that not knowing English is not a learning difficulty. Children for whom English is an additional language require learning activities that reflect their potential achievement level; not work that is below their level of attainment simply because they are not yet fluent in speaking, reading and writing English. This is discussed further in Chapter 3.

Case study

One of the ethnicities most discriminated against in the UK is Gypsy Traveller peoples.

In 2005, the *Sun* newspaper ran a front page headline that called for 'War on Gypsy Free for All'; the accompanying story launched a campaign to 'stamp on illegal camps'. The *Sun* vehemently defended this campaign, claiming that it was not racist, but spoke for millions of householders who had had, or faced having, their communities 'ruined' by illegal camps.

In 2009 the same newspaper ran a story under the headline 'Gypsies Ruined our Kids' School' (Francis and Jackson 2009). This story claimed that because of the significant rise in the number of Traveller children now attending a particular school in Essex, the quality of the schooling on offer to non-Traveller children had declined. The journalists described the Traveller site these children came from: 'Dogs roamed free and kids were unsupervised. One who looked about ten was driving a Volvo. The residents there refused to talk to us' (ibid.).

What is your initial response to these comments? How do they accord with what you know and think about Gypsy Traveller people?

The media is very powerful in projecting and supporting particular values, attitudes and beliefs. However, journalists are not always interested in telling all sides of a story. While the *Sun* claimed that it had 'wide support from its readers' (Barkham 2005), newspapers more interested in telling both sides of the story talked to Gypsy Travellers about the *Sun*'s campaign and reported:

> A [Gypsy Traveller] woman living on a site in Kent was so worried by the *Sun*'s attitude that she contacted the police yesterday and asked for their protection. Other Gypsies said their children were frightened when they read headlines apparently declaring 'war' on them.
>
> (ibid.)

On reflection – that is, thinking about the other side of the story – it is hard to believe that anyone would actively support a campaign that frightened children like this. Such persecution of Gypsy Traveller people is not new and, as when any discrimination goes unchecked, it can – and has in the past – reach terrifying proportions:

> The European Gypsy community was part of Nazi Germany's race extermination holocaust in the late 1930s and up to 1945. During this time Gypsies were used for medical experimentation at Dachau, Buchenwald and Sachsenhausen . . . experiments with 'Zyklon B gas crystals . . . were tested – fatally – on 250 Gypsy children.'
>
> (Channel 4 2008)

It is estimated that 23,000 German Gypsies were sent to Auschwitz (Knowles 2009: 138).

Nomadic peoples are an ancient ethnic group, often pre-dating settled cultures. All nomadic peoples have a rich and long cultural heritage. There are many reference sources that provide information about nomadic Traveller groups; below is a list of some UK Gypsy Traveller websites that will help develop your understanding in this area of inclusion, particularly if you are interested in learning more about children from Gypsy Traveller families:

http://www.romanysociety.org.uk/
http://www.travellerstimes.org.uk/

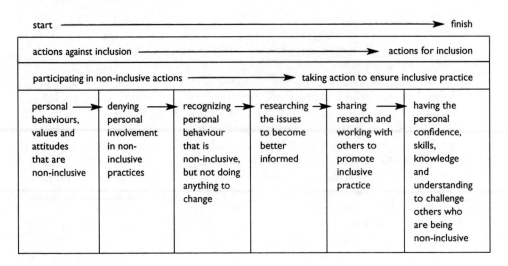

personal behaviours, values and attitudes that are non-inclusive	denying personal involvement in non-inclusive practices	recognizing personal behaviour that is non-inclusive, but not doing anything to change	researching the issues to become better informed	sharing research and working with others to promote inclusive practice	having the personal confidence, skills, knowledge and understanding to challenge others who are being non-inclusive

Figure 1.1 Professional development: the journey to new understandings

Source: Adapted from Adams, Bell and Griffin 2007

Reflecting on values, attitudes and beliefs about people and children from backgrounds different to our own can be painful and challenging. However, if we are to provide an inclusive learning environment for the children we work with, it is part of our required professional development to review our beliefs and work practice to ensure that it is not us who are causing barriers to children's learning. Understanding how our values, attitudes and beliefs can create barriers to children's learning – and learning different ways of thinking and behaving so as to ensure that those barriers are removed – is not necessarily something that happens quickly. Usually these aspects of personal development take time, reflection and sometimes research. It is useful to think of this kind of professional develop-ment as a journey. Some of the ideas that you encounter in the rest of this book will be new to you and some will be very familiar. We are all on different journeys and at different stages in that journey. Above is what Adams, Bell and Griffin (2007) call an 'action continuum'. It describes the journey we take to better understanding of new and often challenging ideas.

Thinking about our discussion about Gypsy Traveller people and reflecting on your own views about Gypsies, where would you say you were on the continuum above? You may be at the point where you have researched the background of Gypsy Travellers and are sharing your knowledge and understanding with others to ensure that any Gypsy Traveller children you work with in school, or may work with at some point, are learning in an inclusive environment which will enable them to enjoy and achieve. If you feel you might still be somewhere near the beginning of the journey, you might need to do further research in order to develop.

Make a positive contribution

The aim for this outcome of the ECM agenda requires schools to enable children to:

> engage in decision making and support the community and environment; engage in law-abiding and positive behaviour in and out of school and to develop self-confidence and successfully deal with significant life changes and challenges.
>
> (DCSF 2008)

The subsequent chapters in this book cover many of these aspects, particularly in terms of how children with the need under discussion can be enabled to 'develop self-confidence'. Removing barriers to learning and providing an inclusive environment is a large part of helping children develop self-confidence. Children who are healthy, safe and enjoying and achieving will have confidence. Self-confidence is also part of having resilience, which is about knowing how to tackle 'and successfully deal with significant life changes and challenges' (ibid.).

A further aspect of enabling children to achieve this outcome is about allowing them to 'engage in decision making' (ibid.): this is about children having a voice and being part of the day-to-day decisions that are taken about them, or that have an effect on their lives. People sometimes confuse the idea of listening to 'children's voices' with 'doing what children want'. Part of growing up and learning to live in society is about being able to voice one's own ideas and opinions, expecting others to respect them and knowing how to listen to and respect others. If children are not given the opportunity to develop these skills they may become withdrawn or aggressive, as they will believe that their views do not count and will feel marginalized or rejected. They will not develop the skills to allow them to voice ideas and opinions effectively. They will not believe that they will be listened to when they need to 'speak out' to defend themselves or when they need to seek help. The NSPCC states: 'children who are listened to are usually well adjusted and self-confident, while those whose needs are ignored may be withdrawn or difficult and suffer from low self-esteem' (NSPCC 2009).

Many schools have made improvements in this regard and have established school councils which give children the opportunity to be part of the decision-making processes in school. The current citizenship curriculum provides many opportunities to engage children in decision-making activities and to help develop skills for negotiation and team work. In terms of making a contribution to the wider social context, this can begin locally within the classroom or school context itself. Some of these ideas are further explored in Chapter 9.

Activity

Below are a few ideas for activities to try in the classroom to give children a 'voice' and encourage them to make a positive contribution to their community.

- In some curriculum areas it is possible to give children a choice about how they want to record their learning. For example, if you are working on a history-based topic, give children the choice of making a model related to the learning being explored, or designing a poster, doing a drama or making an information leaflet. Do not require all children to have the same 'product' from the learning activity.
- Negotiate classroom rules as an ongoing process. Having once agreed a set of rules, come back to them regularly and discuss with the children if they are working. Ask if they need to be modified, and if anyone can think of good examples that show that the rules are working. Allowing children the choice and the opportunity to go through the process of discussing and negotiating is as important, in these instances, as having a finished outcome.
- Set up 'buddy' schemes where particular children have the responsibility at certain times to ensure that no one in the playground is being excluded and everyone has someone to play with.
- Encourage links between classes in different age phases, where children can share their work with each other or read together.

Achieve economic well-being

Particularly for primary schools, this outcome can seem very long-term, especially regarding aims stating that schools are required to enable children to:

> engage in further education, employment or training on leaving school; be ready for employment; live in decent homes and sustainable communities, have access to transport and material goods and live in households free from low income.

> (DCSF 2008)

However, these aims do serve to remind primary schools of how long-term education is, and how important it is to get each stage right for each child, as each stage is a foundation for the next phase the child is moving on to. Therefore, if barriers to learning are not overcome at the earliest opportunity there will be a knock-on effect regarding children's access to learning in the future, and eventually in terms of their access to economic well-being.

A further way primary schools make a very large contribution to achieving this outcome and these aims is by ensuring that the parents and carers of the children are able to work, which, in turn, improves the economic well-being of the child.

Good practice in enabling families to achieve economic well-being

Many schools, as a result of the ECM agenda, have become 'extended schools' or provide a range of childcare and additional activities which enable parents and carers to be in employment, or to be seeking employment. For example, they might offer childcare facilities between 8.00 a.m. and 6.00 p.m., including breakfast clubs, for both children and their parents. Some schools have before-school and after-school activities, including additional fitness and PE activities or homework clubs, plus a whole range of more 'traditional' after-school activities.

Schools are expected to work with the community to share access to their buildings and facilities and this can work both ways. Most schools have very good IT facilities, but not all schools have access to good outdoor environments, either for PE or for learning about nature and the environment. Therefore, schools are encouraged to allow access and training for those in the community who want to develop their IT skills, who want support in developing their literacy and numeracy skills, or who want to use the school hall for dance and fitness classes. Equally, schools are encouraged to look to the community for facilities to provide activities for the children, such as the use of local leisure centre facilities and staff expertise.

In particular, schools should be working with parents to understand their needs and should consider providing:

- parenting programmes using structured, evidence-based programmes, as well as more informal opportunities for parents to engage with the school and each other;
- family learning sessions to allow children to learn with their fathers and mothers and information sessions for fathers and mothers at the beginning of primary and secondary phases.

(DCSF 2007)

Schools have access to additional money from local authorities to support these initiatives and to pay any staff involved. Teachers and teaching assistants are not expected to run these activities as part of their usual employment; however, if they do wish to be involved they can be contracted and paid separately.

Further support that schools are working with local authorities and children's trusts to deliver includes:

- access to health services (e.g. speech and language therapy, sexual health advice and support, Child and Adolescent Mental Health Services, and drugs and substance misuse advice and support), SEN and disability services, behavioural support (e.g. from educational psychologists, education welfare officers and behaviour and education support teams); and
- support from youth workers, family support, mentors, social care workers and counsellors.

(DCSF 2007)

Case study

The ECM outcomes do not 'stand alone'; they are all interlinked and inter-related. We can see this more clearly if we look at a specific example; in this instance, that of looked-after children, or Children in Care (CiC). Looked-after children have particular needs when it comes to ensuring that they are included and are being enabled to *enjoy and achieve* at school. The very fact that some children are looked after or CiC will mean that they may need particular support in areas that relate to being healthy and staying safe.

A looked-after child may be particularly vulnerable in terms of emotional and mental health, and a child who has suffered physical, emotional or sexual abuse will need support in dealing with these experiences and in knowing how to keep safe from possible further abuse. That is, schools need to be very aware that children who have suffered abuse will not necessarily be able to recognize appropriate boundaries in terms of others' behaviour towards them – or their own behaviour. This can make them vulnerable to further abuse, or may lead them to behave inappropriately towards others. Such children often do not trust anyone and may need time to learn trust, which requires a particular approach to engaging them in learning from the adults around them. Children who have been victims of physical abuse may feel that physical aggression is the way to get what you want or the only way to protect oneself. Again children need to un-learn these lessons and develop other ways of dealing with situations.

The research shows that looked-after children are among those who *enjoy and achieve* least well at school – which then has a long-term effect in terms of *achieving economic well-being*. It is also the case that a disproportionate number of the prison population is comprised of people who have been CiC. Similarly, many looked-after children go on to develop drug and alcohol-related problems as teenagers and adults (DCSF 2009).

A school that has a strong inclusive ethos enables children and their families to achieve some if not all of the ECM outcomes in their day-to-day lives. Such schools also equip children with the skills, knowledge and understanding that allow the outcomes to be achieved in both the short term and the long term. The following chapters of this book develop and explore, to a deeper level, many of the ideas introduced in this opening chapter. Taking on board the ideas discussed in this book and developing your own practice in the light of what you have read will not only ensure that the children you work with are included, but will also ensure that they are helped to meet the outcomes of the ECM agenda.

Bibliography

Adams, M., Bell, L. A. and Griffin, P. (2007) *Teaching for Diversity and Social Justice*, 2nd edn. New York and London: Routledge.

Barkham, P. (2005) 'Gypsy Groups Report the *Sun* to the Police'. *Guardian*, 10 March. http://www.guardian.co.uk/media/2005/mar/10/pressandpublishing.localgovernment.

DCSF (2007) 'Extended Schools Building on Experience'. London: DCSF.

—— (2008) 'Every Child Matters Outcomes Framework'. London: DCSF.

—— (2009) 'Improving the Educational Attainment of Children in Care (Looked After Children)'. London: DCSF.

Dear, P. (2005) 'Gypsy Campaign Raises Ethics Issues'. BBC, 11 March. http://news.bbc.co.uk/1/hi/uk http://news.bbc.co.uk/1/hi/uk/4337281.stm /4337281.stm (accessed 23 January 2010).

DfES (1999) *The National Curriculum Handbook for Primary School Teachers*. London: HMSO.

—— (2001) *Inclusive Schooling*. London: DfES.

—— (2003a) *Aiming High: Understanding the Educational Needs of Minority Ethnic Pupils in Mainly White Schools*. London: DfES.

—— (2003b) *Aiming High: Raising the Achievement of Gypsy Traveller Pupils*. London: DfES.

—— (2004a) *Removing Barriers to Achievement: The Government's Strategy for SEN*. London: DfES.

—— (2004b) *Every Child Matters: Change for Children*. London: DfES.

—— (2005) *Leading on Inclusion*. London: DfES.

—— (2006) *What to Do if You're Worried a Child is Being Abused*. London: DfES.

Francis, N. and Jackson, K. (2009) 'Gypsies Ruined our Kids' School', *Sun*, 4 April. http://www.thesun.co.uk/sol/homepage/features/article2360398.ece (accessed 23 January 2010).

Knowles. G. (2009) *Ensuring Every Child Matters*. London: Sage.

Macpherson, W. (1999) *The Stephen Lawrence Inquiry Report*. London: HMSO.

NSPCC (2009) *Listening to Children*. London: NSPCC.

Ofsted (2003) *Handbook for Inspecting Nursery and Primary Schools* (ref. HMI 1359). London: Ofsted.

—— (2004) *Special Educational Needs and Disability: Towards Inclusive Schools* (ref. HMI 2276). London: Ofsted.

Osler, A. (2003) *Citizenship and Democracy in Schools: Diversity, Identity, Equality*. Stoke-on-Trent: Trentham Books.

Websites

http://audit.healthyschools.gov.uk/Themes/default.aspx

http://news.bbc.co.uk/hi/uk/2698295.stm

Chapter 2

Children for whom English is an additional language

Kathy MacLean

Introduction

This chapter aims to provide practical advice to the reader in order to enable an inclusive and collaborative approach that supports the learning of children for whom English is an additional language (EAL). It aims to ensure that the diversity of children's linguistic needs and experiences is understood and reflected in the readers' planning so that cognitive challenge is appropriately high. The chapter also aims to develop knowledge that will help readers to select and prepare appropriate teaching resources and learning activities for the provision of contextual and linguistic support across the curriculum.

In this chapter, *EAL children* refers to children whose mother tongue is not English and who may live their lives in two or more languages. This means that they may '. . . have access to, or need to use two or more languages at home and at school. It does not mean that they have fluency in both languages or that they are competent and literate in both languages' (Hall 1992).

Case study

It cannot be assumed that only one language is spoken in any given home. Children may be exposed to a number of languages. Zainab, a child in my Reception class some years ago, spoke Tigre at home with her family but her parents regularly spoke Saho to each other. She was also learning Arabic at the Mosque. Jessica's mother, who was Malay Chinese, and her father, who was Ghanaian, had only English as their shared language. Both parents spoke English as their second language; neither was fully fluent in English but this was the language that was spoken with their children. The children would also hear their parents use their first languages (Cantonese and Twi) with other family members. Though Zainab did not speak Saho, and Jessica did not speak either of her parents' first languages, both children could understand conversations which took place in these languages. André, with a German-speaking mother and English-speaking father, was spoken to in each language by his respective parents.

Careful questioning will elicit information about a child's linguistic exposure. In Jessica's case, her exposure to non-fluent models of English out of school led to confusion and slowed her acquisition of English fluency. Having accurate information about languages spoken and understood by families is important, for in British homes, as in some regions of the world, several languages may be used.

Children learning English as an additional language are not a homogeneous group; they come from diverse regions and backgrounds. Some may be from families who have travelled from another country out of choice, for business, academic or diplomatic reasons. Others may be from families who have migrated out of choice for economic reasons, an example being the most recent Polish arrivals. Some may be from families who are refugees or asylum seekers; currently such children are likely to be from Somalia or Afghanistan.

Children learning English as an additional language (EAL) are likely to have a range of experience and fluency in learning English. Some may have recently arrived and be new to the English language and British culture; some children may have been born in Britain but have been brought up with languages other than English; while yet others may have had years of learning in English. In some classrooms a range of languages may be represented; in others children for whom English is an additional language may be the linguistic majority. In some schools in Tower Hamlets, for example, 98 per cent of the children have Bengali or Sylheti as their mother tongue, while in most other areas of Britain there are far fewer EAL learners. Both situations have their own challenges, for both adults and children.

Learning a language is a social process; at the heart of the experience is the EAL learner with his or her mother tongue and previous experience of learning, dependent on a child's particular aptitude and style. EAL learners are affected by attitudes towards them and the language they speak; how their cultural practices, religion and ethnicity are viewed from within the school and beyond. Social and cultural experiences have an impact on children's progress in acquiring English, as well as their general cognitive and academic ability. The child of a visiting academic or diplomat may view an experience of British school as an opportunity to learn English as an addition to his or her repertoire, while maintaining a firm grasp of the mother tongue. However, a child from another immigrant group may view the experience differently; particularly if his or her own language has low status in the host community.

Creating an inclusive culture

In order to learn effectively, children need to feel 'safe, settled and valued'. The ethos and environment created in the class and by the school are crucial. A child will have a sense of belonging if his or her linguistic, cultural, social, religious and ethnic background is positively valued, reflected and included in the curriculum. Evidence of this will be seen in displays and the print environment as well as in the content of the curriculum. An environment in which children from minority ethnic groups feel safe also depends upon how the school implements its policies on equalities, behaviour, bullying and racism. Taking racist incidents seriously and responding effectively is crucial.

Activity

Powerful messages are conducted through the physical environment of the classroom. The type of materials used in displays should reflect diverse groups, ensuring that there are images of people from different ethnic, cultural and religious backgrounds and that these images are not stereotypical or tokenistic and give positive messages. Religious events and cultural festivals from the children's home country should be recognized and celebrated by ensuring that they are included in the curriculum as well as in school assemblies.

Celebrating the linguistic diversity of the class and children's bilingualism can be done in a variety of ways. For example:

- List the variety of languages spoken in the classroom.
- Make a display with children's photographs and add a comment from each child in his or her mother tongue.
- Write the same sentence or saying in a range of languages.
- Display a map of the world, showing the places where a language is most spoken and where children's families originate.
- Research a 'language of the week' – a particular language spoken in the class or the school. The speakers of the language have the chance to act as 'experts'.
- Display examples of writing in different scripts and languages.
- Provide opportunities to listen to and share stories in a range of languages.

Resources

Resources play an important part in supporting the EAL learner, and artefacts from different cultures and how they are used in the school can say much about how that school values diverse culture. Some artefacts, by their nature, can only be used in particular ways; a copy of the Koran cannot be merely passed around as an object of interest, for example, but has to be treated with reverence and respect, and Muslims only handle the Koran following ritual washing. Other resources could include having musical instruments from a range of cultures in the school's collection; such a collection should be accompanied by opportunities to learn about the instruments and how to use them appropriately.

Role-play areas afford an opportunity to reflect aspects of life from diverse cultures. This can be done through a supply of fabrics, headwear and other accessories from a range of cultures being made available for 'dressing up'. Kitchen and eating utensils that children use in their own homes can be kept in the 'home corner' – for example: a board for rolling out chapattis or Chinese bowls with chopsticks. Dolls, puppets and masks can also be used in the classroom to reflect a wide range of cultures.

Ideally, a classroom should be equipped with at least one text in the first language of every child who studies there. There is a growing range of dual-language texts available, and children can be encouraged to bring in newspapers, comics and magazines in their home languages to contribute to the class collection. Ensure that the graphic or writing area in the classroom includes a range of writing materials and examples of writing in a range of languages and scripts. Similarly, a listening area should be developed to provide easy access to story tapes and CDs with rhymes and songs in children's first languages.

Planning for children for whom English is an additional language

English language acquisition

Learning a new language takes time and passes through distinct phases. Jim Cummins (2001) identifies the following three phases in the development of language proficiency:

1 conversational fluency;
2 discrete language skills;
3 academic language proficiency.

'Conversational fluency', also referred to as basic interpersonal communicative skills (BICS), is developed by EAL children through exposure to the language of school and the environment in between one and two years. BICS refers to children who have acquired a vocabulary of high-frequency words and simple grammatical structures, enabling them to manage well in social situations. Developing the 'discrete language skills' – which include the specific language skills required for literacy and grammatical knowledge – usually needs to be taught, since, as with all language acquisition, these children need more direct teaching and scaffolding. Becoming fully fluent in a language, or *acquiring cognitive academic language proficiency* (CALP), can take between five and seven years. This level of language acquisition is the language associated with higher-order thinking skills such as evaluating, justifying, forming hypotheses, deducing, arguing a case, identifying criteria and analysis. A child who has this level of language proficiency is able to use more demanding vocabulary and is able to write and understand increasingly complex texts.

While EAL children are learning to speak the English language, they are also required to learn to manipulate language functions (how language is used in particular situations) – for example, the language we use to 'chat' is very different from the language we use to explain or instruct. The framework developed by Cummins is very useful in exploring this area of language acquisition, as it illustrates the 'cognitive and linguistic demands' which are made in the classroom and which we may need to be aware of when thinking about the needs of children for whom English is an additional language. It is a very helpful tool for thinking about the learning needs of these children and ensuring comprehensible and meaningful input for them. The emphasis of the framework is to ensure that children are engaged in learning which is contextual, or embedded – that is, the learning tasks themselves generate meaningful use of language. This means that children can learn appropriate language for and in a given context; for example, tasks which give opportunities for negotiating meaning and scaffolding learning. Children can then move on to tasks which are 'context-reduced' and heavily reliant on linguistic cues – for example, 'imagine you are walking along a . . .'

This framework enables us to identify the demands that classroom activities place on the child and at the same time can be used as a planning tool that enables the teacher to ensure that the cognitive challenge remains high. This framework can be used to support children for whom English is an additional language across the curriculum.

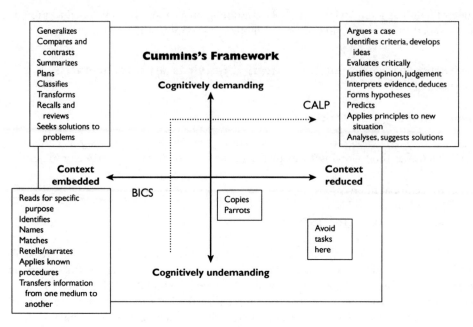

Figure 2.1 Cummins's framework for identifying classroom demands

Source: Hall (1995).

Planning for children who are new arrivals and new to English

Welcoming new arrivals

Planning for 'new arrivals' is crucial; there must be a supportive environment into which children are received. From the first point of contact, children and parents must feel that they are welcome in the school. On entering a school that values and promotes, visually and physically, the rich cultural and linguistic diversity of its pupils, both adults and children receive a clear message: 'You are welcome here!'

'New arrivals' form a diverse group; children that arrive may be of any age and arrive at any time during the academic year. Not only this, but they will arrive with varying educational needs based on their previous experience: they may have had full schooling in another country; no schooling; or very little previous schooling. Schooling they have had might have been uneven, and the education system they know may be very different from the one in Britain. These children will be from a range of linguistic, national, cultural and religious backgrounds. They and their families may experience feelings of loss and isolation as well as cultural disorientation. In some cases, the family may feel optimism and excitement about the challenges and opportunities offered by their new life. These feelings will vary depending on the circumstances of their migration. Families may have experienced extreme hardship and trauma before arrival in the UK; children may well have been separated from one or both parents, and from other loved ones.

All class teachers should be aware of the challenges and issues facing new arrivals, and should consider how the child can be most effectively welcomed and supported so that he or she is able to settle easily into learning. If the school has effective admission and induction arrangements, this process is made easier. Those working with the child should have clear information about the child's country of origin, and the languages spoken at home and to the child. Other pertinent information includes which languages children are able to read or to write, previous educational experience, faith, and whether there are any health or disability issues. The school should be able to provide welcome booklets, leaflets or CDs in children's first languages, containing easy, accessible information, well supported by photographs and pictures. A school's local authority will be able to provide support in obtaining the above materials if necessary. It is good practice for these resources to be accessed by those who will work with the child before he or she arrives at the school.

Activity

Working with all children to support a 'new arrival':

- Talk to the class about how they can help to support the new child.
- Gather information with the class on the country that the child comes from and the language or languages spoken.
- Elect a class buddy. Class buddies who share the same language are an obvious advantage, but language is not the only criterion – a buddy with a different language who is empathetic and willing may be more appropriate. Being a class buddy can be a heavy burden, so it may be a good idea to have a number of children who are able to take on that role and apply a rota system.
- Develop a code of practice with the class for 'buddying' and supporting new arrivals to the class.
- Make a photograph album or a booklet that outlines routines and display it in the classroom.
- Ensure that there are signs and labels in the child's first language.

It is not necessary to withdraw new arrivals from the classroom. Learning English through the curriculum gives a meaningful context for all EAL children, including new arrivals, and provides them with access to the curriculum. This can be achieved in the classroom through careful planning for scaffolding language and learning, with support from additional adults when available.

Those working with the child need to ensure that they have differentiated their planning to meet the needs of new arrivals, particularly if they have low fluency in English. Identifying the language that children need in order to participate in a lesson is the first step in planning for such children, followed by planning how the key language can be modelled, and what activities and strategies can be used to scaffold the understanding needed for a specific learning activity.

Activity

Checklist of good practice for scaffolding the learning of new arrivals for whom English is an additional language:

- Use visual prompts such as pictures, photographs, tables, charts, maps, concept maps, Venn diagrams, timelines, real objects, artefacts and actions.
- Make learning activities into collaborative tasks – for example: sorting activities, role play and drama.
- Make sure that there are lots of practical learning tasks with planned opportunities for speaking and listening.
- Use games which rely on repetition or careful structuring of language.
- Identify key vocabulary or constructions and teach them explicitly within a meaningful context.
- Make sure that bilingual adults and bilingual dictionaries are available.
- Use bilingual strategies such as paired work in the first language.
- Model vocabulary in relevant contexts.
- Use assessment for learning (AFL).

Remember, hearing English used and listening to a skilled speaker of the language in a range of meaningful contexts is an important key for developing fluency in English.

The role of talk in learning

Children learn about language through using it and hearing how others use it; children talk to make their needs known and to make sense of the world. Language is an important tool for learning and responding to experience. The classroom provides a space where the teacher and children are partners in developing knowledge and understanding. It is an apprenticeship in which the learners receive guidance and scaffolding through language acquisition and the curriculum (Gibbons 2001). Active involvement in exploratory talk makes learners focus on the language structures they need to use and they are pushed to perform at a higher level.

Activity: engaging children in exploratory talk

Design a learning activity that includes the following elements:

- Children work in small groups to share and discuss information.
- Each member of the group is expected to contribute and offer relevant information for discussion and joint consideration.

- The emphasis of the activity needs to be on justifying suggestions and points made.
- Proposals may be challenged and counter-challenged, in which case reasons need to be given and alternatives offered.
- The group must be expected to reach an agreed conclusion, solution or outcome.

Note: the focus of such activities is on the language of reasoning and can take place in any language (Mercer 2000: 98).

The importance of talk as a tool for learning is crucial to the achievement of children for whom English is an additional language. Involvement in collaborative talk gives bilingual children the opportunity to listen to language models, to evaluate their language use and to participate in specific language use. The work of the National Oracy Project (1990–1992) (Howe 2003) was a major curriculum development which provided a body of classroom-based research evidence that demonstrated the necessity of talk in helping children to understand new concepts and ideas across the various areas of the curriculum. The project outcomes emphasized the relationship between spoken language and learning, and the researchers claimed that talk is a fundamental part of learning in that it enhances thinking and learning (Corden 2000).

A classroom that supports talk is one:

- Where children feel able to make mistakes, be tentative and 'think aloud' without being judged.
- Where children's own language, way of talking and right to be silent are respected.
- Where children's opinions are taken seriously.
- Where teachers listen to pupils rather than constantly questioning them.
- Where the dominant voice is not always the adult.
- Where the environment and organization encourage collaboration between children.
- Where tasks that require purposeful talk for their success are set.
- Where children need to talk and listen to each other.
- Where there is sometimes opportunity for the talk to develop beyond the immediate task.

Collaborative learning

Collaborative learning takes place when a group of two or more children engage in a task or problem that they explore together in order to develop their understanding and learning. The collaborative talk generated by the task is a key aspect of this approach. Good quality talk will capture the interest of the participants, and in turn promote critical thinking. Research has shown that collaborative learners achieve higher levels of thought and retain information for longer than learners working in isolation. To ensure that collaborative activities are successful, it is important to plan the grouping of children, and this should be devised according to cognitive rather than linguistic ability. This enables the language of the less fluent EAL learners to be scaffolded by the more fluent learners and native English speakers. As Vygotsky's zone of proximal development shows, what a child can do with support today, he or she will do alone tomorrow (Harry 1996). Through working in this way, the shared learning situation gives learners opportunities to discuss their learning and extend their thinking. This approach benefits all children but has particular benefits for children who are learning English as an additional language.

Advantages of group work

- More and greater variety of language directed at and from the EAL learner.
- Increased language output through interaction with other speakers and more turn-taking.
- Increased language learning through children needing to clarify their own meanings.
- Language learnt is used and heard in an appropriate context and with a meaningful purpose.

Considerations when planning for collaborative group work

- The group task must *require* talk, not just encourage it.
- The task must be at a cognitively appropriate level.
- As far as possible, language-learning tasks should be relevant to what is being learnt generally in the classroom.
- The activity will work better if there is an agreed set of rules for behaviour and all the children in the group are involved.
- If roles are assigned to each member of the group – for example: time keeper, recorder, reporter, someone who keeps the task going – this will ensure that everyone has an opportunity to contribute.
- The response to the task can draw on children's first language – they can discuss, read or write in their first language, before they report the outcome in English.
- Involve beginner English learners in tasks less dependent on language, such as experiential science or mathematics activities, where they are able to experience success and participate more easily.

Types of collaborative activity

In thinking about learning that will support children learning English as an additional language, try incorporating some of the following activities:

- *Matching* – including identifying, labelling, naming, describing and measuring objects, words and letters.
- *Sorting* – again, through using objects or letters and words that can be classified or grouped under an agreed definition, or can be described by generalizing about their characteristics ('these are all red things'), or compared and contrasted ('these are all cars, but two are red and two are blue').
- *Sequencing* – designing activities that require discussion about how to sequence objects.
- *Making things* – for example, preparing food and describing the process, writing instructions for doing the cooking, putting a list of tasks in chronological order – so that things happen in the correct sequence.
- *Ranking activities* – evaluating, judging, applying criteria, selecting, comparing, assessing relative size, importance, value or other measures.

Reading

All reading involves the orchestration of three kinds of knowledge in order to make meaning of text. First, this includes semantic knowledge, or understanding of the wider context that the words relate to, so that the reader can make sense of and give meaning to the text. Second, the reader needs syntactic knowledge and understanding of how a language works – or how words fit together to make grammatical sense. Finally, the reader needs graphophonic knowledge of the language; that is, the language's alphabet, and the sound–letter, or phoneme–grapheme, relationship. EAL children who are already fluent readers of their first language will have less difficulty in learning to read in their second language than those who are not literate, since they will have an understanding of semantics, syntax and graphophonic knowledge. When you are introducing EAL children to reading, you also need to be aware that children's picture books, including 'reading scheme' books, are written on the assumption that children are familiar with the cultural aspects of the story and are fluent speakers of the language. Therefore, if the culture shown in the books is new to the child, he or she will struggle not only with the complexities of learning to read, but also with making sense of unfamiliar picture clues.

Reading aloud

This is a key strategy. When read to by experienced readers, children hear how the language is constructed and key into the tunes of the language on the page. There are particular benefits for children for whom English is an additional language, in that the universality of stories told and heard provides them with transferable skills and knowledge. Storytelling is a global pastime and children who have heard stories in any language will, however unconsciously, recognize the structure of narrative. Telling stories or reading stories aloud is a good way of introducing children to the tunes and rhythms of a new language. It will also introduce them to the way in which the language is spoken and to its grammatical structure, and will broaden their vocabulary.

It is important to choose appropriate texts to suit your purpose and the needs of the child. Reading good quality texts and following up the reading activity with engaging in text-related activities will encourage and motivate children to read more. Having outlined the importance of narrative texts or storybooks, particularly to help children engage with the semantic and syntactic aspect of the language, using non-fiction texts is also an important way to engage children's interest in reading. Working alongside children to help them find a non-fiction text about something that interests them allows you to learn more about their interests. Discussion about the text and pictures helps to develop children's spoken-language and reading skills.

The use of phonic approaches is currently a commonly used strategy in schools, for the teaching of reading to all children. EAL children will respond to this strategy in a similar way to other children; however, without an understanding of semantics and syntax they are likely to struggle to understand what they are reading. For this reason, pre-reading activities other than phonic activities are key. If a child is able to come to a text knowing what it will be about then he or she is more likely to be successful in being able to 'read' the words and understand the meaning of the text.

Pre-reading activities

Using illustrations

Make time to talk about the illustrations or pictures in the books. These can be shown on the interactive whiteboard, or if the children are in groups they can be given laminated colour copies of the illustrations to share and talk about. In undertaking activities like this, ensure that the composition of groups is such that children for whom English is an additional language are working with children who can model the use of fluent English.

Before beginning to read the book, allow the children to examine the cover illustration in pairs and discuss what the book is about. Ask questions: Who is the main character? What kind of story might it be? Encourage the children to generate questions or 'puzzles' on 'Post-it' notes.

Show part of an illustration to generate discussion and questioning, and then reveal the rest of the image. Discuss with the children how or whether this affects their previous interpretation, or does it answer or raise additional questions?

Sequencing illustrations

Give children a set of illustrations or visuals from the story, or some text, and ask them to put them in the possible order and explain how they have decided on the order. Now get them to tell the story or describe the process in the sequence selected.

Storytelling

Tell the story simply, either referring to the illustrations as you narrate or by using story props; these can be illustrations on a magnet board, objects linked to or representing characters from the story, puppets or your own line drawings.

Drawing the 'story'

After reading a new text, try representing the story physically and graphically, using story-boards, diagrams or story maps; this supports retelling. Becoming more familiar with a story enables the reader to understand its shape, and to consider how it fits together.

Story circles

Another technique that works with longer stories is forming a story circle with a specific number of children. Each child is assigned a chunk of the story, so the story is passed around the circle. This act of joint retelling in a mixed group scaffolds children for whom English is an additional language and builds their confidence in using spoken language. The retelling can be followed by discussion about particular characters and their roles in the story. The use of illustrations will also add further support.

Drama and role play

The use of drama techniques is a powerful pedagogic tool for developing understanding of texts, and exploring character relationships and thematic concerns. Through devices such as 'hot seating' and 'freeze framing', pupils are able to rehearse the dramatic devices that bring alive the narrative since 'drama creates the immediacy of lived experience' (Bassi 1999) and gives teachers and children a vehicle for exploring stories in an active way.

Drama activities that can be used to explore text and develop language skills

- *Role play* – encourage children to 'take on' characters from the story and tell their version of events, or work with other children being other characters to 'tell' parts of the story. Or children can simply 'be' the character.
- *Hot seating* – ask a child to be one of the characters from the story. Invite the other children to ask questions, which he or she must answer in character.
- *Freeze framing* – individuals or groups of children dramatize part of the story. On the word 'freeze' the children stop moving and form a 'frame' of that part of the story. Other children (or you) can then ask them about what they are doing at that point in the story, how they feel, what they are going to do next, etc.

- *Character in role* – this is like role play, but it requires the child to imagine the character in a different setting and be able to act out or discuss what he or she thinks the character might do then.
- *Witness* – can a child imagine being present at some or all of the events in the story and dramatizing or telling the event(s) from their point of view? Or being a witness to what they saw.
- *On trial* – this can follow on from the previous activity. Imagine asking the main characters to explain the events, through questioning from other children, and involve witnesses (as above) in being questioned to support the main character's story, or to show that they are lying about what happened.
- *Debate* – hold debates about the events in the story. Should characters have done what they did?
- *Mantle of the expert* – ask children to imagine that they have some particular knowledge and understanding about events in the story, or can provide an insight that the other characters don't know about. How does the input of the expert change the understanding of what happened?
- *Press conference* – hold a press conference where characters from the story have to explain themselves. Ask the other children to be 'the press', asking questions and wanting an explanation.

Active reading

If children are to create meaning from texts, they need opportunities to actively engage with them: to make decisions, take forward, try out and discuss their ideas. The use of activities such as concept maps, inference grids, Venn diagrams and other graphic organizers of ideas helps children develop English language skills, and these are good strategies for collaboration. They also encourage the use of important strategies, such as skimming, scanning, close reading, organizing, prioritizing and justifying. Engagement with these tasks involves a high level of challenge, conversion of information from one form to another and metacognition (thinking about thinking).

Writing

Writing can be a challenging task for any child. For EAL children there are often additional hurdles to overcome. They may have little or no experience of writing; or they may be familiar only with writing in a different language and even in a different script. Learning to write cannot be divorced from talking or from reading. The processes are inextricably linked. Written language, however, is not just talk written down. It is deliberately constructed to create meaning. Vygotsky (Harry 1996) referred to the process between thought and writing as being a long journey, for when written language is the final outcome of what began through thinking, it has to be carefully constructed and structured. When children adapt and reform their inner speech into a written form they have to be able to take account of the transitions necessary to make their meaning accessible to their audience. The opportunity to explore and practise this transition orally increases the successful transformation from thought to writing.

Learning written language from oral stories

Listening to stories and involvement in role play scaffolds the learning of pupils for whom English is an additional language; through storytelling they begin to acquire knowledge about story structures and become familiar with grammatical features. They develop story grammars and knowledge of the formal style and vocabulary which is characteristic of certain forms of writing. The opportunity to rehearse a story or any piece of work before writing is particularly helpful for the bilingual child. Children for whom English is an additional language need an environment where they can talk aloud, and where they can rehearse their thoughts.

Case study

Abijola was in a year 5 class, working on telling stories before beginning to write them. Abijola came from Nigeria and his first language was Yoruba. He had been learning in English for a few years. He was a quiet, serious boy, keen to work and to do well in school, but found writing difficult. His comprehension was poor and his experience of written language quite limited. His teacher felt that his inclusion in the activity would develop his self-confidence and encourage him to express his opinions.

Abijola's main concerns were with his spelling and punctuation. He described himself as not being a good writer as he was unable to write at length and rarely finished a writing task. His first writing sample was an unfinished, sparse narrative in a series of sequential actions with undeveloped context and setting. As part of pre-writing activities he was engaged in oral storytelling and drama techniques like those described above.

As a result of using these pre-writing activities, he wrote a short story in the fairy tale genre. In contrast to his earlier work, he used descriptive language to set the context and to identify the protagonists. Abijola also showed control of the narrative voice. The action in his story was developed and moved forward coherently, bringing it to a satisfactory conclusion, which indicated his growing experience as a writer and his ability to imagine a fictional world. The activities also increased Abijola's confidence: he participated more actively in the sessions and began to describe himself as someone who enjoyed writing stories.

Other pre-writing activities: story boxes

A story box is a vehicle for telling, retelling or constructing a story. It is usually about the size of a shoe box, and contains a small number of objects related to a story. The box can be covered with decorative paper, which may be themed to reflect the story. The shape may be altered by cutting away the sides and creating a land or seascape using a variety of materials. The box may also be accompanied by a copy of the story.

This resource may be used with individuals or set as a collaborative task. Including objects related to the country or culture of children for whom English is an additional language creates a link with their prior experience and stimulates engagement and learning.

Case study

Ali, a Somali boy who had been learning English as an additional language for two terms, was given the opportunity to use a story box which had been themed to represent a Somali landscape with a flat-topped acacia tree. There was also a hunter, a toy hyena, a snake and a toy lion.

Using the story box, Ali was stimulated to tell a story to the teaching assistant working with him. It was a story based on a traditional Somali story that he knew. The story was shared with the class who then, through a shared writing exercise, created a written text.

Writing in role

Barrs (1994) proposes writing in role as an effective way of giving children the opportunity to create writing in new genres. She confirms that in dramatic play, when children are extended by the creative process, they draw on the social processes they have seen and heard in other parts of their lives. They can assume adult voices and show how much they have learned about different registers from listening and from reading.

Activity

Ask children to discuss what characters represented in an illustration might be thinking. This, alongside the use of drama techniques described in the section on reading, can help children progress to writing in role.

Making books and publishing

Publishing written work and making books encourages children to develop as writers. It is helpful to children at all stages; it also creates a unique and meaningful text that can be used in the classroom. Research conducted by Dr Lynne Cameron (Cameron and Besser 2004), 'Writing English as an Additional Language at KS2', indicated aspects for particular concentration.

To develop their confidence, skills, knowledge and understanding of writing in English, EAL children need extensive opportunities to encounter and work with a range of genres of written English. They will require direct teaching about more advanced tenses that show relative times of events, and experience in how to write with more advanced linguistic features – such as subordinators, conjunctions (and, then, because, etc.) – in order to create more varied sentences. They will also benefit from support with trying out various story-ending techniques and help with development of story setting, character and plot, and with sense of audience – thinking about the imagined readers of their stories. Although their spoken language may be developing well in terms of range of vocabulary and fluency, their capacity to write with the same fluency may not keep pace with their spoken language and they need to be shown how to write using specific grammatical patterns and how to use modal verbs, adverbials and prepositional phrases.

Supporting developing writing skills

- Ensure that all children are clear about the aims and purpose of the writing task.
- Provide children with examples of the type of text that is to be produced; for example, a leaflet, letter or report.
- Discuss the features of the text.
- Through questioning and discussion determine the conventions for that genre of text. For example, what are the specific features of report writing that are different from the features of story writing, or narrative?
- Model some of the writing – show the child how to turn 'thoughts/ideas' into writing. Show the child how to re-draft an initial idea. For example, if you were writing a report about a football match, you might write: 'The match took place on Sunday; it was raining hard so the pitch was muddy.' If you were writing a story, you might write: 'Aziz jumped out of bed on Sunday morning. He was excited, as it was the cup final match against Bury Wanderers. He pulled back the curtains and groaned – it was pouring with rain.'
- Compose part of the text as a shared writing activity (see above).
- Scaffold first attempts through collaborative active reading and talk.
- Move on to independent writing.
- Publish the finished piece, if appropriate, either by displaying it on the wall or compiling it is a book with other class work.

The writing process

All writing and writers need to go through three distinct phases in achieving a 'finished' piece of writing. The word *writing* itself refers to both the process of doing the writing and the finished article or piece of writing.

Phase 1

Before writing, children need to explore ideas and have something meaningful to write about. Generating ideas to write from can come through talking and playing with stories in many of the ways already explored, including through drama activities, drawing and storyboarding ideas. Children might also be engaged in 'events' that they can then write about. A school trip, for example.

Phase 2

As children are engaged in the writing, they need the opportunity to work with proficient writers who can support them through modelling and sharing writing. They need the opportunity to have feedback on what they have written through a response or editing partner. This partner reads their work aloud and continues to talk and share ideas about their writing, particularly if they need to 'shape' the writing for a particular purpose or audience.

Phase 3

Producing a worthwhile piece of writing, however old the child is and however familiar with writing English, takes time and effort. Given the effort that goes into producing a good piece of writing, the final draft needs to be celebrated. This can be achieved by displaying the work, publishing the writing in a class book, performing the writing for others to hear and enjoy or talking about how the piece of writing was put together.

Assessment

Assessment is a fundamental part of the learning process. It enables you, as the manager of the learning process, to check that children have learnt what you intended and enables you to decide where their learning needs to go next. In terms of assessing a child for whom English is an additional language, the initial assessments you need to make are ones that will provide you with the information given below.

• Where is the EAL learner's starting point in relation to children of the same age whose mother tongue is English? Making this assessment will help you to establish the sorts of strategies and activities the EAL learner needs to start with. Once you have established this, you may want to undertake specific assessments that will explore knowledge and understanding in particular areas of language. For example, the EAL learner's spoken English may be in advance of his or her reading in English – or he or she may be able to write but need work on developing use of adjectives and descriptive language.

- EAL children need to be learning English as well as all the other knowledge and understanding in the relevant aspects of the National Curriculum. It is important to have an accurate assessment of their knowledge and use of English as this is the medium for learning in British schools, but their level of proficiency in using English may be well below their ability to comprehend and understand other aspects of the curriculum. Therefore, the two must not be confused. A child for whom English is an additional language is not the same as a child who cannot learn or a child who has a special educational need.

Where possible, an assessment of understanding and skills in a child's first language will provide a better understanding of their cognitive ability when new to English or ensure that additional needs are clearly identified. Both assessment for learning (AFL), (see Chapter 9) and assessing pupil progress (APP) provide useful opportunities to assess progress made by EAL learners in English and mathematics. These approaches enable teachers to recognize and record uneven profiles and different rates of progress in the different language modes, and this is particularly useful for children who are learning English as an additional language.

Bilingual approaches

Maintenance and support of children's first language improves their chances of success in subsequent language learning. Additional benefits include raising the status of EAL learners by allowing them to demonstrate their linguistic expertise, and increased intellectual and academic progress for those who maintain literacy and fluency in their first language. Exposing monolingual children to other languages increases their knowledge about language. Bilingual strategies are easier to implement when bilingual staff with appropriate language skills are available. However, with careful planning, it is possible to use the support of bilingual parents and colleagues. In one school, parents got involved in dual language storytelling sessions on a regular basis. The parent read or told stories in their first language in partnership with the class teacher, who read or told the same story in English. After each session the stories were taped so that a bank of material available for wider use was created.

Bilingual strategies involve the appropriate use of first language or mother tongue for learning and teaching before, during and after lessons. The use of bilingual strategies must be carefully planned with the adults who are responsible for input in the first language. A range of bilingual resources are available for use in the classroom. Bilingual dictionaries, word lists and glossaries are available for purchase, as are first-language resources such as recorded stories, storybooks, DVDs, posters, newspapers, magazines and calendars. It is also possible to purchase first-language number lines and other such learning aids. Bilingual staff and parents can give support in identifying bilingual resources for use in ICT and on the Internet.

Storytelling in first language

Children can listen to the story told or read in their first language, either by a bilingual member of staff or by an invited parent or carer. This can be done in mixed groups, which sends a clear message to the rest of the class about the value placed on the child's mother tongue. Making audio recordings of storytelling or reading is an excellent way of building a bank of stories in children's first languages, which can be copied and made available for use in listening areas.

Bilingual approaches used before the lesson are most often to prepare children for specific content or concepts. These include pre-teaching content and concepts in first languages, or reinforcing content and concepts in first languages. Bilingual strategies used during the lesson can involve appropriate interventions in first languages. These may include paired or group work in first languages (for example, working with linguistic partners for discussion in first languages as a precursor to writing exercises) or support from an adult who shares the same mother tongue. After the lesson there may be opportunities for reflection in the first language on the learning that has taken place, what was understood or what aspects may have been puzzling.

Bilingual and monolingual staff can plan activities which enable bilingual children to present in their first language to others, orally or in writing, or to undertake first-language activities to help develop conceptual understanding and content knowledge (either the whole class or in groups or as individuals). The use of bilingual strategies builds a bridge between experience in first languages and new experiences in the second language.

Case study

Cherrystones Primary School was concerned about the reading development of children for whom English is an additional language, particularly in the area of comprehension skills, so staff compiled a general guidance leaflet about supporting reading development and questions that could be asked about texts. This was translated into a range of languages and sent home with dual-language texts. As the work developed, the teachers involved realized that their understanding of multilingual development and the issues in reading two languages simultaneously was developing. They also saw that the children were developing skills in transferring concepts and skills between their languages, as well as transferring strategies at decoding and context level.

Through this work the staff realized how the children were developing sophisticated metalinguistic awareness: that is, while learning new vocabulary in both languages, they also developed understanding of the different phonics and word order in different languages. Their sense of their own bilingual and bicultural identities was evolving as was their interest and pride in the language and culture of home, and they became more balanced bilinguals. Additionally, some parents became more closely involved with schools as their own skills in English developed.

(Adapted from Lancashire County Council 2009)

In summary, while English is the medium through which most education in Britain is conducted, for many children and families it is only one of the languages they use. For EAL children to become fluent in English they need a school environment that supports the development of language skills in their widest sense; a school with an ethos that reflects an understanding of and a respect for the long and rich cultural histories of all languages. In such a supportive environment EAL children will be more confident to work with the skills, knowledge and understanding of language they have, and can begin to apply them to the task of learning English. Given a supportive environment to learn in, the teaching and learning strategies explored here will not only enable EAL learners to become proficient users of spoken and written English, but will also benefit all children learning to speak, read and write English.

Bibliography

Barrs, Myra (1994) 'Genre Theory: What is it All About?' In Stierer, B. and Maybin, J. (eds) *Language, Literacy and Learning in Educational Practice*. Clevedon: Open University.

Bassi, L. K. (1999) 'How Storytelling Affects the Stories Children Write'. In Brock, A. (ed.) *Into The Enchanted Forest*. Staffordshire: Trentham Books.

Cameron, L. and Besser, S. (2004) *Writing in English as an Additional Language at Key Stage 2*. Nottingham: DfES.

Corden, Roy (2000) *Literacy and Learning through Talk*. Buckingham: Open University Press.

Cummins, J. (2001) *Negotiating Identities: Education for Empowerment in a Diverse Society*, 2nd edn. Ontario, CA: California Association for Bilingual Education.

Gibbons, P. (2002) *Scaffolding Language*. Portsmouth, NH: Heinemann.

Hall, D. (1995) *Assessing the Needs of Bilingual Pupils*. London: Routledge.

Harry, D. (1996) *Introduction to Vygotsky*. London: Routledge.

Howe, A. (2003) 'Talk is vital'. www.literacytrust.org.uk/Pubs/howe.html (accessed 26 February 2010).

Lancashire County Council (2009) 'Talk partners: A guidance booklet for schools', Naldic Working Papers, November.

Mercer, N. (2000) *The Guided Construction of Knowledge. Talk Amongst Teachers and Learners*. Clevedon: Multilingual Matters.

Chapter 3

Reassessing gender issues in the primary classroom

Barbara Thompson

Introduction

When this book was first published in 2006, I wrote that the focus of gender and achievement in the classroom had shifted dramatically over the last 20 years. The language of educational inequality has changed from a concern, from some, about the disadvantages faced by girls to a national focus on the underachievement of boys. Four years later these debates show no signs of diminishing, but rather have become more complex and more hotly contested. The emphasis of this chapter will be to provide an overview of some of the most prevalent of these debates because they are powerful, prevalent in popular educational discourse, and, as I will argue, in many ways flawed.

Gender and achievement in education became a discussion point through the feminist research of the 1970s and 1980s, which focused largely on the marginalization of girls in the classroom by teachers and by boys. Numerous commentators (Lobban 1975; Clarricoates 1978, 1980; Delamont 1980; Spender 1982; Lees 1983; Browne and France 1985) argued that classrooms were places for boys that happened to have girls in them. For example, Spender (1980), in a study of teacher time, discovered that, conversant with gender issues as she was, Spender herself spent far more time interacting with boys than with girls. Stanworth (1981) discovered that teacher expectations were higher for boys than for girls, and Arnot and Weiner pointed out that: 'Because of their underlying beliefs about gender behaviour, teachers act out, unconsciously, a hidden curriculum in favour of the boys and to the detriment of girls' (Weiner 1987: 160).

However, from the mid-1990s to date, much of the concern related to gender issues and schooling became focused on the perceived underachievement of boys. The increased educational achievement of girls, far from receiving public accolade, is seen almost to be an indicator that 'something is wrong'. There appears to be what Epstein describes as a 'moral panic' engendered by the failure of some boys to achieve academically, whipped up by a media frenzy that things are not as they should be (Epstein *et al.* 1998). A headline in the *Guardian* on 26 August 1995 announced: 'Girls Doing Well While Boys Feel Neglected', and Chris Woodhead, then Chief Inspector of Schools, is reported to have said that the underachieving boy is one of the most disturbing problems facing the education system (*Times Magazine*, 30 March 1996). Epstein *et al.* (1998: 3) refer to the comments of a feminist colleague who remarked that boys were 'not doing better than girls any more, like they should'!

In 1996 the Office for Standards in Education (Ofsted) and the Equal Opportunities Commission (EOC) published *The Gender Divide: Performance Differences Between Boys and*

Girls at School. Jackson (1998: 77) argues that: 'Although the book's foreword stressed that any national debate about education and gender must take account of both sexes', most responses to the booklet put the spotlight on boys' performance. As a result of intense media interest and the attention of an inspectorate directed to boys' underachievement, millions of pounds of government money has been spent on developing strategies to remedy 'the problem of boys'. In many schools the curriculum has been adapted to be more 'boy-centred' and money has been spent on resources to persuade boys to attain academically, as the *Guardian* headline of 11 July 1996 announced: 'Schools Urged to Focus on Low Achieving Boys'. However, for some feminists, including myself, more recently there has been an emerging concern that girls are once more in danger of returning to the status of Spender's 'invisible women' in contemporary classrooms (1981).

All those working in education need to provide genuinely inclusive learning opportunities for both sexes. To do so, they need to understand the shifts in debates about educational inequality, from a concern with girls' disadvantage raised in the main by feminist teachers and researchers, to the national outcry about boys' disadvantage. Related to this is the necessity to understand changes in the theory of gender and education. I would also argue that, in order to understand why some stereotypes about males and females remain so persistent, it is useful to understand where some of these stereotypes originated and how they have become deeply embedded in popular discourse. Therefore the next sections of this chapter are presented as follows:

- a brief historical overview of gender inequality and education;
- a brief discussion of the 'hidden curriculum' and how it may operate in some classrooms;
- a critical interrogation of the main concerns related to boys' underachievement;
- an exploration of emerging concerns related to girls in the contemporary classroom.

In order to develop your understanding of these issues, a series of questions and practical activities will be provided. These are designed for personal study and with a view to developing good practice.

Setting the scene: why is an understanding of history important for our understanding of contemporary gender issues in schools?

Our notions of what girls and boys 'can' and 'should' do are in many cases shaped by historical stereotypes, and education is no exception. Despite particular periods in history – for example, Anglo-Saxon and Elizabethan times, when the education of girls was given more credence than at most other times – in general the ideology of female educational provision has been that it should be both inferior to and different from that provided for men. As Kamm states:

> For the vast majority of girls of all classes, marriage was the real goal. If a girl stayed at home under her mother's eye, if she went to a village school, or boarded in a convent, or with a noble family, her prime consideration was to find a suitable husband.
>
> (1965: 28)

The nineteenth century saw a complex debate surrounding the nature of girls' education. Whereas some middle-class parents advocated the setting up of small private girls' schools, controversy raged over the wisdom of educating girls at all. Burstyn points out: 'The ideal to be produced by schools in the 19th century was one which rested in the prototype of the frail, protected woman of the middle classes' (1989: 145). Lewis describes the idealized notion of womanhood revealed by such writers as Ruskin and Coventry Patmore:

> A woman's fundamental task was to create a haven of peace, beauty and security for their husbands and children. The home was to be a sanctuary in which the wife reigned as guardian 'angel' in the words of Patmore, or as a Queen in the imagery of Ruskin.
>
> (1984: 81)

Official educational policy reinforced a separate and sexist education, which for girls was centred on preparing them for marriage and motherhood. For example, the Norwood Report argued: 'The grounds for including domestic subjects in the curricula are . . . firstly that knowledge of such subjects is necessary equipment for all girls as potential makers of homes' (1943: 127).

Activity

- How much do you think the ideology of marriage and motherhood continues to influence the life/educational choices of girls and boys today?
- Interview some older members of your family or friends about what influenced their educational opportunities and their choice of career.
- Repeat this exercise with younger people. What are the differences in their responses? Are there any similarities in what older and younger people say? Is there any sign of a lingering ideology of domesticity for some girls and women?

Historical perspectives on boys and educational achievement

Concern with boys' underachievement is nothing new. In his 1693 educational treatise, 'Some Thoughts Concerning Education', John Locke was addressing boys' underachievement and was concerned by young gentlemen's failure to master Latin despite spending years studying it. In 1923, the Board of Education stated: 'it is well known that most boys, especially at the period of adolescence, have a habit of healthy idleness' (1923: 120).

From the late nineteenth century, Cohen (1998) argues that there was a concern with the finite limitations of the body and a concern with the notion of 'overstrain'. The schools inquiry commission, the Taunton Commission, of 1868, was the first public assessment of the performance of boys and girls. It is interesting that the board noted girls' greater eagerness to learn than boys', but framed its discussion not in terms of how boys would keep up with girls but in terms of girls' over-conscientiousness and the fear that they would overstrain themselves. Cohen argues that:

The eager and achieving girl had become pathologized, while boys' underperformance was an expression of their 'traditionally' boyish ways . . . 'Overstrain' is thus a critical construct for a history of boys' underachievement, because it contributed to producing the underperformance of boys as an index of their mental health.

(1998: 27)

The differentiated education of boys and girls has a long history and, as we will see, old stereotypes remain deeply embedded in some places even when official policy has moved forward.

Towards gender equality in education?

The passing of the Sex Discrimination Act in 1975 saw boys' and girls' entitlement to the same curriculum in law. It could have been assumed, therefore, that gender discrimination in education was to be a thing of the past. Interestingly, however, the Department of Education and Science (DES) was remarkably reluctant to include education in the 1975 Sex Discrimination Act and was resistant to the implementation of major changes in schools designed to eradicate gender inequality (Arnot 1987; Skelton and Francis 2003). The studies of the 1970s and 1980s revealed that gender discrimination operated in schools at many different levels, indicating that education was a patriarchal institution dedicated to maintaining and reinforcing gender discriminatory practices and upholding the status quo. For example, the role models that children observed in school were found to be gender differentiated; women were more likely to teach younger children and have more pastoral responsibilities. Men, on the other hand, were found more often in the older age bands teaching technological subjects and were more visible in administrative and curricular responsibilities (Acker 1983). David (1984: 197) showed that the ethos of the school was dedicated to reinforcing notions of traditional male and female societal roles: 'The whole "hidden curriculum" of the school points to the different work of mothers and fathers . . . Mothers who take paid employment either have to find part-time work to suit school hours or make elaborate arrangements to cover childcare.'

The hidden curriculum of schools

Roland Meighan (1981) argues that the classroom is a 'haunted' place, pervaded by the messages of the 'hidden curriculum'. This he defined as all the other things that are learnt during schooling in addition to the official curriculum, or the subjects studied. The hidden curriculum involves such things as: teachers' attitudes; how much time they give to boys or girls; and who does the monitors' jobs – for example, boys carry PE equipment, girls water plants. Delamont (1983) argued that everyday life in school is permeated by sexist routines and practices. She noted that cloakrooms and playgrounds were often sex segregated, with boys dominating playground space. Registers were also often separated by gender, with boys' names being called first. Delamont also found that teachers frequently use gender to discipline children, with girls gaining approval for being neat, tidy and docile, while boys were complimented on being tough, brave and strong (ibid.). Girls were more likely to gain approval for wearing dresses rather than trousers and were often told, 'You've done enough fussing. I know you're all film stars' (ibid.). Pupils themselves monitored their peers' behaviour. Girls or boys who behaved in an inappropriate manner were either greeted with hostility or ignored. Teacher attitudes were also seen to be deeply gender differentiated, with many teachers stating a preference for teaching boys.

Kohlberg (1974) stated that children from about the age of 6 are 'fully fledged chauvinists'. They have a certain idea about what is correct behaviour. Even primary school children will choose not to work in mixed groups, and by age 9 the two sexes may vigorously avoid each other.

Activity: find out whether there is a 'hidden curriculum' operating in your school

- Carry out some research in your school to find out if attitudes to gender have changed. Use Sarah Delamont's headings to find out whether there is still a hidden curriculum operating in the primary school where you are based today.
- What issues have changed since Delamont carried out her research?
- Are there any aspects of her 'hidden curriculum' that still operate today?
- Investigate the interactions between boys and girls and adults in the classroom. Are there any differences? Does it make any difference if the adult is a man or a woman?

Continuing resistance to gender equality in education

Despite a wealth of evidence that pointed to the fact that practice in many classrooms was different for girls and boys, education still remained strangely unwilling to engage with issues of gender diversity. In her research into the attitudes of primary teachers, teacher trainers and teacher-training students towards gender issues, Thompson (1989) found that the predominant attitude of many education professionals was that of either complacency or hostility. Many of the teachers and teacher educators whom she observed and interviewed were complacent that gender inequality was not a concern in schools because child-centred education meant that everyone was treated 'as equal'. One of the teachers in Thompson's research commented, 'I don't see what all the fuss is about; we treat them all the same anyway' (ibid.: 68). Skelton (1989) also referred to the fact that a belief in child-centred methods caused 'gender blindness' in the PGCE students with whom she conducted her research. Other teachers and teacher educators in Thompson's research were found to be hostile to the idea that the issue of gender should have anything to do with the training of primary school teachers, as it was not an appropriate issue (1989: 74). One student had been refused permission by a member of college staff to undertake a special study on gender. Another student had had permission for a similar study refused by her teaching practice school. Her tutor had commented: 'It's very difficult in a public sector like education, which at its root is very resistant to change, very conservative . . . schools are sensitive to subjects like gender.'

More recent research by Skelton and Francis (2003) argues that the position of girls in primary schools has altered very little. They illustrate this argument with reference to teacher perceptions of girls' abilities and behaviour in the classroom. One of the lingering stereotypes about boys is that they are innately clever but unwilling to work, whereas any success that girls have is frequently put down to hard work and diligence rather than brilliance. Skelton and Francis (2003: 8) refer to some very able girls in Renold's (2000) study who were not seen by their teachers as clever but as 'bossy' and 'overconfident' and, in one case, 'not as clever as she thinks she is'. In contrast, boys in Maynard's (2002) study were regarded as having 'innate if untapped potential'. In terms of behaviour, Skelton (2002) found that girls who demonstrated behaviours that were not considered 'feminine' were described as 'pushy'. Reay (2001b) found that teachers described girls who were misbehaving as 'a bad influence' and 'spiteful little madams', whereas boys who exhibited the same types of behaviours were described as 'mucking about' (see Skelton and Francis 2003: 9). Nonetheless, as has been seen, any concern with how girls were positioned in classrooms quickly became eclipsed with the widespread outcry about boys' perceived failure to achieve academically. The next section of the chapter explores this complex and contested issue.

Activity

Listen to what adults who work in your school, including teachers, say about girls and boys. Are there differences in the way in which they talk about, or behave towards, them?

Failing boys: moral panics and simplistic statements

As we have seen, concern about the failure of some boys to engage with academic work is nothing new, so the question must therefore be asked: 'Why are we now so concerned with the underachievement of boys when for years there has been a covert acceptance that "boys will be boys" and "real boys don't work"?' (Epstein *et al.* 1998: 96). Mahony (1998) links this current preoccupation within the broader context of the introduction of market forces into education and increased competition within a globalized economy. She refers to the comments of Anthea Millett, chief executive of the Teacher Training Agency, who said:

> Everybody is now agreed that the top priority in education is the need to raise pupils' standards of learning . . . And there is a widespread awareness that, in a competitive world, constant progress is necessary just to maintain parity with other nations.

The introduction of the National Curriculum in England and Wales in 1988 was part of the increasing drive to reform and standardize education and to introduce market forces into schools (Ball 1994; Clarke and Newman 1997; Tomlinson 2005). The National Curriculum compelled boys and girls to take the same core curriculum subjects for the first time and, as part of a new drive to measure and audit performance, also introduced standardized tests at the end of key stages 1 and 2 (SATs). These initiatives led to the production and publication of league tables of GCSE results at secondary level and test results at primary level, which meant, in turn, that both the general public and educationalists could interrogate performance. As a result of this, for the first time, the extent of girls' success was revealed. Emphasis on boys' underachievement began in the mid-1990s with the publication of league tables related to schools' performance in SATs (standard assessment tasks). This happened in 1994 for secondary schools and in 1996 for primary schools.

Francis comments: 'Girls have been performing increasingly well in terms of attainment at GCSE level and their achievements at this level now equal or excel those of boys in all subjects' (2000: 7).

Like Epstein *et al.* (1998), I am not arguing that we should be unconcerned that boys do not appear to be performing as well as they should; however, what is of concern is that the achievement of girls has never been celebrated. In fact, as Francis (2000) points out, 'girls' improvements are often presented in the media as having been at the expense of boys'. As Arnot *et al.* (1999) observe, the improved achievement of girls has been problematized, leading to the denigration, rather than praise, of teachers' success with girls.

Furthermore, the notion that 'all boys underachieve' has been challenged as overly simplistic by commentators such as Epstein *et al.* (1998), Lingard and Douglas (1999), Francis (2000) and Forster *et al.* (2001). Exam results indicate that, in fact, performance is improving for both boys and girls, although boys' results are not improving as fast as those of girls. Furthermore, as Skelton and Francis (2003) argue, just as not all boys underachieve, neither do all girls succeed. The binary divide between boys and girls masks the differences between boys and boys and girls and girls. Skelton and Francis state:

> Groups such as middle-class white boys and Indian and Chinese boys continue to achieve highly. White working class, African Caribbean and Bangladeshi boys tend to underachieve in the British education system . . . white working class girls underachieve compared to their middle-class counterparts.
>
> (2003: 5–6)

It is clear that issues related to the perceived underachievement of some boys and the perceived success of some girls are by no means as clear and straightforward as they may appear at first sight. The statements advanced by some government organizations and reported by some sections of the media mask a situation which is infinitely more complex than that implied by headlines such as 'Girls Doing Well While Boys Feel Neglected' (*Guardian*, 26 August 1995).

Activity: attitudes to the 'problem of failing boys'

- What is the attitude of those who support the learning and teaching of children about the 'failing boys' issue?
- What sort of strategies have been introduced to help to remedy the situation? For example, have reading materials been changed in order to reflect an emphasis on more 'boy-friendly' materials? Is the emphasis on one or both genders?

Understanding gender theory . . . why is it important?

So far this chapter has explored some of the key issues related to gender diversity in the education of girls and boys. It has argued that, historically, education has been reluctant to engage with issues of gender inequality, including an unwillingness to include gender in the Sex Discrimination Act (1975). It has also noted the moral panic about boys' underachievement and pointed out that, in most cases, the success of girls seems to have attracted little popular acclaim. Although recent legislation (the Equality Act of 2006 and the Gender Equality Duty of 2007) has placed a legal duty on organizations to promote gender equality, old stereotypes remain remarkably persistent, and in order to understand why this may be the case, an understanding of gender theory may be helpful. The following section of the chapter explores some important theoretical perspectives and links these specifically to the issue of boys' underachievement.

The nature/nurture (culture) debate

Gender issues tend to arouse strong feelings and many of these are related to one's standpoint on 'the nature of gender'. By this I mean whether one believes that gender difference is based on biological differences and is therefore 'natural' and unchanging, or whether one believes that gender identity is socially constructed and is likely to change over time (or a mixture of the two). This is called the *nature/nurture debate* and it is very long-running and hotly contested.

Activity

What is your initial reaction to the nature/nurture debate? Which do you think is more important in a child's development?

Gender theory and the gap in gendered achievement

Francis and Skelton (2005: 75) provide a useful analysis of contemporary theories which have been advanced as explanations for the 'gender gap' in the United Kingdom. These are that:

- Boys and girls are naturally different and this explains discrepancies in achievement.
- Boys and girls have different learning styles.
- Pupils' constructions of gender produce different behaviours which impact on achievement.
- Schools are feminized and this disadvantages boys.
- Assessment procedures are biased towards boys.

These are explored in the next part of this chapter.

Some biological explanations for the 'gender gap'

One 'common sense' explanation for differences in gendered achievement takes an essentialist biological perspective which argues that boys and girls are born with different abilities and interests, and that this impacts on achievement. Evolutionary psychologists argue that gender differences simply reflect biological differences. This would argue that we are all predestined to certain gendered behaviours that are fixed and inevitable and will not change (Birkhead 2001). Neuroscientists such as Gurian (2002) offer a range of biological explanations for gender differences including the fact that the brain is 'wired differently', with boys and girls using different parts of the brain. However, these notions have been challenged as overly simplistic, and as Slavin points out:

> The most important thing to keep in mind about this debate is that no responsible researcher has ever claimed that any male–female differences on any measure of intellectual ability are large compared to the amount of variability within each sex. In other words, even in areas where . . . gender differences are suspected, these differences are so slight and so variable that they have few if any practical consequences.
>
> (1994: 130)

Francis points out that:

> there is yet no evidence to show that those (extremely slight) tendencies to differences in the brain are related to gendered patterns in educational achievement – whereas the evidence that achievement is affected by social factors is overwhelming.
>
> (2005: 79)

It is also of paramount importance to remember that the brain is a tensile organ that can develop in the same way as other organs (Paechter 1998). The argument here is that if different parts of the brain are given more stimuli, they are more likely to develop in different ways. So, for example, if boys are given toys that develop spatial awareness, then these skills are likely to be well developed.

Another 'popular' biologically based notion is that boys and girls have different learning styles (Duffy 2003; Maby 2004), and a 'natural' inclination towards certain subjects because of their different biological make-up. Traditionally curriculum subjects have been labelled as 'more suitable' for boys or girls, with boys favouring 'hard' subjects such as science, mathematics and information technology and girls leaning towards English and modern languages. Following on from this, it is argued that boys respond better to learning tasks involving rules and abstract facts, whereas girls respond to more 'open-ended' tasks and tasks which involve 'real life' situations (Murphy 1989; Arnot et al. 1998). However, it would seem to be fairly obvious that if learning was biologically driven there would be no female mathematicians, scientists or IT technicians, which clearly is not the case. Nonetheless despite evidence to the contrary, gendered discourses about learning and achievement are deep-seated and seem currently to be gaining in popularity. Indeed we seem to be engaged in a 'biological backlash', where theories about brain difference are once more predominant.

As Francis points out, 'in recent years there has been a re-emergence in arguments supporting brain difference' (2005: 79). As part of this biological resurgence, initiatives such as 'accelerated learning' in primary schools (the ALPS approach) have been enthusiastically taken up by many schools. Smith and Call (1999: 33) inform us that the ALPS approach is founded on 'nine brain-based principles'. It is not my intent to enter into debates related to brain-based techniques, but to note that 'common sense' assumptions about brain-based and gendered learning patterns and styles seem to have become part of popular discourse. In my years as a teacher trainer, I have frequently heard headteachers making sweeping statements to students to the effect that 'all boys' need kinaesthetic learning styles, and that girls are 'naturally' better at reading and writing. Statements such as these have become part of popular educational discourse but are made without reference to critical analysis and without any acknowledgement that these issues may be complex, contested and problematic. Even Gurian (2002) admits that there are as many differences between boys and boys and girls and girls as there are between girls and boys (Francis and Skelton 2005). The whole notion of learning styles in itself is problematic, and recent research (Coffield *et al.* 2004) has pointed to the fact that, just as there is little evidence to support the notion of gendered learning styles, there is little evidence to support the effectiveness of matching teaching styles to learning styles, and current strategies related to learning styles are misplaced. Francis and Skelton (2005) and recent research by Hughes (2007) have indicated that what matters for the achievement of both genders is good teaching that engages pupils rather than essentializing how boys and girls learn.

Socially constructed gender roles and impact on achievement

In contrast to those theorists who believe that gender differences are innate, there is an opposing body of thought which holds that society has a powerful role in influencing how we construct our identities (Davies 2003; Francis and Skelton 2005; Thompson 2006). Gender relational theory argues that how people create their identities is situational and relational, affected by such issues as class background, ethnicity, age and life experiences. In other words, we become who we are through the situations that we encounter and through social interactions. This theory accounts for the fact that not all girls and boys or women and men behave in stereotyped ways. For example, not all girls are quiet, hard-working and good at literacy, and not all boys are boisterous, like football and are good at maths. Gender relational theory argues that gender identities are socially constructed and boys and girls are active in creating their own identities according to dominant discourses. The construct of femininities in classrooms resides in being sensible, mature and self-effacing, whilst masculinity is associated with being demanding and assertive. For all age groups, the effect of peer group pressure is of paramount importance in creating the dominant discourses in classrooms and much research has been carried out into how primary and secondary pupils police each other's behaviour and punish those who fail to conform with established 'norms' (Lees 1992; MacNaughton 2000; Skelton 2001; Reay 2003). The dominant discourse in both primary and secondary schools currently appears, for the most part, to be that of an 'anti-academic laddish culture' which has a negative impact on achievement (Francis and Skelton 2005: 100). It could be argued that these dominant discourses are unhealthy for both boys and girls, but particularly for boys who want to achieve and are put under tremendous pressure to conform to an anti-school culture. My own observations of peer-group pressure bear out these arguments. Whilst working with a group of children who had failed their GCSEs I observed the efforts of a group of boys who had no interest in their resits to disrupt the studies of a friend who stood a good chance of success. It took a concerted effort on behalf of some teachers to persuade this boy not to give in to peer-group pressure not to work.

The feminized school?

Another 'popular' reason put forward for the underachievement of boys is that schools, particularly primary schools, are perceived as a feminized environment and in some way 'alien' to boys. Ralph Tabberer, chief executive of the Teacher Training Agency, has said: 'Many would be male primary teachers are dropping out of training or leaving the profession because they feel isolated in schools where nearly all the staff are female' (*Independent*, 23 April 2002).

This implies that there was a time when primary teaching was not a female-dominated profession. Indeed teaching, along with other caring professions such as nursing and social work, is one of the few professions traditionally deemed suitable for women because of its links to mothering and caring (Acker and Feuerberger 1996). However, although recent years have demonstrated a small increase in numbers of women and a small decrease in males entering the profession, Hutchings (2001) notes that male teachers are statistically more likely to become a headteacher than are their female colleagues.

As has been discussed earlier in this chapter, Delamont's (1983) analysis of the hidden curriculum as it operates in schools indicates that schools are patriarchal institutions. Since then, far from schooling becoming more 'feminized', more recent research suggests that, with the introduction of educational reform (Clarke and Newman 1997), it is more likely that schools have become increasingly masculinized. Educational reform has meant that schools, as well as other educational institutions, have entered the marketplace and have been forced into competition with each other. In a culture of target setting, audit and inspection, management styles, whether carried out by men or women, have become more masculinized, involving more diktat and less collaboration in the bid to survive in the educational marketplace (Reay and Ball 2000; Thompson 2001). As Francis and Skelton argue, 'the teacher's role has become increasingly focused on ensuring pupils achieve prescribed stages at certain ages in public tests' (2005: 93).

Haywood and Mac an Ghaill (2001) argue that schools have adopted an increasingly authoritarian system with increased surveillance and testing regimes which, far from producing a 'feminized' environment, have re-masculinized schooling.

Assessment procedures and teaching practices . . . biased in favour of girls?

Another argument put forward by some of those concerned with boys' underachievement is that testing procedures are biased in favour of girls. This is because, particularly in English, GCSE assessment is based on coursework, which, as Bleach (1998: 14) argues controversially, suits the 'diligent and plodding approach that is characteristic of girls'. Some elements of the media have called for a return to unseen examinations in the style of O Levels, which preceded GCSEs. However, Bleach (1998) notes that girls currently outperform boys in both coursework and 'sudden death' examinations. What does seem to be emerging from the research is that attitude and behaviour have more of an impact on assessment than any bias in assessment procedures (Mansell 2004). It could be that media and teacher 'obsession' about boys' underachievement has created a self-fulfilling prophecy, where boys 'know' that the dominant discourse is that to succeed at school is not for them.

Invisible girls and demonized boys . . . the twenty-first-century schooling scandal?

The current situation regarding gender equality in schools is worrying. We seem to be caught in a situation where boys are being constructed and are constructing themselves as 'anti-academic', a situation which is not helped by the barrage of media headlines that are likely to reinforce these perceptions. Recently I was concerned to see a session at an educational conference entitled 'What shall we do about the boys?' I have also been disturbed to hear students asking what they should do about having a 'boy heavy' class. My answer to both these questions is to say that 'you teach them', and this is not meant to be a flippant response. Hughes's (2007) research on gender and achievement in mathematics in a primary school showed that what is effective for raising achievement for both genders is effective, interesting teaching.

The other worry about the intensive focus on boys' underachievement is that girls run the risk of once more slipping off the educational radar. Not only do girls face the problem of becoming once more 'invisible' in the classroom (Spender 1981), but many teachers are under pressure to replace resources with those deemed to be 'boy friendly'. For example, a female headteacher of my acquaintance was in despair because she was being put under pressure to replace all her reading materials with ones that 'boys would find more appealing'.

Case study 1: how would you react in a situation such as this?

You are an NQT in your first teaching post and are attending a staff meeting about achievement; the focus of the meeting is, unsurprisingly, boys' underachievement. However, because of your knowledge about gender issues and your own investigation of gendered performance statistics on 'RAISEonline' you feel that the discussion should be about gender, rather than solely about boys' achievement. You also know that some girls in your class have underachieved quite significantly in mathematics. How would you try to persuade your colleagues that the 'achievement issue' is more complex than it may, at first sight, appear?

The fact is, of course, that not all boys are achieving, just as not all girls are achieving. It is true that many white middle-class girls are meeting with success in classrooms, but as we have seen earlier, in general this success has not been celebrated and the achieving girl has largely been ignored unless positioned in opposition to the 'moral panic' around the underachieving boy. Outcries about the feminization of classrooms and assessment techniques, flawed though many of these are, seem to go so far as to blame girls and women for boys' underachievement (Epstein *et al*.1998). Lucey (2001) argues that the presentation of the white middle-class girl as 'having it all' is an illusion. Lucey (2001) and Walkerdine *et al.* (2001) point out that being academic, with its long-time association with lack of sex appeal and femininity, means that being a high-achieving girl can lead to anxiety and has been linked to self-harm and eating disorders (Reay 2001a; Walkerdine 2003). If the achievements of middle-class white girls have not been celebrated, as Francis and Skelton point out (2005: 108), while working-class girls are, in general, outperforming working-class boys, they are still, in the main, underachieving. In terms of minority ethnic achievement, Mirza (1992) argues that girls tend to be either ignored or problematized. As she notes, the educational performance of British African-Carribean girls has been conflated with that of British African-Carribean boys, while the achievements of minority ethnic girls are linked to notions of a ruthlessly oppressive home culture (Archer and Francis 2007). Despite the changes in the overall pattern of gendered performance, there remain some traditional similarities in the subject choices of boys and girls that are significant in resistant pay gaps between men and women. Although Francis (2000) found that both girls and boys named English as their favourite subject and many girls like mathematics, when speaking of most disliked subjects stereotyped patterns remain. Lucey (2003) points out that by 11 boys have an advantage in mathematics and science, and this is maintained through GCSEs, A Levels, degree subjects and employment.

The importance of teacher attitudes

Reay (2001b) argues that one subtle yet influential influence impacting on girls' subject choices is the attitude of teachers. As has been noted earlier in this chapter, there is evidence that some teachers have markedly different attitudes to the behaviour and expected performance of boys and girls (Reay 2001b; Skelton 2002; Skelton and Francis 2003). So, if teachers have different expectations for both the behaviour and the achievement of boys and girls and perceive their approaches to school work differently, it is quite likely that some teachers will consciously or unconsciously steer children to what they see as appropriately gendered subjects.

Making a difference

I would argue that the practice of gender equality in some classrooms is in danger of re-visiting earlier inequalities. Recent legislation (Gender Equality Duty 2007) provides a basis for gender equality in law; however, as we have discussed in this chapter, issues related to the gender gap in achievement seem in some cases to be based on populist and unsubstantiated arguments. No matter where you are in the journey towards understanding gender relations in education, it is important to be aware that what you do as an individual to promote equality is crucial. Understanding and challenging inequality can be difficult, time consuming and stressful, but having the commitment to do so is vital.

As we have seen, in an attempt to address the 'problem of boys' there is a danger of rushing headlong into simplistic and arguably ineffective 'solutions'. From my own experience of working with teachers and trainees over a number of years, I have noticed an increasing number of trainees wanting to carry out studies on 'boys' underachievement' with a view to 'doing something about it', but having no awareness of the complexity of the situation. Skelton and Francis (2003: 15) believe that before teachers can develop gender-relational strategies for working with primary children, they need to examine their own preconceptions of gender as well as examining those of the children.

They suggest that those who work with children in schools might raise their own awareness by asking the following sorts of questions.

Activity: find out about your own preconceptions regarding how boys and girls 'should' behave. Ask yourself:

- Do I expect children to behave differently according to their gender?
- Do I want children to behave differently?
- Do I think that there are ways of being a 'proper boy' or a 'proper girl'?
- How do I feel when children act differently to how, stereotypically, boys and girls 'should' behave?
- Do I think of boys and girls as being homogeneous groups?
- Do I attempt to challenge the ways in which boys and girls practise gender in the classroom?
- What messages about gender are being given in the curriculum materials that I use?
- Are the toys that children play with giving them messages about the 'correct' way to be a boy or a girl?

In addition . . . get involved!

Put gender issues as an item on a staff meeting agenda . . . you never know, there might be other teachers who think the same way that you do.

Conclusion

To intervene actively and to confront stereotypical thinking in both children and adults can be both time consuming and challenging. However, not to do so means that girls and boys may not achieve as well as they could and may not be educated in a genuinely inclusive educational environment. As someone who is engaged in teaching children, at whatever level, it is your job to take steps to make sure that this does not happen.

Bibliography

Acker, S. (1983) 'Women and Teaching: A Semi-Detached Sociology of a Semi-Profession', in S. Walker and L. Barton (eds) *Gender, Class and Education*. London: Falmer Press.

Acker, S. and Feuerberger, G. (1996) 'Doing Good and Feeling Bad: The Work of Women University Teachers'. *Cambridge Journal of Education*, 26 (3), 401–22.

Archer, L. and Francis, B. (2007) *Understanding Minority Ethnic Achievement*. London: Routledge.

Arnot, M. (1987) 'Political Lip-Service or Radical Reform?' in M. Arnot and G. Weiner (eds) *Gender and the Politics of Schooling*. London: Unwin Hyman.

Arnot, M. and Weiner, G. (eds) (1987) *Gender and the Politics of Schooling*. London: Unwin Hyman.

Arnot, M., Gray, J., James, M. and Ruddock, J. (1998) *A Review of Recent Research on Gender and Educational Performance* (Ofsted Research Series). London: The Stationery Office.

Arnot, M., David, M. and Weiner, G. (1999) *Closing the Gender Gap*. Cambridge: Polity Press.

Ball, S. J. (1994) *Education Reform: A Critical and Post-Structural Approach*. Buckingham: Open University Press.

Birkhead, T. (2001) *Promiscuity: An Evolutionary History of Desire*. Cambridge, MA: Harvard University Press.

Bleach, K. (ed.) (1998) 'Why the Likely Lads Lag Behind', in K. Bleach (ed.) *Raising Boys' Achievement in Schools*. Stoke-on-Trent: Trentham Books.

Board of Education (1923) Report on the Differentiation of Curricula Between the Sexes in Secondary Schools. London: HMSO.

Browne, N. and France, P. (1985) 'Only Cissies Wear Dresses: A Look at Sexist Talk in the Nursery', in G. Weiner (ed.) *Just a Bunch of Girls*. Milton Keynes: Open University Press.

Burstyn, J. (1986) in V. Beechey and E. Whitelegg (eds) *Women in Britain Today*. Milton Keynes: Open University Press.

Clarke, J. and Newman, J. (1997) *The Managerial State*. London: Sage.

Clarricoates, K. (1978) 'Dinosaurs in the Classroom: A Re-Examination of Some Aspects of the "Hidden Curriculum" in Primary Schools'. *Women's Studies International Quarterly*, 1 (4), 353–64.

—— (1980) 'The Importance of Being Ernest . . . Emma . . . Tom . . . Jane: The Perception and Categorisation of Gender Conformity and Gender Deviation in Primary Schools', in R. Deem (ed.) *Schooling for Women's Work*. London: Routledge & Kegan Paul.

Coffield, F., Moseley, D., Hall, E. and Ecclestone, K. (2004) *Should We Be Using Learning Styles? What Research Has to Say to Practice*. London: Learning and Skills Research Centre.

Cohen, M. (1998) 'A Habit of Healthy Idleness: Boys' Underachievement in Historical Perspective', in D. Epstein, J. Elwood, V. Hey and J. Maws (eds) *Failing Boys?* Buckingham: Open University Press.

David, M. (1984) 'Women, Family and Education', in *The World Yearbook of Education: Women and Education*. London: Kogan Page.

Davies, B. (2003) 'Death to Critique and Dissent? The Policies and Practices of New Managerialism and of "Evidence-Based Practice"'. *Gender and Education*, 15 (1), 91–103.

Delamont, S. (1980) *Sex Roles and the School*. London: Methuen.

—— (1983) 'The Conservative School', in S. Walker and L. Barton (eds) *Gender, Class and Education*. London: Falmer Press.

Department of Education and Science (1975) Sex Discrimination Act. London: HMSO.

Duffy, M. (2003) 'Achievement Gap' (TES Friday). *Times Educational Supplement*, 15 November 2003, 15–18.

Epstein, D., Elwood, J., Hey, V. and Maw, J. (1998) *Failing Boys? Issues in Gender and Achievement*. Buckingham: Open University Press.

Equality Act (2006) London: HMSO,

Forster, V., Kimmel, M. and Skelton, C. (2001) 'Setting the Scene', in W. Martino and B. Meyenn (eds) *Teaching Boys: Issues of Masculinity in Schools*. Buckingham: Open University Press.

Francis, B. (2000) *Boys, Girls and Achievement*. London: Routledge Falmer.

—— (2003) 'Introduction: Boys and Girls in the Primary Classroom', in C. Skelton and B. Francis (eds) *Boys and Girls in the Primary Classroom*. Maidenhead: Open University Press.

—— (2005) 'Explaining Gendered Achievement', in B. Francis and C. Skelton, *Reassessing Gender and Achievement. Questioning Contemporary Key Debates*. Abingdon: Routledge.

Francis, B. and Skelton, C. (2005) *Reassessing Gender and Achievement. Questioning Contemporary Key Debates*. Abingdon: Routledge.

Gender Equality Duty (2007) London: HMSO.

Grocott, M. (1989) 'Civil Service Management', in I. Taylor and G. Popham (eds) *An Introduction to Public Sector Management*. London: Unwin Hyman.

Gurian, M. (2002) *Boys and Girls Learn Differently!* San Francisco: Jossey Bass.

Haywood, C. and Mac an Ghaill, M. (2001) 'The Significance of Teaching English Boys: Exploring Social Change, Modern Schooling and the Making of Masculinities', in W. Martino and B. Meyenn (eds) *What About the Boys?* Buckingham: Open University Press.

Hughes, C. (2007) 'Girls' Underachievement'. Unpublished MA (Ed) dissertation, University of Chichester.

Hutchings, M. (2001) 'Towards a Representative Teaching Profession: Gender'. Paper presented at the University of North London, 11 December.

Jackson, D. (1998) 'Breaking out of the Binary Trap: Boys' Underachievement, Schooling and Gender Relations', in D. Epstein, J. Elwood, V. Hey and J. Maw (eds) *Failing Boys? Issues in Gender and Achievement*. Buckingham: Open University Press.

Kamm, J. (1965) *Hope Deferred: Girls' Education in English History*. London: Methuen.

Kohlberg, L. (1974) 'Stages in the Development of Psychosexual Concepts and Attitudes', in A. Oakley (1981) *The Division of Labour by Gender*. Milton Keynes: Open University Press.

Lees, S. (1983) 'How Boys Slag Girls Off'. *New Society*, 66 (1091), 51–3.

—— (1992) *Sugar and Spice*. London: Penguin.

Lewis, J. (1984) *Women in England 1870–1950: Sexual Divisions and Social Change*. Sussex: Wheatsheaf Books.

Lingard, B. and Douglas, P. (1999) *Men Engaging Feminisms*. Buckingham: Open University Press.

Lobban, G. (1975) 'Sex Roles in Reading Schemes'. *Educational Review*, 27 (3), 202–10.

Locke, J. (1989 (1693)) *Some Thoughts Concerning Education*, edited by J. S. Yolton and J.W. Yolton. Oxford: Clarendon Press.

Lucey, H. (2001) 'Social Class, Gender and Schooling', in B. Francis and C. Skelton (eds) *Investigating Gender*. Buckingham: Open University Press.

Lucey, H., Brown, M., Denvir, H., Askew, M. and Rhodes, V. (2003) 'Girls and Boys in the Primary Maths Classroom', in C. Skelton and B. Francis (eds) *Boys and Girls in the Primary Classroom*. Maidenhead: Open University Press/McGraw-Hill Education.

Maby, T. (2004) 'How to Turn Boys onto Studying, Independent Education and Careers'. *Independent*, 21 October, 4–5.

MacNaughton, G. (2000) *Rethinking Gender in Early Childhood Education*. London: Paul Chapman Publishing.

Mahony, P. (1998) 'Girls Will Be Girls and Boys Will Be First', in D. Epstein, J. Elwood, V. Hey and J. Maw (eds) *Failing Boys? Issues in Gender and Achievement*. Buckingham: Open University Press.

Mansell, W. (2004) 'Teachers Mark Down Bad Boys'. *Times Educational Supplement*, 26 March, 3.

Maynard, T. (2002) *Exploring the Boys and Literacy Issue*. London: Routledge/Falmer.

Meighan, R. (1981) *A Sociology of Educating*. London: Holt, Rinehart and Winston.

Millett, A. (1996) Chief Executive's Annual Lecture. London: Teacher Training Agency.

Mirza, H. (1992) *Young, Female and Black*. London: Routledge.

Murphy, P. (1989) 'Gender and Assessment in Science', in P. Murphy and B. Moon. (eds) *Developments in Learning and Assessment*. London: Hodder and Stoughton.

Norwood Report (1943) Report of the Committee of Secondary Schools Examination Council on Curriculum and Examinations in Secondary Schools. London: Board of Education/HMSO.

Office for Standards in Education and Equal Opportunities Commission (1996) *The Gender Divide: Performance Differences Between Boys and Girls at School*. London: HMSO.

Paechter, C. (1998) *Educating the Other*. London: Falmer.

Reay, D. (2001a) 'The Paradox of Contemporary Femininities in Education: Combining Fluidity with Fixity', in B. Francis and C. Skelton (eds) *Investigating Gender*. Buckingham: Open University Press.

—— (2001b) 'Spice Girls, Nice Girls, Girlies and Tomboys: Gender Discourses, Girls' Cultures and Femininities in the Primary Classroom'. *Gender and Education*, 14 (4), 153–66.

—— (2003) 'Troubling, Troubled and Troublesome: Working with Boys in the Primary Classroom', in C. Skelton and B. Francis (eds) *Boys and Girls in the Primary Classroom*. Buckingham: Open University Press.

Reay, D. and Ball, S. (2000) 'Essentials of Female Management: Women's Ways of Working in the Education Market Place?' *Educational Management*, 28 (2), 145–59.

Renold, E. (2000) '"Square-Girls", Femininity and the Negotiation of Academic Success in Primary School'. *British Educational Research Journal*, 27 (5), 577–88.

Skelton, C. (ed.) (1989) *Whatever Happens to Little Women?* Milton Keynes: Open University Press.

—— (2001) *Schooling the Boys*. Buckingham: Open University Press.

—— (2002) 'Constructing Dominant Masculinity and Negotiating the Male Gaze'. *International Journal of Inclusive Education*, 6 (1), 17–31.

—— (2005) in B. Francis and C. Skelton, *Reassessing Gender and Achievement. Questioning Contemporary Key Debates*. Abingdon: Routledge.

Skelton, C. and Francis, B. (eds) (2003) *Boys and Girls in the Primary Classroom*. Buckingham: Open University Press.

Slavin, R. (1994) *Educational Psychology: Theory and Practice*, 4th edn. Boston: Allyn and Bacon.

Smith, A. and Call, N. (1999) *The ALPS Approach*. Stafford: Network Educational Press.

Spender, D. (1980) *Man Made Language*. London: Routledge and Kegan Paul.

—— (1981) 'Education: The Patriarchal Paradigm and the Response to Feminism', in D. Spender (ed.) *Men's Studies Modified: The Impact of Feminism on the Academic Disciplines*. Oxford: Elsevier.

—— (1982) *Invisible Women: The Schooling Scandal*. London: Writers and Readers.

Stanworth, M. (1981) *Gender and Schooling*. London: Women's Research and Resources Centre Publications.

Thompson, B. (1989) 'Teacher Attitudes: Complacency and Conflict', in C. Skelton (ed.) *Whatever Happens to Little Women?* Milton Keynes: Open University Press.

—— (2001) 'A Thankless Task? Women Managers in Initial Teacher Education'. Unpublished paper presented at the annual conference of the British Educational Research Association, Leeds.

—— (2006) 'Gender Issues in the Primary Classroom', in G. Knowles (ed.) *Supporting Inclusive Practice*. London: David Fulton.

Tomlinson, S. (2005) *Education in a Post-Welfare Society*, 2nd edn. Maidenhead: Open University Press/McGraw Hill.

Walkerdine, V. (2003) 'Reclassifying Upward Mobility: Femininity and the Neoliberal Subject'. *Gender and Education*, 15, 237–47.

Walkerdine, V., Lucey, H. and Melody, H. (2001) *Growing Up Girl. Psychosocial Explorations of Gender and Class*. London: Palgrave.

Chapter 4

Children who are gifted and talented

Gianna Knowles

Introduction

The aim of this chapter is to explore what it means when we say a child is gifted or talented. It discusses a range of research to provide a guide for what behaviours gifted and talented children might display. The chapter also explores the Department for Children, Schools and Families (DCSF) definition of gifted and talented, since it defined the terms in a specific way, which can cause confusion. The last part of the chapter discusses what constitutes barriers to learning for these children. In some ways it seems at odds with the very terms 'gifted' or 'talented' that such children should experience any barriers to learning. Indeed, far too often they have been seen as the 'lucky' ones. It can seem unfair that while some children struggle for years to try to gain some proficiency in reading, writing or basic mathematics, gifted children seem to have no problem in competently completing work that is well in advance of what children of their age can normally achieve; or where some children struggle to make any meaningful marks on paper, a talented child can draw objects that look extraordinarily true to life. However, research has shown that where children do not have their gift or talent recognized and planned for, such neglect can lead to children failing to reach their potential, often becoming bored and disaffected. In the saddest cases these children become so disruptive that they are excluded, or so bored that they simply refuse to attend school.

What do we mean by gifted and talented?

Before exploring who the gifted and talented children might be and how best they can be supported in schools, what is meant by gifted and talented must be explored. The DCSF (now the Department for Education (DfE)) definition of gifted and talented is:

'Gifted and talented' describes children and young people with an ability to develop to a level significantly ahead of their year group (or with the potential to develop those abilities):

- 'gifted' learners are those who have abilities in one or more academic subjects, like maths and English;
- 'talented' learners are those who have practical skills in areas like sport, music, design or creative and performing arts.

Skills like leadership, decision-making and organisation are also taken into account when identifying and providing for gifted and talented children.

(www.direct.gov.uk 2010)

However, while the then DCSF made a distinction between 'gifted' and 'talented', many experts use the terms interchangeably. Therefore, when discussing the terms, it is necessary to be sure whose definition is being used.

Case study

Eddie is now 14. He could walk at 10 months and displayed highly developed speech and reasoning powers at an early age. For example, as a 3-year-old, he would say in discussions: 'I want to make three points: point one . . .', and he would explain his first argument; 'point two . . .', and he would explain the second reason, 'and point three . . .'. As a young child he was not interested in learning to read; however, he was very able in work with numbers at an early age.

When he was 4 Eddie could already tell the time. Until this point Eddie had never slept through the night, but once he made the connection between numbers on a digital clock and how they measured how long he needed to be asleep he slept through. At age 6 he initiated a discussion about infinity, having worked out for himself that if you begin counting from 1 along the number sequence *1, 2, 3, 4,* etc., there will always be one more number, and you could go on forever.

However, throughout nursery and school he has found it difficult to find children of his own age to form close friendships with. He has friends with whom he enjoys practical activities – football, riding his bike and playing at game consoles – but often turns to adults for company and conversation. He finds it difficult to deal with the 'robust' nature of school life, and the unpredictability of others' behaviour – both pupils and teachers – to the point where the thought of having to go to school makes him very anxious.

Having outlined how the DCSF approach differentiates between gifted and talented children, the next few sections of this chapter will explore other concepts which are often used in discussions of the subject; for example, intelligence and creativity. Having discussed these terms of reference, it will then be possible to more helpfully explore how gifted and talented children can be supported and included in school.

Intelligence

Currently, the concept of intelligence held by most Western psychologists is that it involves 'the ability to carry out abstract problem solving' (Gardner *et al.* 1996: 2). The ability to think in terms of abstract ideas and concepts involves the aptitude to grasp relationships and patterns, particularly where such relationships and patterns cannot be detected by other methods – for example, through the senses. The senses can be used to see colours and hear music, but abstract thinking is needed to solve abstract and logical reasoning problems such as those below.

1   Insert the word that completes the first word and begins the second:

PRACT(. . .)BERG

2   Find the odd word out:

BLOW
NOPOS
LETAP
DHATUMB

3   Insert the missing word:

ORBIT(RILE)WHEEL
ARSON( )STEMS

4   Insert the missing number:

196(25)324
329( )137

5   What is the next number in the series?

18   10   6   4   ?

(Eysenck 1966: 25)

Being able to solve the problems in the example above tests only a part of what the brain is capable of; in this instance abstract thinking and logical reasoning. At the present time, in Western societies, the ability to carry out such tasks is often used as a measure of intelligence, sometimes so as to award an individual an intelligence quotient, or IQ score. However, in terms of thinking about an inclusive school and an inclusive society, it is important to consider that abstract and logical reasoning abilities are only part of a child's capabilities. Further to this the notion that abstract and logical reasoning abilities are the only abilities that denote intelligence is also a cultural convention. Different concepts of intelligence exist between different psychologists and different cultures.

The needs of different cultures vary and change over time. In a society like Britain's, where wealth and success is dependent on those who can rapidly assimilate and process information and perform certain problem-solving tasks quickly and efficiently, the detection of potential problem solvers is important. Similarly, the identification and cultivation, through the school system, of such abilities will be paramount.

Since the 1980s there have been challenges to the Western cultural notion that only the ability to be proficient at abstract problem solving denotes intelligence. The strongest challenge has come from Howard Gardner in his work on multiple intelligences (Gardner 1993). In *Frames of Mind* (1993: 8), Gardner argued for the existence of several intellectual competences, which he referred to as *intelligences*. Gardner suggested that humans possess 'one or more basic information-processing operations' designed to deal with specific kinds of input (ibid.: 63). We might recognize a particular input as belonging to an area of experience we can name as a conventional curriculum subject – for example, music, or a bodily kinaesthetic area such as dance or football. In most people, one such intelligence will be more pronounced than the others. The notion that we might define intelligence in a range of ways and that children may have a *dominant intelligence*, or preferred way of learning and demonstrating what they have learnt, is now more widely accepted. Indeed as part of the National Strategies support materials, there is 'the multiple intelligence quiz' (www.nationalstrategies.standards.dcsf.gov.uk 2010). The test is designed to help children and teachers determine an individual's predominant intelligence. The eight intelligences are: linguistic, logical-mathematical, visual-spatial, bodily-kinaesthetic, musical, interpersonal (working with others), intrapersonal (quiet, reflective, preferring to do things alone) and naturalist (interested in the environment, plants and animals) (ibid.). Working with these intelligences, or learning styles, in the classroom is discussed further in Chapter 9.

Although traditionally the marker of a gifted and talented child is that he or she possesses the capacity to reason in an abstract, logical way more efficiently, or faster, than other children of a similar age, the assessment of intelligence may be more complex than previously thought. Therefore, in terms of supporting gifted and talented children in the classroom we need to be aware of a range of factors. Firstly, that a child may be gifted in terms of academic subjects, or that they may be talented in terms of performance abilities. Secondly, that giftedness or talentedness may be manifested in a range of ways, not just through a narrow scope of subjects such as language and mathematical ability.

How can we tell if a child is gifted or talented?

In 2010 the Qualifications and Curriculum Development Agency stated, 'being gifted and talented covers much more than the ability to succeed in tests and examinations. For example, gifted and talented learners may demonstrate leadership qualities, high-level practical skills or a capacity for creative thought' (www.qcda.gov.uk 2010). They also warned that where gifted and talented children go unnoticed they may actually underachieve.

While the QCDA agreed that checklists to 'spot' gifted and talented children can be helpful, it warned that these must not be used as the only ways to assess a child for gifted or talented status. As much as it is possible to generalize about children, those who may be gifted or talented are likely to:

- think quickly and accurately;
- work systematically;
- generate creative working solutions;
- work flexibly, processing unfamiliar information and applying knowledge, experience and insight to unfamiliar situations;
- communicate their thoughts and ideas well;
- be determined, diligent and interested in uncovering patterns;
- achieve, or show potential, in a wide range of contexts;
- be particularly creative;
- show great sensitivity or empathy;

- demonstrate particular physical dexterity or skill;
- make sound judgements;
- be outstanding leaders or team members;
- be fascinated by, or passionate about, a particular subject or aspect of the curriculum;
- demonstrate high levels of attainment across a range of subjects, within a particular subject, or aspects of work.

Schools also need to be aware that because gifts and talents can 'lie outside the standard curriculum', again, they can go unnoticed (www.qcda.gov.uk 2010). Or children may not be given the opportunity to develop their talents in school; for example, if they are talented in music or dance.

Activity

All Special Educational Needs and Disability (SEND) policies should make reference to gifted and talented children. Next time you have an opportunity to look at a school's SEND policy, ensure that you are aware of:

- How the school identifies and monitors the achievement of gifted and talented children.
- What happens in individual classrooms to meet the needs of gifted or talented children.
- What additional provision there is for gifted and talented children, particularly for those in performance areas of the curriculum.

Case study

While undertaking some literacy work with a year 6 class, a teaching assistant noticed how interested two children were in the writing activity, which involved looking at newspaper articles. The TA herself was also interested in writing, and talked to the teacher about working with the children to write a class newsletter. The teacher agreed that this would be a good extension activity for the children, who were in the high ability group for literacy.

The TA and the two children produced the first newsletter, which turned out to be so popular they decided to do another one. Now the newsletter is published twice a term and contains articles covering news about the whole school. The children who were engaged in writing the first edition have moved on to secondary school, but the newsletter continues to be written and published by year 6 children who show a particular interest or ability in writing, planning and organizing the newsletter.

Creativity

Many writers on intelligence and gifted and talented status believe that beyond a certain threshold of intellectual ability there is an additional skill called 'creativity'. The defining attributes of creativity 'can be described as combining the following five characteristics: using the imagination; a fashioning process; pursuing purpose; seeking originality; and judging values' (Wilson 2005: 18). Particularly, it would seem, creativity is evidenced by an ability to generate something new or innovative, often through interaction with others' ideas, or with current knowledge and understanding. It is about reflecting on what is known, or exists already, and being able to create new links between ideas, or to find solutions to problems (ibid.). The more popular use of the term 'creativity' is often linked to the notion that for someone to have a creative idea it must be entirely original. However, in the classroom, children will be very creative without necessarily *inventing* new things. To view creativity as resulting only in a product is to focus only on the measurable output of the creative process. All thinking is creative if an idea is new to an individual, or if it involves solving a problem or making sense of a complex idea.

The Qualifications and Curriculum Development Authority's (QCDA) definition of creativity

The QCDA stated that there are four principles to creativity and being creative.

1   thinking or behaving *imaginatively*;
2   that this imaginative activity is *purposeful*;
3   that these processes must generate something *original*; and
4   that the outcome must be of *value* in relation to the objective.

(www.curriculum.qcda.gov.uk 2010, my emphasis)

In a classroom, children use their imagination to generate images and ideas, and many children do this. But creativity requires that these ideas must be acted upon: a piece of art created, a dance idea explored, an approach to solving a mathematics problem tried out, a poem written, a new football team formation tested, food ingredients combined in a different way. If the idea and the action are new to the child, then in the sense of how the term creativity is being explored here, the ideas and actions are original.

The QCDA also stated that part of the creative process requires that the product or the action can be critically evaluated; that those working with children in these creative ways

> need to help pupils judge the value of what they and others have done through critical evaluation. This means asking questions such as, 'Does it do the job?', 'Is it aesthetically pleasing?', 'Is it a valid solution?', 'Is it useful?' and sometimes teachers' and pupils' views about what is worthwhile and valuable may differ.

(ibid.)

Creativity, like intelligence, is one of a range of factors we need to consider when thinking about children's gifts and talents. However, we can see from the QCDA's definition of what constitutes creativity, that for children to have the opportunity to explore their creativity and to demonstrate how creative they are, they will need a range of experiences to be provided for them. If the main experience for children in school is of learning literacy and numeracy, only those who are particularly able in those subjects will ever have their gifts or talents noticed. In the same way, if we are really interested in knowing which children are gifted or talented, and believe creativity to be part of being gifted or talented, creativity will not be found through giving children conventional intelligence tests, since these measure only particular ways of thinking and conventional knowledge, rather than the imagining and generation of new or original ideas (Porter 1999: 28).

Cognitive (thinking) skills

This chapter has already introduced the idea of thinking skills in relation to the discussion about intelligence and creativity. This section explores what is meant by thinking skills and abstract and logical reasoning. Then, through a more detailed analysis of the terms, it helps the reader distinguish between intelligent behaviour and gifts or talents. Cognition refers to our ability to process information; it is essentially the brain's capacity to acquire, store, retrieve and apply knowledge. In gifted children it would seem that their cognitive abilities are more efficient or better able to undertake these activities than is usually the case with children of a corresponding age.

Determining which children are gifted in terms of cognitive ability: knowledge acquisition, storage, retrieval and application

We have already explored how, until recently, gifted children were seen as those who were particularly skilled in terms of their cognitive ability. While we have seen that gifts and talents may be broader than this, it is still important to know what the cognition of children gifted in this area looks like, particularly since we will need to be able to recognize it in such children.

Cognitively gifted children are those who are seen as having a wider and deeper knowledge base than their peer group, despite the two having experienced similar learning opportunities. This may be because gifted children are faster at acquiring knowledge and more efficient at storing and retrieving it. Children who have this capacity become increasingly more competent in particular subject areas, because of this ability to acquire and recall knowledge with such efficiency. Similarly, having acquired a broader and deeper knowledge base than is usual for children of a similar age, gifted children are then able to apply it to abstract and complicated subjects; for example, time (Porter 1999: 57). A further indication that children are gifted in these capacities, over and above what might be expected for children of their age, is the ability to use and apply metacognition. Metacognition in gifted children is the ability to focus: the ability to define the particular nature of a task and select the information and skills that are needed to complete it, including the use of metamemory to scan for relevant information and possible, already stored solutions. It also includes the ability to apply knowledge or previously tried solutions in an innovative way; to synthesize information – that is, take information from a range of perhaps seemingly unrelated sources and work it together to find a solution (which may involve, or appear to involve, creativity). Children who are gifted in this way will also be able to elaborate on and develop ideas and to evaluate – that is, test – whether a solution to a problem is viable (Porter 1999: 57). Again, the model we have just explored is very similar to the QCDA's definition of creativity.

Measuring gifts or talents

> High performance in tests does not mean gifted.
>
> (Sternberg and Davidson 2005: 55)

Regard this as a health warning about using particular types of test as the only measure of intelligence. Similarly, this is a warning about using correlation between performance outcomes in tests as the only measure of ability. To look at the results a child scores in any particular test or end of key stage task is to start with the outcomes first, and if they are far above average for what is expected for that age range, the temptation is to trace that outcome back to 'gifted' ability.

However, tests are very particular in what they measure. For example, one of the skills a times table test measures is recall and memory of a particular set of facts. That these facts, in this instance, are mathematical does not necessarily mean that a child who does well in such tests is a gifted mathematician. For example, a good score, even an above average score, in a times tables test cannot be used as the sole evidence for claiming that the child is therefore a gifted mathematician who understands the concept of numbers, multiples and factors. To establish if a child is a gifted mathematician, the fact that he or she scores well in times tables tests might be an indicator of a gift, but would not be the only evidence required. For example, the child's understanding of such concepts as multiples and factors would have to be investigated through an activity: it would be possible, for example, to observe how a child applies knowledge and understanding of multiples and factors in a problem-solving activity.

'The Department for Children, Schools and Families (DCSF) developed a suite of National Quality Standards for Gifted and Talented (G&T) Education in England' (DCSF 2009). The standards are recognized by Ofsted as benchmarks for good practice in identifying and meeting the needs of gifted and talented children (Parkman 2007: 6).

A summary of the standards

A school that is working with or to meet the standards with regard to provision for its gifted and talented children will have in place, or be developing, the procedures and practices summarized below (www.nationalstrategies.standards.dcsf.gov.uk).

Gifted and talented children are *identified* through an agreed school understanding of what it means to be gifted and talented. Systems are in place in all year groups, which screen children annually against a clear set of criteria. A range of evidence to establish if a child is gifted or talented is collected, and those deemed gifted or talented are monitored on an ongoing basis. This information is also used to identify exceptional achievement or underachievement. Those children who are recognized as gifted or talented reflect the school's social and economic diversity. For example, if one-third of the school is comprised of children from an Asian heritage, one-third of the children deemed gifted or talented will be from that group. The gifted and talented policy is seen as being integral to the school's inclusion policy.

Having identified which children are gifted or talented, schools provide for their gifted and talented children a stimulating *learning environment* where the teaching and learning strategies are diverse and flexible. Teaching and learning is differentiated and challenging and includes independent learning, breadth, depth and pace. There is also a focus on new technologies and personalized learning.

Levels of *attainment and achievement* for gifted and talented pupils are comparatively high in relation to the rest of the school and inspection evidence indicates that gifted and talented provision is very good or excellent.

The *curriculum* provided is flexible, with opportunities for enrichment and diversity in subject/topic choice. Children are enabled to work beyond their age and/or phase, and across subjects or topics, according to their aptitudes and interests. The curriculum offers *personalized learning* pathways for pupils which maximize individual potential.

Monitoring and assessment strategies employed by the school are used to plan for progression in pupils' learning and to ensure challenge and sustained progress. Dialogue with children provides focused feedback, including peer and self-assessment, which is used to plan future learning. Systematic oral and written feedback helps children to set challenging targets. Information about gifted and talented children is passed on, and acted on, when children transfer to new schools.

The school recognizes the importance of clear *leadership* in creating the ethos and managing the provision for gifted and talented children. For example, the head-teacher actively champions gifted and talented provision; related staff development is provided and the school sets high expectations, recognizes achievement and celebrates the successes of all its pupils. It budgets for resources to support gifted and talented children.

Parents/carers are aware of the school's/college's policy on gifted and talented provision, contribute to its identification processes and are kept informed of developments in gifted and talented provision, including through the school profile. There are opportunities for pupils to learn beyond the school/college day and site (extended hours and out-of-school activities).

The DCSF definition of gifted ability is useful, up to a point. It helps schools identify children who have 'high ability in one or more academic subjects' – but the downside of this definition, as we have seen, is that it determines giftedness in a way that is often dependent on the outcome of test results, or predicting how well a child might achieve in tests. The other problem with this definition of gifted ability is that it is no predictor of potential, other than in particular curriculum tests used by the British education system. It is no indicator of how a child's ability in any particular subject or field might develop later in life.

A last word on talent

The DCSF defined talented children as being those who have a 'High ability in sport, music, visual arts and/or performing arts' (www.direct.gov.uk/ 2010). Many experts, writing about gifts and talents and about performance, do not limit themselves to meaning 'performance' in the way suggested by the DCSF. That is, children who are talented are said to be so when their unusually proficient outputs are related to performance endeavours. However, many of the attributes we have explored in relation to gifts would seem to also apply to talents. That is, a child may be talented if he or she is able to perform at a level above what might be expected; is able to understand the knowledge base of the area of endeavour faster than might be expected for a child of that age. A talented child may be one who is creative and innovative in the area of endeavour, and who is able to demonstrate skills in the area at a level higher than might be expected for a child of that age.

As discussed above, we have seen how one of the markers for identifying a gifted child is that he or she possesses the capacity to reason in an abstract logical way, and can do so more efficiently than other children of a similar age, or faster and with greater effect than is the norm. We have also seen how the focus of what is thought of as intelligence is dependent on the presence of these attributes, particularly as they relate to specific academic curriculum subjects. However, it is possible to argue that a talented musician possesses a faster and above-average ability, in terms of what is usually expected for his or her peer group, to reason in an abstract way – but musically – as does a talented dancer, or a child who is good at art or sports. To perform any act requires the application of skills, knowledge and understanding, and to perform it unusually well – that is, to be talented in that performance – is to have the above-average ability to think in abstract terms and apply skills, knowledge and understanding creatively.

As a child gifted in mathematics can solve mathematical problems, sometimes without being able to articulate how, so a talented dancer may be able to interpret through physical movement an idea or concept without being able to explain how. One of the greatest services Gardner's work on multiple intelligences has done for the gifted and talented debate is to change, particularly in the West, the notion that some abilities are of greater value than others; that is, that a child who is gifted in an academic subject is more special than a child who is talented in a performance-based subject. Through Gardner's work it is increasingly apparent that *intelligence* can be manifest in any number of ways; and it is only when the potential of a talented dancer is spotted, developed and encouraged that the potential can be realized – as with a child who, early on, demonstrates a gift in mathematics. It is not possible to score goals in football, or netball, or to produce an outstanding piece of art without being able to think in an abstract way – to understand the possibilities of the application of known skills, knowledge and understanding and to apply them in a novel or creative way.

If some gifted children go undetected in schools, then how many more talented children are failing to be detected in schools, particularly where the focus of the curriculum may be on literacy and numeracy at the cost of marginalizing dance, drama, many aspects of PE, and music? As Cross and Coleman, in Sternberg and Davidson (2005), state:

> Some talents are developed entirely outside of school, whereas others are developed in schools to a considerable extent. Some talents are in domains that schools have key roles in developing, others may have no direct relationship to a school's curriculum.
>
> (Sternberg and Davidson 2005: 52)

Barriers to learning

It seems at odds with the notion of gifts and talents to think in terms of gifted or talented children experiencing barriers to their learning, or to the fulfilling of their potential. However, we have already explored how limited notions of what may constitute gifts or talents, or a restricted curriculum, can mean that some gifted and talented children can be overlooked. Gifted and talented children who are not being appropriately 'stretched' in their learning may become bored and frustrated. As children get older this can result in behavioural problems and truancy.

Children who are gifted or talented can experience other barriers to learning as well. For example, a gifted child's social skills may often be advanced compared with age peers. Where this happens the child may become frustrated with age mates, as they may be unable to play at the level the gifted child is playing at. This can lead to the gifted child resorting to solitary play and, in some cases, becoming friendless and isolated. In some instances this can lead to bullying. Again, perhaps surprisingly, gifted children can sometimes appear to be emotionally immature. This may indeed disguise their giftedness (Porter 1999: 52). Since 'a gifted child's highly attuned nervous system contributes both to advanced learning and an increase in their emotional sensitivity. Again, this may disguise their giftedness' (ibid.: 26).

Case study

Eddie always refers to adults if he wishes to talk over anything he has learnt at school or picked up from the television. Where the information may cause him distress he can become seemingly morbidly obsessive or emotionally very dependent and 'clingy' towards trusted adults. For example, watching news reports about such events as those in New York on 11 September 2001, and the subsequent war with Iraq, made him very upset. As a gifted child he could understand the import of what he was seeing, but did not have the experience in terms of age to put it into a context. Therefore he became very insecure and in need of a trusted adult's presence.

The gifted child is able to take on board and understand more information than is usually the case for children of the same age. For example, a child picks up knowledge and information from a whole range of day-to-day contacts. Information may be collected incidentally from such sources as the television, overheard news reports, adult conversations or conversations between older children, newspapers, magazines, etc. Sometimes the child will pick up information that is distressing, as he or she is able to understand the content but is too young to put it into the context of life experience which would enable them to manage it. It may also be the case that children are unable to discuss this kind of information with their age peers. Although friends often are a source of comfort, because they do not process the same information at the same level, they dismiss events more readily than the gifted child. Because gifted children may feel overwhelmed and confused by some of the information they are trying to deal with, they may seek constant reassurance from adults and appear over-sensitive or clingy. Porter discusses the work of Jackson and Butterfield (Porter 1999) and Roeper (ibid.) in this area, stating that while the ability to gain and retain knowledge is usually thought of as advantageous, 'it can propel gifted children into examining abstract issues before they have the emotional maturity to cope' (Porter 1999: 54).

Similarly, talented children may be able to perform in such a way that the adults around them fail to support children in coping with their talent. A talented child may react in a way markedly different to their peer group when exploring a work of art, piece of music or dance. Children may become very involved in the experience, and if the cause of this is not recognized, such children can be labelled as being 'over-sensitive', 'highly strung' or 'dreamers'. In the same way, children who possess a particular sporting talent may become bored and frustrated by working with children who do not match their level of performance. In the worst cases, where a school does not recognize gifts or talents within an inclusive ethos, children who are markedly different from their peer group because they are gifted or talented can become isolated from the group, and in some instances can become victims of bullying.

Assumptions about children's home backgrounds can lead to schools failing to recognize children who are gifted or talented

Some studies of gifted children, particularly those focusing on identifying gifts in young children, have found that a preponderance of those children identified by schools as being gifted come from home backgrounds that can be described as middle class (Porter 1999: 53). Two things may be happening here: the first factor to consider is that some children come from home backgrounds that are aware of, and engage with, those societal norms that are recognized, prized and rewarded by schools – for example:

- punctual and regular attendance at school;
- the ability to converse articulately in the language in which learning is conducted – in this instance, English;
- parental interest in the child's schooling, attendance at parents' meetings and supervision of homework; and
- parental involvement with reading at home, regular bedtimes, healthy diet, monitored television watching and playing of electronic games, etc.

Where young children are already socialized into behaviours recognized by school, it may be more straightforward for a school to identify gifts. A young child who comes to school from a home background that is less able to provide these conditions, or who has limited understanding of the language the learning is conducted in and the culture the subjects are derived from, may present difficulties which mask their gifts. That is, if the first factor is to do with what is happening at home, the second factor is to do with what is being expected by the school. That the school does not recognize gifts in some children, because of behaviours they are bringing from home and their apparent difficulty in dealing with the school environment, means that the school identifies gifts by how well adjusted children are to school life, rather than in terms of potential to learn at a faster rate or perform above the average for age peers. The school, through the content of the tasks it presents, may also make assumptions about the cultural background of the child and assume prior knowledge and understanding that the child does not possess. For example, not all cultures contain the same fantasy creatures, like fairies or dragons. Therefore, if a child has not grown up hearing stories about fairies and dragons, or seeing them in pictures or on television, and is asked to write a story containing such creatures, that child may appear to be working at a level lower than expected.

Case study

In a multi-ethnic inner-city school, one of the mothers approached the headteacher asking if she could run an after-school dance club. She had been a talented dancer as a child, having trained in classical Indian dance, but as a teenager had moved into modern Indian dance in the 'Bollywood' style. The mother said that she knew that her daughter Somy and her friends were interested, and she felt that her daughter had a talent for dance, but the school had no facilities to develop such a talent.

Initially the headteacher was resistant, but the mother persisted. The club proved very successful, with first girls, and after a while some of the boys, joining it. The children who wanted to dance came from a variety of cultural backgrounds. The club represented the school at a number of community arts events and always danced at school open days and summer fêtes. The club gained sponsorship from a local business and was able to travel to wider dance events.

Somy has left primary school now. However, her mother continues to run the club and Somy now does some of the teaching. Because of her talent, which was 'spotted' at one of the club's performances, Somy was encouraged to apply for a grant to fund a trip to India to take some classical Indian dance training. Somy takes her GCSEs this year and is undecided about what to do next. She is unsure about whether to pursue dance in Britain or to try to raise the money to return to India for more classical training. However, she is very clear that if her mother hadn't seen her talent and persuaded the school to let her run a dance club she would not have had the opportunity to realize her talent.

Activity

In the next PE lesson you are a part of, note how the children who are particularly talented in this area are planned for and supported in the session. Is there specific planning to ensure that their needs are met – that is, are they given challenges and activities to work on that extend their current level of performance?

In the next art lesson you are a part of, note how the children who are particularly talented in this area are planned for and supported in the session. Is there specific planning to ensure that their needs are met – that is, are they given challenges and activities to work on that extend their current level of performance?

In the next few lessons you are a part of, look to see if the gifted children are provided with challenges and learning experiences that challenge them. Are they simply expected to do 'more of the same' or have appropriate extension activities been planned for them?

Some children may be gifted in areas outside conventional curriculum subjects – for example, in personal, social, citizenship and health education (PSCHE) – and, just as children gifted in terms of mathematical understanding need challenges, so, too, do children gifted in this area. Many schools are good at recognizing gifts in traditional curriculum subject areas and providing for these children; however, providing for a child who has an above-average understanding in terms of non-conventional curriculum subjects can be more challenging. Just as children develop knowledge and understanding of English and mathematics, so, too, do they pass through stages of development in terms of moral understanding. In his work Kohlberg described children as moving through a range of developmental stages from babyhood to adolescence, and these stages are linked to the development of moral skills, knowledge and understanding, just as Piaget outlined a range of stages linked to cognitive development. For Kohlberg, children begin at stage 1, where they behave in an egocentric way, not understanding that their actions can have a consequence for the welfare of others. They progress to stage 2, where they know that there are correct and incorrect ways to behave, but only because this is what they have been told. It is not until stage 3 that they begin to understand that rules about behaviour have reasons behind them, and at stage 4 they can understand how rules are part of wider society's collective functioning. Children who are particularly gifted in this area may also be able to explain and explore differing moral points of view and be able to reason philosophically in ways far in advance of their peers (Reimer et al. 1990). Problems occur for these children when they are able to grasp notions out of step with those of their peers. For example, a child who is gifted in this area may be at stage 3, while his or her peers may be at stage 1 or 2. The gifted child understands notions of sharing, while the children around him may not. The gifted child may be in a peer group where children only share when an adult tells them to, and other children will grab egocentrically at desired objects; the gifted child can become upset and frustrated because he or she *can* understand how to share, indeed *why* sharing is important. These experiences may leave the gifted child feeling isolated from their friends and let down by the adults who seem to be indulging the 'naughty' children who are grabbing.

Conclusion: a different sort of differentiation

Borland, in Sternberg and Davidson (2005), writes:

> along with my colleagues in the gifted-education field, I believe that high-achieving or high-ability students are among those who are the most ill-served when curriculum and instruction are not differentiated.
>
> (Sternberg and Davidson 2005: 2)

Cross and Coleman (Sternberg and Davidson 2005) agree with this statement, adding that:

> having a group with unrealized potential is unacceptable because students are supposed to perform near their potential. The typical reply to this situation is to assert that the child has some problem that is inhibiting his or her development.
>
> (Sternberg and Davidson 2005: 56)

With regard to ensuring an inclusive curriculum that meets the needs of gifted and talented children, schools must guard against the pitfalls described by Cross and Coleman below:

> Environments that are unresponsive to rapid learning have inadequate resources relevant to a domain and provide no models for development and inhibit advanced development. Impoverished environments have the most pervasive negative effect . . . some contexts promote the development of the individual more than others.
>
> (Sternberg and Davidson 2005: 60)

This chapter has examined what is meant by gifts and talents, and it has sought to explore what barriers to learning and achievement a gifted or talented child might encounter. Gifted and talented children possess incredible potential, but as Sternberg and Davidson state, unless the context is there for a child to thrive, the gift or talent may never be realized, and, to date, there has been an ongoing concern in the field of gifted and talented education about the underachievement of such children (ibid.: 60). Many schools now have procedures for identifying gifted and talented children and have enrichment programmes to help children to realize their potential. However, while most schools have become very effective in providing for children who have difficulties grappling with learning at the level deemed the norm for their age, many schools still have a long way to go to provide an effective curriculum differentiated to meet the needs of the gifted and talented.

Bibliography

DCSF (2009) 'The Classroom Quality Standards for Gifted and Talented Education: A Subject Focus'.

Eysenck, H. J. (1966) *Check Your Own IQ*. London: Penguin.

Gardner, H. (1993) *Frames of Mind*. London: Fontana Press.

Gardner, H., Kornhaber, M. and Wake, W. (1996) *Intelligence: Multiple Perspectives*. Fort Worth, TX: Harcourt Brace.

Gross, U. M. (2005) *Exceptionally Gifted Children*, 2nd edn. London: Routledge/Falmer.

Parkman, M. (2007) *National Quality Standards in Gifted and Talented Education User Guide*. Mouchel Parkman, available at: http://nationalstrategies.standards.dcsf.gov.uk/node/195324?uc=force.

Porter, L. (1999) *Gifted Young Children: A Guide for Teachers and Parents*. Buckingham: Open University Press.

Reimer, J., Pritchard, D., Paolitto, D. and Hersh, H. R. (1990) *Promoting Moral Growth from Piaget to Kohlberg*, 2nd edn. Prospect Heights, IL: Waveland Press.

Sternberg, R. J. and Davidson, J. E. (2005) *Conceptions of Giftedness*, 2nd edn. Cambridge: Cambridge University Press.

Wilson, A. (2005) *Creativity in Primary Education*. Exeter: Learning Matters.

Winstanley, C. (2004) *Too Clever by Half*. Stoke-on-Trent: Trentham Books.

Websites

www.curriculum.qcda.gov.uk/key-stages-1-and-2/learning-across-the-curriculum/creativity/whatiscreativity/index.aspx (accessed 17 February 2010).

www.direct.gov.uk/en/Parents/Schoolslearninganddevelopment/ExamsTestsAndTheCurriculum/DG_10037625/ExamsTestsAndTheCurriculum/DG_10037625 (accessed 16 February 2010).

www.nationalstrategies.standards.dcsf.gov.uk/node/83386 (accessed 16 February 2010).
www.nationalstrategies.standards.dcsf.gov.uk/node/96614?uc=force_uj (accessed 17 February 2010).
www.qcda.gov.uk/1960.aspx (accessed 17 February 2010).

Chapter 5

Children with autism and Asperger's syndrome

Diana Seach

Introduction

We are now seeing an increased prevalence of children being diagnosed with autism and Asperger's syndrome. The National Autistic Society (NAS) statistics (2007) suggest that one in a hundred children are likely to fall somewhere on the autism spectrum, although many fewer will actually receive a formal diagnosis. Lathe (2006) suggests that the inclusion of autism-related conditions in the diagnostic criteria may be the reason why rates appear to have increased. Whilst there is no concluding evidence as to the reasons for the increase in the number of individuals (including adults) receiving a diagnosis, it has meant that schools have had to look carefully at how they provide for children with autism and Asperger's syndrome.

The Inclusion Development Programme (2009), as part of the Labour government's strategy for promoting equality and opportunity for pupils with special educational needs, aims to support schools in raising awareness of the autism spectrum to ensure effective access to education. Our understanding of the autism spectrum has altered considerably over the years, and whilst research has played a large part in this, the views of parents and individuals with autism and Asperger's themselves have also contributed to a shift in our thinking. Inclusion and inclusive pedagogy has also brought about developments in the language used to describe individuals who think and respond in ways that we might describe as different to our own. In the past few years, the description of individuals as having an 'autistic spectrum disorder' or ASD has been challenged by those individuals as failing to reflect how they regard themselves: as understanding the world in a different, rather than a 'disordered' way. Similarly, the more recent use of 'autism spectrum conditions' or ASC maintains a focus on medical diagnosis, which may inappropriately lead to autism being regarded as an illness and therefore curable. In light of this, I will refer to children as having autism or Asperger's syndrome (AS), and follow the terminology used in the Inclusion Development Programme (2009) to describe their position on the autism spectrum.

A predominance of behavioural and cognitive approaches to teaching children with autism are now being reconsidered in the light of more inclusive practice, and I intend to discuss this further within this chapter. Nind (2000) points out that interactive approaches which focus on a facilitative approach to teaching are equally valid, and yet rarely acknowledged in terms of supporting children's access to the curriculum.

In this chapter I will be highlighting how important it is to focus on children's learning needs in relation to their developmental profile, rather than in terms of deficits in skills.

As Beaty (cited in Knowles 2006) states: 'to ensure full inclusion it is essential that practice is rooted within an understanding of developmental theory' (Knowles 2006: 51). This gives us a much greater opportunity to recognise each child's strengths and abilities and how they can be used to enhance the child's learning and interactions with others. To illustrate this, the following conversation was recounted to me by a parent.

Mum: What did you learn at school today?
Tommy: Nothing.
Mum: Your teacher told me that in maths you were learning numbers up to 20.
Tommy: I already know my numbers up to 100 so there's no point in only learning up to 20.

What is the autism spectrum?

Autism is recognised as neuro-developmental delay or damage that can present with varying degrees of severity and varying levels of intellectual functioning. In the DSM-1V-TR (2000), the latest version of the American Psychiatric Association's Diagnostic and Statistical Manual, the different subtypes of autism and Asperger's syndrome and related conditions are described using a set of generalised criteria. These include examples of behaviours that show significant differences in the development of social interaction, communication and more flexible ways of thinking and behaving. These core features have been described as the 'triad of impairments' (Wing 1996), with a set of separate and well-defined characteristics that are frequently described as deficits. However, as I shall describe in the following sections, these core features are both inter-related and developmental, and will manifest differently between individuals due to the underlying cause or aetiology; hence, the *autism spectrum* (see Figure 5.1). Whilst these criteria are useful tools for diagnosis, they also need to be considered within the socio-cultural context specific to the individual.

The diagram in Figure 5.1 is in no way intended to be a complete picture of the autism spectrum, but it serves to illustrate how a whole range of factors will impact on children's developmental potential. In addition, some children will also experience physical and psychological difficulties such as epilepsy, attention deficit hyperactivity disorder (ADHD), mental illness and digestive problems. It is through careful observation and awareness of the particular difficulties experienced by individuals that practitioners can gain a greater understanding of their unique developmental profile.

Current brain research has played a key role in understanding what happens in the neural development of those with autism and why some individuals develop with significant difficulties in language and communication, social engagement and responding to the feelings of others (Boucher 2009). For example, a greater emphasis is now being placed on studying the different areas of the brain and how they affect emotional responsiveness, face recognition and sensory processing. As it is not possible to discuss this research in detail here, further references are recommended at the end of this chapter.

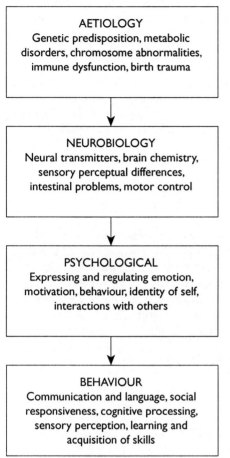

AETIOLOGY
Genetic predisposition, metabolic disorders, chromosome abnormalities, immune dysfunction, birth trauma

NEUROBIOLOGY
Neural transmitters, brain chemistry, sensory perceptual differences, intestinal problems, motor control

PSYCHOLOGICAL
Expressing and regulating emotion, motivation, behaviour, identity of self, interactions with others

BEHAVIOUR
Communication and language, social responsiveness, cognitive processing, sensory perception, learning and acquisition of skills

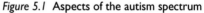

Figure 5.1 Aspects of the autism spectrum

What does it mean when a child has received a medical diagnosis of autism or Asperger's syndrome?

Where there is evidence of more severe neurological damage, developmental assessments and a subsequent diagnosis of autism usually occur before a child reaches school age. In such cases many children will attend school with a statement of special educational needs. However, there will be a number of children – particularly those who are higher functioning or who have Asperger's syndrome – where their difficulties become more evident as a result of their increased participation in the social learning environment of school. This means teachers in key stages 1 and 2 having to spend time in discussions with parents and other professionals to decide how they can best support such children's learning. For practitioners it can be difficult to know what resources they need during this assessment period, and therefore regular discussions with parents are essential.

In seeking to provide an inclusive environment for a child who has a diagnosis of autism or Asperger's syndrome, school staff need to ensure that they remember that, despite the diagnosis, the child's individual personality will also influence how he or she behaves and relates to others. This will affect any assessment of the impact of the condition on the child's ability to learn and interact with others. Schools also need to be aware that different families respond in different ways to the diagnosis, and not always in the ways that professionals expect. Staff also need to be aware that a child with autism or Asperger's will not have global delay in all areas of development, but may have additional learning needs such as dyslexia or dyspraxia, or problems with motor co-ordination and sensory processing. The most important thing is that the school focuses on the personal and developmental needs of the child rather than the deficits associated with the diagnosis, so that teaching can be personalised – albeit in ways which may be very different from methods used for others who do not have autism.

Case study

Because I was supporting a boy with Asperger's in the classroom, I was given some training about autism. I worked with Simon for a whole year and really got to know him. I became really interested in autism and learnt a lot from his parents. When the headteacher asked me to support another boy in another class I thought it would be fine, as I'd worked well with Simon and he'd made lots of progress. How wrong I was! Phillip was a different story altogether, and now I'm struggling to understand what I can do to help him.

Teaching Assistant

This comment highlights how difficult it is to have a 'one size fits all' approach to teaching children on the autism spectrum. In the following sections, I have therefore described the features of autism from a developmental perspective rather than using a deficit model. At the end of each section there are some examples of inclusive practice that may or may not already be evident in your school setting. They are intended to provide a better understanding of the impact that having autism has on children's learning in the classroom, and describe some practical and positive ways to support all children's learning and developmental potential.

Communication and language

Communication arises from a desire to interact with another person. This is evident from early childhood and is fundamental to how children develop an understanding of the 'self' and gain knowledge of others and the world around them. Any disturbance in functioning, such as in autism, is likely to impair this sense of relatedness and the subsequent ability to interpret or understand one's own emotional states and those of others. Similarly, the use of eye contact, taking turns and sharing attention are fundamental to how children learn what communication is. Understanding the pragmatics of communication is the basis for the development of speech and language, and is essential for developing skills in relating to others (Potter and Whittaker 2001). Trevarthen (2004) suggests that without this innate desire to engage in the rhythmic act of communicating our learning and interaction with

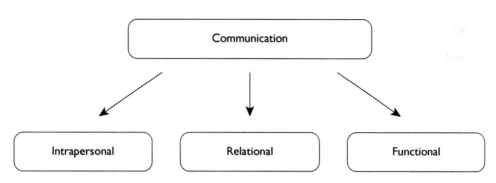

Figure 5.2 Teaching communication skills

others become impaired. Approaches to teaching communication skills need to ensure that they don't just focus on the functional use of communication but also help children to express themselves and relate to others in meaningful and positive ways.

Children who are less competent in communication will be reliant on others to teach them, so that all aspects of their learning are supported. Behavioural approaches to teaching communication have tended to focus on what the child needs to do in order to respond in ways that meet the adult's expectations. To give rewards for communicating undermines the natural process of engagement that is fundamental to the development of the skill of inter-relating. As Nind and Hewett state, communication as a first-hand experience is irreplaceable – far more effective than a learned experience – and therefore 'the reward for communicating is communicating' (Nind and Hewett 1994: 67).

Teaching communication is a two-way process involving the child and his or her relationship to:

- the environment;
- the adults in the classroom;
- peers.

The provision of a communication-rich environment will help children to make connections with their own internal states, as well as develop a sense of a shared cultural identity. In their research, Potter and Whittaker (2001) found overriding evidence that children with autism benefit most from an environment which provides opportunities for them to develop spontaneous communication. The importance and frequency of these communicative opportunities should enable children to:

- gain and maintain the attention of an adult in positive ways;
- request and initiate an adult's help;
- express emotions;
- influence the feelings and actions of others;
- follow the ideas of others;
- gain independence;
- develop interdependence.

Activity

Have you seen classrooms that are communication-rich environments? Consider the points above and use examples from your own practice in relation to this table. Are there any changes you would like to make or anything you would like to add?

Clearly defined areas	Labelled resources and equipment	Interesting displays	Visual timetable	Group and individual work areas
Computer access	Task preparation	Task discussion	Supportive information	Opportunities for social interaction

Visual systems of communication

In most classrooms today teachers and teaching assistants are using a wide range of methods to support children's communication and language development. The use of visual systems of communication, computerised communication aids and interactive whiteboards has had a significant impact on how children learn and have access to the curriculum. Language, like thought, is a symbolic form of communication that is dependent upon shared meanings and can be represented in a variety of different ways, using pictures, signs and symbols.

Case study

Before we were advised to use picture symbols to help Jack understand what was happening, he would just run around the classroom not knowing what to do. He never picked up cues from the other children when they sat down on the carpet or lined up at the door. When he wanted to go outside and it wasn't playtime he would start to scream or find something to throw, which wasn't very nice for the other children. As a staff, we didn't know what we could do to help him understand, we thought it would take some time and that he would get used to the routines eventually. With help we were advised to start with a few picture symbols and every time we were going to start a new activity we showed him the picture. It was amazing. Within a week he knew what they were for and stopped running around the room. The great thing was that all the other children would look at the pictures too to see what was on the timetable. It's become a really essential part of our wall display in the classroom.

Teacher in year 1

As this example shows, children who are less confident in using language may feel that withdrawing from verbal communication is preferable and that other forms of expression and non-verbal behaviour are more effective. Spoken language, as a means of conveying messages to others, is regarded as the most important measure of communicative competence. Williams (1998) describes her early experiences in learning about language as a sensory experience linked to feelings about objects and people rather than the words or labels she was given. As she got older her understanding changed. As she describes:

> When I was 10, I could hear sentences just fine, even repeat them back as I'd heard them, but I could only process a few disjointed words in each sentence. Words were cues for my monologues and not part of a dialogue.
>
> (Williams 1998: 243)

Whilst some children with autism may have limited skills in verbal communication, those who are higher functioning or who have Asperger's syndrome are likely to be extremely competent in their language use. However, as Powell and Jordan (2001) suggest, this can mask their difficulties with social communication and comprehension. Using an augmented communication system – for example, visual information – may still be relevant but it will need to match the child's level of functioning and not replace a system that the child is already using. As practitioners we can refer to other professionals for guidance on the most effective methods for individual children but we also need to be careful that an over-reliance on one particular system doesn't reduce the child's ability to be spontaneous or to engage in positive interactive experiences with their peers.

The adult's role

Regardless of whether a child has a language delay or difficulties in processing language, the adult's role is to provide a model of interaction that acknowledges the developmental path towards helping children to become more competent communicators. Rather than restrict our language to 'short sharp phrases' or instructions, we need to help children to value the expressive use of language as a tool for relating. They need to experience more relaxed forms of language, such as occurs in conversations and humorous situations. Griffiths (2002) also suggests avoiding the over-use of prompts and questions as this can lead to less spontaneous communication and generalised interaction. It also helps to use confirmation rather than too much repetition, as repetition can cause children to block out and lose the meaning of what is being said to them. In order for children to develop greater understanding of how to relate to others, they need reassurance that their efforts to communicate are valued.

'Where's Mrs Clarke?'
'She's not in today.'
'Where's Mrs Clarke?'
'I told you she's not here today.'
'Where's Mrs Clarke?'
'Don't keep asking me, I've told you she's not here, she's sick.'

As a communicative partner we have a responsibility to assist the child sensitively and empathetically in using more effective means of communication.

'I understand that you are upset because Mrs Clarke is not in today. Mrs Clarke cannot come to school today because she is sick. She needs to stay at home and get better. Perhaps if we sit down together and write her a letter, she would know that you are missing her. I'm sure that would make her very happy.'

Activity

The next time you have the opportunity to consider how a school is promoting positive communication in the classroom, look for the aspects of good practice suggested below.

- Before children begin a task, do they understand what they are being asked to do?
- Are ideas communicated through means other than verbal language? For example, through using objects, pictures, photos, symbols and words and in different formats, such as labels, lists, information sheets, cartoons, posters and computers?
- Are language skills taught to enable children to use language to make relationships and relate to each other? That is, are children encouraged to make use of the intra-personal, relational and functional aspects of communication to express themselves, through using language to say, 'You look sad today, what's the matter?' Or, 'Please let me have the bike when you have finished playing on it.'
- Children who have difficulties using language will use their behaviour to express how they are feeling about themselves, others and their environment. What strategies do you see children being given to enable them to let you know how they are feeling?
- All children enjoy opportunities to relate to others in a more relaxed and less demanding way. Are play, drama and games being used to help children with autism or Asperger's syndrome learn how to interact with others?

Social interaction

Experts in the field of autism have stressed for many years that children with autism are not asocial (Frith 1991; Wing 1996; Jordan and Powell 2001; Attwood 2006). As highlighted in the previous section, it is more relevant to consider how differences in social behaviour are linked to difficulties in communication and the child's level of intellectual functioning. From early infancy it is the emotional connection that adults develop with the child which leads to increased social understanding and engagement with others. Stern (2003) points out that the relationship between the infant and its caregiver develops through the reciprocal, emotional patterning of their interactions. This sensing or reacting to social stimuli in meaningful and positive ways leads to significant changes in the child's cognitive development (Vygotsky 1978). It is not that parents of children with autism fail to socially stimulate their child but that the child's capacity for interaction may be affected by the extent of the neurological damage. The greater the child's difficulty in interpreting and making sense of others' social behaviour, the more likelihood there is that they will withdraw, preferring their own company and focusing on their own interests. Studies by Hobson have also shown that how we socially engage with others is fundamental to how we develop empathy with others: 'We need to realise that one of the most powerful influences on development is what happens *between* people' (Hobson 2002: 7).

Children need to feel secure in their interactions with others in order to learn from them. If they are uncertain they may respond by:

- not seeking out others to develop friendships;
- not wanting to interact with others; or
- making attempts to interact that are considered by others to be inappropriate.

Williams (1996) describes how when she was younger, most of her approaches to her family members and other people were an attempt to establish control. Because social interaction was something she found confusing, like many children with autism and Asperger's syndrome she developed interests in objects and activities to compensate and to establish a sense of connectedness. Classrooms are designed as social environments in which to learn, but for many children with autism and Asperger's syndrome they can be confusing and frightening places. As a consequence these children may find it difficult to focus on activities, and so learning becomes more difficult.

Case study

Since starting at school, May has had an interest in playing in the sand tray with some plastic animals. If we didn't take her to other activities I think she would have stayed there all day. We tried to encourage other children to play with her but as soon as they went near her she moved away from them and spent her time looking out of the window. Then we had an autism advisor come and observe her. She suggested putting plastic animals in other places around the classroom and in the outside area. When May noticed them she would spend a few minutes playing with them with other children near her. Now she will accept other children being close to her. She still likes to spend time at the sand tray but at least she is moving around the classroom a lot more and developing an awareness of the other children, even if she is not playing with them.

Teacher in a Reception Class

The extent to which a child develops social understanding will depend on the individual's abilities, the context in which the interaction takes place and the way in which relationships are established. Very few studies have looked at how social and cultural differences affect social development in children with autism and Asperger's syndrome, but this also needs to be taken into account, particularly when planning social skills programmes for children. In a report for the NAS, 'Missing Out? Autism, Education and Ethnicity' (Corbett and Perepa 2007), parents from black and ethnic minority (BME) communities were less satisfied with their child's academic and social progress compared with their white British counterparts. One of the reasons identified related to how the developmental milestones were used in diagnosis, particularly with the criteria for social communication, which are culture-specific to white, mainstream British groups. The recommendations were that schools needed to take much more account of how autism-specific social skills are being taught in schools and whether they are appropriate and relevant for the individual based on his or her cultural background.

The 'Removing Barriers to Achievement' document (DFES 2004) states that all children should have opportunities to learn, play and develop alongside each other, within their local community of schools, with shared responsibility and a partnership approach to their support. However, in the *Make School Make Sense* report (Batten *et al.* 2006), parents stated that their children received very little in the way of social skills training. If their son or daughter with Asperger's syndrome was coping well academically, then they received less social support but they were still very vulnerable to being bullied, made fewer friends and spent a lot of time alone.

Schools tend to adopt their own social skills programmes, depending on the resources they use or the additional support offered for children with autism. Where children have access to a separate unit or class within the mainstream school, often social skills training will take place with groups of children who also have additional learning needs. Some schools have adopted the Nurture Group scheme, where children are selected to spend a regular amount of time with a specially trained support worker and teacher. The focus of these sessions is to provide a safe and relaxing environment and to support children's social learning through developmentally appropriate games and activities. Impact studies (Sonnet 2008; Scott and Lee 2009) showed significant improvements in children's social and emotional development and learning in the classroom. However, they also acknowledged that other factors such as the number of sessions and underlying emotional problems and family circumstances also affected the level of improvements made.

Activity

- What strategies have you seen employed in the classroom to promote social interaction and ensure that all children are included?
- Are there places in the school or classroom where children can go to be part of a smaller group, or be by themselves?
- Who does the child with autism or Asperger's syndrome spend most time with, or does the child prefer to work alone?
- What social activities do all the children in the class enjoy?

Circle of friends and 'buddy' systems

These are two popular schemes, which involve peers within the class providing a support network for the child with autism or Asperger's syndrome. However, adults need to be aware of how the individual themselves wants to socialise and should be careful not to coerce children into becoming friends, since it is the relationship and not the notion of friendship that needs to be recognised (Webster and Carter 2007). Children must have a voice in determining who they want to be friends with. We also need to consider whether children have the skills to join in activities with their peers. Some children may find interactions in the classroom much easier than playing in the playground. This may be because the structure of the classroom situation is less demanding than the unpredictable nature of other children's play. Compared to adults, children are less consistent in their behaviour and can also misinterpret the social behaviour of others. Hence, children with Asperger's syndrome may prefer conversations with adults, which are also more intellectually challenging than those they might have with their peers.

Social Stories™

Two strategies that have been introduced into mainstream classrooms to support the social skills development of children on the autism spectrum are Comic Strip Conversations and Social Stories™. Comic Strip Conversations provide a visual representation, using stick figures or even cartoon characters, to describe certain social situations. Having specific examples can help children to understand social situations from different perspectives. Social Stories™ were devised by a speech and language pathologist, Carol Gray (1994), to provide clear explanations of situations in which children are helped to understand not just their own feelings but those of others. They can also be devised to show children how to behave in certain situations. Whilst there is a great deal of anecdotal evidence to support the benefits of Social Stories™, highlighting their effectiveness with particular personal and social behaviours, studies by Reynhout and Carter (2006) suggest that it remains uncertain whether these skills are maintained, as there are likely to be other interventions running concurrently that are influencing the success of any intervention.

Activity: good practice to look for to encourage children's social participation and inclusion in the classroom

- Do children have an opportunity to benefit from working in different groups and with different adults throughout the day?
- Are children sometimes given a choice about whom they work with and when? This may need to be negotiated to ensure that it fits in with the lesson plan or class activity.
- What social skills programmes are used to help children to learn how to cope in certain social situations? How are they used? There needs to be some caution in teaching these as general skills – consistency is not a human characteristic!
- Are children given opportunities to observe how others behave in social situations?

- Are children helped to recognise situations where they might be vulnerable and can ask for help?
- Recognise that there may be times in the day, such as lunchtime or playtime, that may be more stressful.
- Are parents and carers able to discuss what they consider to be their priorities for their children's social skill development?
- Children with Asperger's syndrome may be acutely aware of their social difficulties and relationships with peers. It may become a great source of distress to them and they may benefit from additional therapeutic support or counselling to help them to manage any anxieties that this may cause.

Remember: all children learn how to positively interact with others through sharing meaningful and enjoyable activities.

Thought and behaviour

The ability to engage with others, socially and emotionally, is what drives language development and thought. In developing greater awareness and knowledge about the 'self' and 'other', the young infant's mind changes from using a concrete way of responding to incoming sensory experiences, to thinking about people, objects and experiences in more complex and flexible ways. Children at this stage no longer relate to experiences in purely literal ways, but develop the capacity to consider others' perspectives as well as their own. The ability to read the minds of others and adapt one's own behaviour is what psychologists have referred to as having a *theory of mind*. Skills such as imitation, sharing attention and emotion regulation are fundamental to the ability to mind read. Hobson (2002) believes that these skills are the basis for symbolic thought and the development of imagination.

Children with autism are often described as having impaired imagination (Wing 1996), but it may be more relevant to consider this in relation to underlying difficulties with the development of social communication and how information is processed. When difficulties with the social aspect of learning arise, children may become less inclined to alter a familiar way of being, and thinking becomes more rigid. Children with autism are on a developmental path but may display behaviours that can be described as 'stuck' in patterns of thinking and interacting with objects and people. There are many different ways in which children process information and therefore this way of thinking cannot be regarded as specific to autism or Asperger's syndrome.

Linked to the development of imagination is the role that play has in helping children to move from an absorption in sensory-motor experiences to being able to represent and redefine objects and experiences in more complex ways. As many developmental psychologists have identified, social engagement in meaningful and enjoyable activities is what drives cognitive development and children's learning potential. Because children have a fundamental need to explore the world in a variety of different ways it is essential that we acknowledge how children on the autism spectrum play. The ability to play imaginatively is not globally impaired in individuals with autism, but they may have difficulty in using the social imagination required when playing with their peers. Other children are less predictable in their actions and may play in ways that some children on the autism spectrum have difficulty in interpreting.

Neurobiological studies are now able to identify areas of the brain that help to regulate behaviour, responses to sensory stimuli, memory and attention. Research has shown significant differences and weaker neural connections in individuals with autism. Many people with autism have described the way in which information is received as a 'sensory overload', resulting in a preference for fixing attention on the details and an overriding desire for sameness (Grandin 2006; Lawson 2008; Williams 1996). Happé's (1999) research suggests that this should not be regarded as a deficit, but as a difference in how information is processed. She also suggests that there are benefits to this way of thinking, particularly in establishing rote memory or specific skills in calculations and spatial awareness. This may be the reason why some people with autism have exceptional (savant) creative abilities, or develop highly focused interests that become the basis for their future employment.

Children with Asperger's syndrome will typically be within the normal to above-average ability range, and may show particular gifts for a particular subject or special talent in a creative or mathematical skill. Often their skills can be hidden by the difficulties that they have with social interaction and maintaining concentration on tasks that they do not enjoy. Staff may therefore want to work with the child and his or her parents or carers to plan an individual programme based on a solution-focused approach (de Shazer 2005). This begins by recognising the child's strengths and skills and working on those areas that the child has difficulties with. These may include:

- personal organisation;
- motivation;
- problems with remembering and recording information;
- doing homework;
- managing frustration and mood swings;
- insisting on rules;
- focused topics of conversation.

A solution-focused intervention concentrates on setting realistic goals with the individual, and, having decided on the area that the individual wants to change, a programme is implemented to support the child in making those changes. By gradually helping the child over a set period of time, the child takes ownership of the programme and recognises his or her own capacity for change.

Activity: good practice to look for in helping children to develop more flexible ways of thinking and behaving

- Does the child understand the meaning and the purpose behind the task he or she is being asked to do? In the same way, while it is important to provide rules or expectations for behaviour, do they make sense to the child?
- Do children have an opportunity to share their skills and talents with others? These may be a skill or talent in a particular subject or knowledge that children can bring to a lesson or activity to enhance their learning.
- Are tasks and activities presented in a way that helps children to organise ideas and concepts? Are children given the opportunity for creative activities that enable them to respond to experiences in more flexible and imaginative ways, including through autonomous thinking and learning?
- Are children given time to process the impact of new situations or changes in their routine?

Sensing, feeling and moving

Sensory perceptual processing is at the core of the development of knowledge and involves not just a response to physical sensations but what the experience comes to represent. For example, we might experience the smell of a meal that immediately takes us back to a childhood memory. Developing self-knowledge also involves a process of increased engagement with objects and people in the child's immediate environment. It is a highly personalised experience and dependent on how different experiences are perceived and interpreted. Many individuals have described similar sensory processing difficulties in response to touch, taste, sound and visual stimuli, and in recent years there has been much more research devoted to physiological explanations for the sensory difficulties experienced by those on the autism spectrum. Sensory integration is the term used to describe the ability of the nervous system to process sensory stimuli through a range of sensory systems. Sensory integration dysfunction (SID) means that children can experience a hyper (over) or hypo (under) stimulation of their senses, making ordinary, everyday experiences difficult or intolerable.

Case study

Aftab was overly sensitive to the noise of cars so he couldn't go out for a walk during the day. At home his mother said that she had difficulties trying to get him to eat soft food. She said: 'it's like he doesn't think its food unless it's crumbly or rough on his tongue – so he eats a lot of biscuits!'

Children who experience low arousal, on the other hand, may show poor responsiveness to particular situations and appear inattentive. This is also where an occupational therapist can help with planning a programme to help increase the sensory sensitivity.

Difficulties with sensory systems can also affect muscle coordination, muscle planning and spatial awareness. Many children on the autism spectrum may also be given a diagnosis of dyspraxia for this reason. They may be more sensitive about joining in with PE or movement activities, or become anxious about their handwriting. Sensory perceptual difficulties can also be linked to sensitivities about wanting things to happen in a certain way, or becoming preoccupied with certain topics, which can lead to excessive worry or anxiety.

Case study

When Alex moved to our school into year 3 we were told that he had an interest in drains and vents and air conditioning units. When it was playtime he wouldn't run around, he would just walk around the parts of the school he was close to, checking out the drains and the vents. One day he saw the caretaker working on the drains and that was the start of a great relationship! Whenever Alex came across something he knew wasn't working properly he had to find the caretaker and let him know. The problem was that he found it difficult to settle down to his work in the morning until he had spoken to the caretaker to check that everything was working OK.

Year 3 Teacher

Whilst those who work with children may develop a good idea of which triggers within the environment might affect a child's responses, it isn't always possible to know what those are. Just the subtle change of a notice on the school noticeboard could upset a child. Feeling insecure or worried that something else might change will make it much harder to concentrate on work. Excessive worry, panic, fear, low or high arousal towards particular stimuli will not only affect children's physiology and behaviour, but also how they feel about themselves through what they are experiencing.

Activity: good practice in supporting children's sensory processing and motor coordination

Carry out a sensory audit of a classroom by asking pupils what they like and don't like about it. However, be careful: as you know there will be some things you can change and some you can't.

In one classroom where this was done the pupils told the teacher they didn't like sitting on the smelly, scratchy carpet so after that she did any plenary work or circle time with them sitting comfortably on their chairs instead.

Whilst you cannot remove all sensory triggers, you can help children to build up a tolerance towards them with a programme of desensitisation. Parents and an occupational therapist will be able to assist with this. They can also help devise programmes for children with low arousal who need help to increase their sensory awareness. Likewise, children may need strategies to calm themselves down in anxious or frightening situations. Teach breathing for relaxation or how to massage their own hands and arms. Drinking water also helps. Mood cards or traffic lights may also help them to let you know their level of tolerance, or a few minutes with a preferred object can help them refocus. In new situations that they are less familiar with children will need reassurance about the people who are going to be there and what the environment will be like. Giving children time to acclimatise, using relaxation techniques or a distraction activity may help them to feel more comfortable.

Children with autism and transition

All children go through a number of important transition points during their schooling. As with all children, teachers will need to provide those with autism with an effective transition programme to ensure continuity in their learning and emotional well-being. Each school will have its own approach and will recognise how sharing information about a child's learning needs and his or her interests and abilities is essential. Children can also get involved in preparing their own 'passport', describing their interests and hobbies, what they like and don't like, how they like to learn and aspects of learning they find difficult. Depending on the child's level of ability this can be done using pictures and words, with adult support in preparing it where required.

Good practice in working with parents

Despite the many advances that have been made over recent years in ensuring that children with autism are supported and included in schools, the report *Make School Make Sense: Autism and Education, the Reality for Families Today*, compiled for the NAS in 2006, has highlighted areas that still need development. In particular the report highlighted the importance of an ongoing dialogue between policy makers, schools, parents or carers and, where possible, children. The following extracts from the report show the importance of dialogue between all those involved in supporting the child – including the children themselves. In discussing a child's access to the curriculum a parent says:

> If I could make one change . . . I would put her in a quieter classroom – not sitting out in the corridor when the noise in the room is unbearable for her. The teacher looked utterly baffled by my comment, 'Is this inclusion?'!!
>
> (Batten *et al.* 2006: 43)

In discussing school staff's knowledge and understanding about the nature of the autism spectrum and the impact this has on children's learning, a parent says, 'If I could make one change . . . every person who comes into contact with my daughter would have some form of training in autism' (ibid.: 42).

In discussing how schools need to be flexible and ensure appropriate provision for individual children, a parent says:

If I could make one change . . . schools would be obliged to put relevant support in place for all pupils with autism. This would involve a proper assessment of their abilities in all areas and may involve thinking 'outside the box' in terms of deciding how best to support them.

(ibid.: 42)

Conclusion

This chapter has explored good practice for children with autism and Asperger's syndrome. Schools have a responsibility to consider what they believe to be the most effective interventions to support children's learning. Schools should not feel under pressure to use practices which they feel do not promote children's inclusion and participation in the school community. Van Acker (2006) guards against the 'bandwagon effect' surrounding the use of many interventions and this may well be the case for schools attempting to follow many of the autism-specific interventions. School staff do, on the other hand, have the capacity to use their own professional judgement to incorporate a range of different approaches and inclusive pedagogical practices that are appropriate to children's development and learning potential. These include access to a broad and balanced curriculum supported by the resources and learning environment that meet the educational needs of the individual. It may also involve additional therapeutic interventions that are increasingly being made available to children in school. Whilst there is potential for flexibility within the curriculum, teachers recognise that statutory assessments can be quite restricting. This can lead to some children not being included in these tests, or the tests, because of the ways in which they are presented, not providing a true reflection of the child's skills and abilities.

This chapter has avoided the use of terms such as 'issues' or 'concerns' in relation to educating children on the autism spectrum in order to offer a more solution-focused rather than problem-saturated approach to their education. However, it is important to recognise that, because of their difficulties in social communication and interaction, children on the autism spectrum can provide the greatest challenge for teachers who want to provide them with meaningful access to the curriculum and opportunities to learn alongside their peers. Exclusion rates for children on the autism spectrum are amongst the highest in the country: one in five children with autism have been excluded from school, and 67 per cent of these have been excluded more than once (Batten et al. 2006: 3).

Parents, along with professionals, recognise that it not acceptable to deny children their entitlement to education; but equally, many parents are concerned that their child should receive an education in a setting where there is a good understanding of that child's learning needs, and one which supports his or her well-being. We also have to make it possible for children themselves to have a say in how they are educated.

I like this school 'cos Mr Freeman lets me sit by the computer. The computer is like my friend. It helps me to get on with my work and finish on time so that Mr Freeman doesn't get cross with me. Mrs Hey [teaching assistant] made me a timetable so I can see when it's my turn to use the computer and sometimes

I do work on it with Dan. That's OK 'cos we can talk and he's good on the computer like me. School would be brilliant if I got to be on the computer all day but my mum says that's not good 'cos I need to learn other stuff like how to line up and go to assembly.

Todd in year 5

Bibliography

American Psychiatric Association (2000) Diagnostic and Statistical Manual of Mental Disorders, 4th edn (DSM–IV–TR).

Attwood, T. (2006) *The Complete Guide to Asperger's Syndrome*. London: Jessica Kingsley Publishers.

Batten, A., Corbett, C., Rosenblatt, M., Withers, L. and Yuille, R. (2006) *Make School Make Sense: Autism and Education, the Reality for Families Today*. London: NAS Publications.

Boucher, J. (2009) *The Autistic Spectrum: Characteristics, Causes and Practical Issues*. London: Sage Publications.

Corbett, C. and Perepa, P. (2007) *Missing Out? Autism, Education and Ethnicity: The Reality for Families Today*. London: NAS Publications.

DCSF (2009) *Inclusion Development Programme: Supporting Children on the Autism Spectrum. Guidance for Practitioners in Primary and Secondary Schools*. London: The Stationery Office.

de Shazer, S. (2005) *More than Miracles: The State of the Art of Solution-Focused Therapy*. Binghamton, NY: Haworth Press.

DfES (2004) *Removing Barriers to Achievement: The Government's Strategy for Special Educational Needs*. London: The Stationery Office.

DfES and DH (2002) *Autistic Spectrum Disorders: Good Practice Guidance*. London: The Stationery Office.

Frith, U. (1991) *Autism and Asperger's Syndrome*. Cambridge: Cambridge University Press.

Grandin, T. (2006) *Thinking in Pictures and Other Reports from my Life with Autism*. New York: Vintage Books.

Gray, C. (1994) *The New Social Story Book*. Arlington: Future Horizons.

Griffiths, F. (2002) *Communication Counts – Speech and Language Difficulties in the Early Years*. London: David Fulton Publishers.

Happé, F. (1999) 'Autism: Cognitive Deficit or Cognitive Style?' *Trends in Cognitive Sciences*, 3 (6): 216–22.

Hobson, R. P. (2002) *A Cradle of Thought*. Oxford: Macmillan.

Knowles, G. (ed.) (2006) *Supporting Inclusive Practice*. London: David Fulton.

Lathe, R. (2006) *Autism, Brain and Environment*. London: Jessica Kingsley Publishers.

Lawson, W. (2008) *Concepts of Normality: The Autistic and Typical Spectrum*. London: Jessica Kingsley Publishers.

Nind, M. (2000) 'Teachers' Understanding of Interactive Approaches in Special Education'. *International Journal of Disability, Development and Education*, 47 (2): 183–99.

Nind, M. and Hewett, D. (1994) *Access to Communication*. London: David Fulton Publishers.

Potter, C. and Whittaker, C. (2001) *Enabling Communication in Children with Autism*. London: Jessica Kingsley Publishers.

Powell, S. and Jordan, R. (eds) (2001) *Autism and Learning: A Guide to Good Practice*. London: David Fulton Publishers.

Reynhout, G. and Carter, M. (2006) 'Social Stories for Children with Disabilities'. *Journal of Autism and Developmental Disorders*, 36: 445–69.

Scott, K. and Lee, A. (2009) 'Beyond the "Classic" Nurture Group Model: An Evaluation of Part-Time and Cross-Age Nurture Groups in a Scottish Local Authority'. *Support for Learning*, 24: 1 (February): 5–10.

Sonnet, H. (2008) *Nurturing Success: How to Create and Run an Effective Nurture Group*. Nottingham: LDA Publications.

Stern, D. (2003) *The Interpersonal World of the Infant. A View from Psychoanalysis and Developmental Psychology*, 2nd edn. London: Karnac.

Trevarthen, C. (2004) *Intimate Contact from Birth*, in White, K. (ed.) *Touch, Attachment and the Body*. London: Karnac.

Van Acker, R. (2006) 'Outlook on Special Education Practice'. *Focus on Exceptional Children*, April.

Vygotsky, L. (1978) *Mind in Society*. Cambridge, MA: Harvard University Press.

Webster, A. and Carter, M. (2007) 'Social Relationships and Friendships of Children with Developmental Disabilities: Implications for Inclusive Settings. A Systematic Review'. *Journal of Intellectual and Developmental Disability*, 32: 200–13.

Williams, D. (1996) *Autism: An Inside-Out Approach*. London: Jessica Kingsley Publishers.

—— (1998) *Autism and Sensing: The Unlost Instinct*. London: Jessica Kingsley Publishers.

Wing, L. (1996) *The Autistic Spectrum: A Guide for Parents and Professionals*. London: Constable.

Useful references

www.aspergerfoundation.org.uk – website committed to providing information on and understanding of Asperger's syndrome with handouts on a whole range of related subjects.

www.attentionautism.com – Gina Davis is a speech and language therapist who has developed a fun and exciting approach to help children gain attention and develop their communication skills.

www.autismeducationtrust.org.uk – part of the National Autistic Society campaign to improve educational provision for children on the autism spectrum.

www.autismresearchcentre.com – based at the University of Cambridge. Includes an overview of projects and publications on a wide range of medical studies and brain research in autism.

www.nas.org.uk – the National Autistic Society website, which provides a wealth of health, education and employment and social information for parents, professionals and individuals with autism and Asperger's syndrome.

Broderick, K. and Mason-Williams, T. (eds) (2005) *Transition Toolkit: A Framework for Managing Change and Successful Transition Planning for Children and Young People with Autistic Spectrum Conditions*. Kidderminster: BILD.

Conn, C. (2007) *Using Drama with Children on the Autism Spectrum*. Bicester: Speechmark Publishing Ltd.

Smith, C. (2003) *Writing and Developing Social Stories. Practical Interventions in Autism*. Bicester: Speechmark Publishing Ltd.

Chapter 6

Supporting children with physical and sensory disability

Victoria Leslie

Students with disabilities are *more like* all other children than they are *different from them* . . . Students with a particular disability . . . as a group are *just as diverse* in their personal characteristics, behaviour, interests, and learning aptitudes as any other group of students. The assumption that they are all the same leads to negative stereotyping of particular disability groups.

(Westwood 2007: 17)

Introduction

This chapter aims to identify and discuss the needs of children with a physical, sensory or learning disability. It explores the legislation in force to support these children, highlights key reports as an integral part of the Every Child Matters agenda, and shows the importance of partnerships between children, parents, schools and supporting agencies. Recent statistics show that there are an estimated 800,000 children in Great Britain who have some form of disability (www.odi.gov.uk 2009), and it is the legislative duty of all schools to consider how they might make provision for including these children.

Before considering how children with physical and sensory disabilities can be supported in schools and benefit from an inclusive education, it is helpful to consider the background to the issues and be aware of the current legislation and its requirements. In 2001 the Department for Education and Skills issued the following guidance to schools:

From September 2002, schools will be required not to treat disabled pupils less favourably for a reason relating to their disability, and to take reasonable steps to ensure that they are not placed at substantial disadvantage to those who are not disabled.

(DfES 2001: v)

The guidance given by the DfES is underpinned by legislation relating to disability; in particular, the Disability Discrimination Act 1995 (DDA), as amended by the Special Educational Needs and Disability Act 2001. These acts make it unlawful for schools and Local Authorities (LAs) to discriminate – without justification – against disabled pupils for reasons relating to their disability. The Disability Discrimination Act defines a disabled person as someone who has 'a physical or mental impairment which has a substantial and long term adverse effect on his ability to carry out normal day-to-day activities' (www.opsi.gov.uk 2009).

The DDA's definition of disability is very broad and includes:

- physical disabilities;
- sensory impairments (for example, those affecting sight or hearing);
- learning difficulties.

A child is considered disabled if any of the conditions above may have an adverse, substantial and long-term effect on the child's day-to-day activities. A long-term adverse effect is described as one lasting 12 months or more. This means that some conditions commonly found in school, such as broken arms or legs, are ruled out of this provision. A substantial adverse effect is 'a limitation going beyond the normal differences of ability' (DRC 2005: 144).

Day-to-day activities are those carried out on a 'fairly regular and frequent basis' (DRC 2005: 145). To understand whether an impairment affects day-to-day activities, broad categories of ability are listed in the 1995 Act. These include:

- Mobility.
- Manual dexterity.
- Physical co-ordination.
- Continence.
- Ability to lift, carry or otherwise move everyday objects.
- Speech, hearing or eyesight.
- Memory or ability to concentrate, learn or understand.
- Perception of the risk of physical danger.

(ibid.)

The *Code of Practice* (2005), published by the Disability Rights Commission, gives a more detailed account of the definition of disability. This code is still current even though the commission's role and functions were taken over by the Equality and Human Rights Commission in 2007.

Having explored the law and how it defines disability, it is important to remember that we are thinking about children who, despite their disabilities, are children first and foremost. Having a disability does not prevent children from learning or wanting to learn and engage in all the activities they see happening around them. It is important to remember that even in cases of severe physical impairment, there is often no impact on a child's cognitive and intellectual ability (Westwood 2007: 34).

Children with physical and mental impairment

The *Special Educational Needs Code of Practice* (DfES 2001) also discusses definitions of disability and includes consideration of children with mental impairment too. Mental impairment includes learning difficulties and an impairment resulting from, or consisting of, a mental illness. Children may suffer from depression, anxiety, stress, psychosis, phobias and obsessive-compulsive disorder and even 'hidden' impairments such as learning difficulties and dyslexia.

Some medical conditions are also covered by this aspect of the *Special Educational Needs Code of Practice*, including those that are likely to change and develop over time; for example, muscular dystrophy. In the same way the DDA covers children with cancer, multiple sclerosis and HIV infection as falling within the definition of disabled, as well as people who are registered blind or partially sighted. As we have seen above, the key to understanding disability lies with the long-term effect on a child's ability to carry out normal everyday activities.

Activity: understanding the DDA's definition of disability

Think about a child you have worked with who is disabled, or who you believe may have some condition which impairs his or her ability to engage with day-to-day activities at school. Read through the list below and note those aspects of disability or impairment which the child is showing.

- *Mobility*: does the child have difficulty getting to or from school, moving around the school or going on school visits?
- *Manual dexterity*: does the child have difficulty holding a pen, pencil or book, or throwing and catching a ball?
- *Physical co-ordination*: does the child have difficulty in undressing and dressing for physical education (PE) and taking part in games and PE?
- *Ability to lift, carry or otherwise move everyday objects*: does the child have difficulty in carrying a school bag?
- *Continence*: does the child have difficulty in going to the toilet or controlling the need to go to the toilet?
- *Speech*: does the child have difficulty in communicating with others or understanding what others are saying?
- *Hearing*: does the child have difficulty in hearing what is being said?
- *Eyesight*: does the child have difficulty in seeing clearly (with glasses or contact lenses where necessary)?
- *Memory or ability to concentrate, learn or understand*: does the child have difficulty with activities in school, including reading, writing, number work or understanding information?
- *Perception of the risk of physical danger*: does the child have difficulty in recognising danger; for example, when jumping from a height in PE, touching hot objects or crossing roads?

Further questions to think about are:

- Do you know if the child's difficulty is caused by an underlying impairment or condition?
- Has the child's impairment or condition lasted, or is it likely to last, more than 12 months?
- Is the child's impairment or condition having a substantial adverse effect?

(Adapted from www.teachernet.gov.uk 2009)

Codes and duties

The *Code of Practice for Schools* (2002), published by the Disability Rights Commission, complements the *Special Educational Needs Code of Practice* (2001). The principle behind the legislation is that disabled people should have the same opportunities as non-disabled people in their access to education. Every aspect of school life is covered by these duties. Responsible bodies must not discriminate in relation to admissions; in relation to education and associated services; or by excluding a pupil.

Ensuring that disabled children are not discriminated against

In their day-to-day experience of school, children who are disabled should have the same opportunities as any child, and those who work with children need to ensure that a disabled child can access all aspects of schooling, including: the curriculum, teaching and learning classroom organisation, all timetabled lessons, usual grouping of pupils, homework, access to school facilities and activities to supplement the curriculum (for example, a drama group visiting the school). Disabled children should also be able to access school sports lessons and events, usual break and lunchtime arrangements, school meals, assessment and exam arrangements, school discipline and sanctions, school clubs and activities, school trips and preparation of pupils for the next phase of education (DRC 2002: 33).

Activity

As you walk around the school and work with the children, make a note of the ways in which disabled children are represented in the school environment. Some particular points to look out for are listed below:

- Is there any evidence that disabled adults work in the school or are invited into the school as voluntary helpers or to talk about their jobs or lives?
- Look carefully at the resources being used by children, particularly books and pictures. Do they show positive images of children and adults with disabilities?
- Are children engaged in activities that encourage them to think about others and to empathise with others?
- Is there evidence of the celebration of successful disabled sports people, for example? Think about the quality of each portrayal as well as the number of times that disability is portrayed.

Whole-school policies and procedures

Schools must publish a Disability Equality Scheme showing how they will promote equality of opportunity for disabled children, staff and those for whom they provide services. Schools must also publish an annual Action Plan showing how they are implementing their scheme. As well as identifying how equal opportunities for disabled people will be promoted, it is crucial that disabled people have a voice within the scheme and are included in its development.

Schools must provide information on their Special Educational Needs (SEN) Policy, their Accessibility Plan and the Disability Equality Scheme, and report on these annually. Despite this legislation being in place for a number of years, the Lamb Inquiry (2009: 45) noted that there is still a concerning level of non-compliance with the requirement to publish a Disability Equality Scheme.

Activity

Following on from the last activity and the discussion about disability so far, the next time you are in a school ask colleagues about what is in place to ensure disabled children are being provided with an inclusive environment. How does the school ensure access to the curriculum?

Think about the following:

- Is the school able to offer disabled pupils access to the wider curriculum – for example: after-school clubs, sporting and cultural activities?
- How have teaching strategies been adjusted to meet individual needs?
- Has there been any relevant in-house training for all staff in the past year?
- What links does the school have with specialist advisors to develop the curriculum for children with disabilities?
- How does the school ensure access to the physical environment?
- Do disabled children have access to all the school's grounds? Take a walk around your school and playground and note accessibility and possible hazards for disabled children – if possible, go with a disabled child and note what he or she says about accessibility.
- How does the school ensure access to written information?
- Are written texts interpreted through supporting adults?
- Is voice recognition software available and used frequently?
- Does the Local Authority (LA) provide specialist guidance on converting written texts into alternative formats? Does your school use this service?

Case study

The Accessible Resources Pilot Project (2009–2011) is currently trialling different curriculum formats for visually impaired and dyslexic children and young people. Children with sight impairment and dyslexia can find textbooks and other school materials difficult to access, so the project is providing electronic versions of texts to be read in a way that suits an individual's need. Since, as the report states:

Books are crucial. Take access to books away from sighted schoolchildren, close school libraries or delay the book until the week after the lesson, and there would be a national outcry! Yet in effect this repeatedly happens to children who can't see as much as their peers.

(RNIB 2006: 5)

Exploring different ways of helping children to access texts is important, since in their desire to ensure that visually impaired children have the necessary learning resources, those providing the resources can sometimes overlook the variety of ways these can be provided. This can mean that children have to wait for resources to be specially prepared and they also have to suffer the indignity of having their resources look different to everyone else's. As one child in the report says: 'I can't stand A3! I absolutely hate it! . . . [A4] is a . . . lot more "normal" . . . The whole point of people modifying things is to make things as normal as possible . . .' (ibid.: 17).

The Children's Plan: building brighter futures

This is a vision for change to ensure that children and young people have the opportunities to grow up in the best imaginable circumstances. It puts the needs and wishes of families first, setting out clear steps to make every child matter.

The Children's Plan (2007) identifies two important priorities for schools regarding children with disabilities. The first is to narrow the gaps in outcomes between children with SEN and disabilities and other children in the population, and the second is to increase parental confidence in the services provided. The Bercow Report (2008), the work on dyslexia being taken forward by Sir Jim Rose (2009) and the Lamb Inquiry (2009) seek to respond to these priorities. The Bercow Report and Rose's work on dyslexia examine the key skill of communication – through speech and language, and reading and writing – whilst the Lamb Inquiry is concerned with parental confidence.

Other strands of the Every Child Matters (ECM) agenda pertinent for children with disabilities are carried forward in the Children's Plan. Examples of this are: investing in facilities for disabled children to take short breaks; ensuring that all families benefit from Sure Start children's centres; expanding provision for school-based parent advisors; creating a Parents' Panel to advise on policies affecting parents; funding for 3,500 playgrounds to be rebuilt or renewed so that they are accessible for children with disabilities; reviewing Child and Adolescent Mental Health Services (CAMHS); producing guidance for Building Schools for the Future to ensure that new schools have space for co-located services and take access requirements into consideration (DCSF 2007: 17–19).

Aiming High for Disabled Children (AHDC)

Aiming High for Disabled Children is jointly delivered by the Department for Children, Schools and Families (DCSF) and the Department of Health. It aims to provide disabled children with the same opportunities as all other children. The joint collaboration puts into practice the idea of the co-working of services in the best interests of disabled children and their families.

AHDC's vision is for 'all families with disabled children to have the support they need to live ordinary family lives, as a matter of course' (DCSF 2008a: 3). It includes a Core Offer for disabled children and families, which is a national set of expectations centring on information, transparency, assessment, participation and feedback. It focuses on meeting individual needs through a tailored and personal response and involving multi-agency working. It is important that schools work with other agencies and share information effectively, since: 'No single agency can deliver any one of the five Every Child Matters outcomes for children and young people by working in isolation' (Bercow 2008: 10).

Case study

Mollie is 10; she has cerebral palsy and is in a wheelchair. She says, 'Because of my weak legs I need help moving around the school. But I am really good at art and love sewing. When I first started at this school, when I was 7, I had come from the special school. I had no friends and all the other children just stared at me and called me 'spastic'. My mum was really upset and cried when she knew. I think she talked to the school . . .

Mollie's mum takes up the story: 'It's always been a battle to get the right provision for Mollie. When I first approached the school a few years ago they were very keen to try and help. But in hindsight I don't think they really realised what they were taking on. Anyway, after a few rather tense conversations things really started to improve. They had all the things in place like a TA to work one to one in class and ramps for the wheelchair and policies coming out of their ears, but they didn't see Mollie as a little girl; they just saw her disability.'

Gradually the school staff realised that they needed to listen to what Mollie was telling them about her needs and how she felt. Part of understanding how to include Mollie was talking to the other children about her condition and working to find ways they could connect with Mollie and not be scared by her 'being different'. Mollie's mum says that 'the staff valued what I said and made Mollie feel included in everything. Now Mollie feels that she is a full member of the class and ever since she has blossomed and loves going to school.'

Achievement for All

Achievement for All (AfA) is a current project that aims to improve outcomes of children and young people identified with SEN and Disabilities (SEND). In the pilot phase, 10 local authorities with 460 schools aim to deliver better educational and wider outcomes for SEND children through a personalised learning approach. It includes careful monitoring and assessment of learning progress, tracking and intervention and engaging with parents. AfA places the vision of the Aim Higher agenda within an educational context. Achievement for All aims to:

- enable children with SEND to be more confident learners and have a positive attitude towards their education

- increase their levels of progress
- work more collaboratively and supportively with parents
- ensure schools have a wider range of successful, inclusive learning and teaching approaches
- ensure schools have an inclusive ethos

(DCSF 2009a: 6)

Case study

George is in year 4 and has a statement for Severe Learning Difficulties (SLD). He is working in all areas of the curriculum quite considerably below what would be expected for a child of his age.

George's parents expressed concerns that much of the work given to George was beyond his grasp. They were particularly worried that in cross-curricular subjects, George was not engaging with the learning, and much of the work was completed by his TA. Homework was often not completed because George was unable to access it.

As a result, George is not making any progress at all. The class teacher admitted that she had no experience of differentiating at George's level. Under the requirements of the DDA, George's entire curriculum must be personalised according to his specific needs.

A meeting between the head, SENCO, class teacher and TAs, and a teacher from the LA with SLD training, identified the following adjustments:

- Training for the class teacher and TAs for children with SLD and using the P scales to monitor progress in small steps.
- Small-step monitoring of George's progress on at least a termly basis.
- Specific help with simplifying each area of the curriculum so that George can often follow the same topic as the rest of the class at his own level.
- Termly identification of the core language and concepts in each topic so that explicit teaching of these can be prioritised.

Personalised learning is a large part of enabling children with SEND to be more confident learners and to have a positive attitude towards their education in practice. In *Removing Barriers to Achievement* (DfES 2004) personalised learning is defined as:

- having high expectations of all children
- building on the knowledge, interests and aptitudes of every child
- involving children in their own learning through shared objectives and feedback (assessment for learning)
- helping children to become confident learners
- enabling children to develop the skills they will need beyond school

(DfES 2004: 52)

Personalised learning covers all aspects of school life and is an essential strategy for children with special educational needs and disabilities.

Raising self-esteem

Children with special educational needs and disabilities can suffer from poor self-esteem. Many schools already use strategies such as SEAL (social and emotional aspects of learning), which not only contributes to all the ECM outcomes and provides a structure to promote emotional literacy for all, but can be used to particularly good effect with SEND children.

Activities

Early Years and Key Stage 1: the treasure box

Resources: box with a lid, mirror, various decorations including a ribbon or string.

Preparation: glue the mirror to the bottom of the inside of the box, decorate the outside and then secure the lid.

Activity: explain that in the box they will see the most wonderful thing in the world. Pass the box around the circle, asking the children to guess what it contains.

Untie the ribbon or string and tell the children that they can peep inside the box to see the most wonderful thing in the world. Tell the children to keep quiet until everybody has seen inside the box. When everybody has had a turn, ask the children what they found when they looked inside the box. Can each child tell you why he or she is the most wonderful person in the world?

Key Stages 1 and 2: heroes

Resources: pictures of heroes.

Activity: the children look at pictures of their heroes and identify what makes each successful. Introduce vocabulary such as persistence, determination, tenacity, resilience, resourcefulness and responsibility. Transfer these skills to members of the class.

Go around the circle, asking children to say something positive about another member of the group; for example, 'I admire . . . because . . . .'

Key Stage 2: child as teacher

Preparation: ask the children to think about an activity in which they are skilful and could teach another child. The children may need warning to bring in resources from home.

Explain to the children that they are going to take on the role of teacher and instruct another member of the class how to:

- tie a knot;
- juggle;
- play chess;
- fold paper (origami);
- or anything else children suggest . . .

Disabled children are more at risk of being bullied

Recent research has shown that disabled children are experiencing bullying to a greater degree than had previously been thought (DfES 2006). A survey by Mencap (Mencap 2007) reported that eight out of ten children with learning disabilities were being bullied, and six out of ten had been physically hurt. Bullying of children, young people and even adults with a disability is perhaps more common than we might want to admit, and this was illustrated by appalling events in Leicestershire in 2007.

Case study

Fiona Pilkington set fire to her car in a Leicestershire lay-by, killing herself and her disabled daughter, who had been taunted by gangs for over 10 years.

According to the BBC report (2009), the mother had repeatedly complained to the police after being targeted by local gangs of youths. Her family told the inquest that her death was 'a final act of desperation' after she could no longer endure the torment any more.

The grandmother spoke of one particular ordeal endured by the family:

'It was Halloween and firework night was coming up. Fiona was dreading them because she knew the children would start throwing things at the house and start putting fireworks through the letterbox.' She added that her granddaughter 'was frustrated because she couldn't go out in the garden without being tormented or teased. We would take her to the park and take her out in the rain because she used to love jumping in puddles.'

Despite dozens of calls to police and the local council little was done to help the family.

On the day they died, the mother rang the police about the gang but she was told to ignore them. Asked why the mother had also killed her daughter, the grandmother said: 'She didn't think anybody would be able to cope with Frankie.'

The horrific nature of this attack follows similar targeted assaults against people with disabilities. In 2006 a young man with epilepsy was preyed upon and tortured in a shed until he died, and in 2007 a woman in her fifties, with physical and learning disabilities, was taunted, urinated on and sprayed with foam as she lay dying in the street.

The Equality and Human Rights Commission is to launch a nationwide inquiry into disability-related harassment that will investigate how public authorities are protecting people with disabilities.

As with all bullying, this harassment 'damages children's self-esteem. It undermines the potential for them to feel safe and secure enough to be able to learn. It can have long-term effects on their mental health' (Lamb 2009: 33). The SEAL resources already referred to above include an anti-bullying theme, and the resource pack 'Make Them Go Away' (DCSF 2009b) provides schools with information specifically about bullying and disability.

Activity

All schools will have an anti-bullying policy; take the next opportunity you have to look at one. Check to see if there is any mention of bullying relating to disabled children. Does the school have a whole-school approach to being positive about disability, including explaining about disability to able-bodied children?

The school's anti-bullying policy should acknowledge that disabled children may:

- find it more difficult than able-bodied children to resist bullies
- be more isolated and have fewer friends than able-bodied children
- not recognize that it is bullying that is happening to them
- have difficulty in being able to report bullying or struggle to remember names and other details about the bullying
- bully others unwittingly, particularly if they have been subject to bullying, since they may believe it to be acceptable behaviour
- find it hard to manage their anger and emotional response to such situations

(DCSF 2009b: 8)

In its statutory Code of Practice, the Disability Rights Commission (DRC) has stated that schools can also promote positive attitudes towards disabled people in lessons such as citizenship, and by ensuring that the views and contributions of disabled children are valued (DRC 2005: 29–30). These approaches help to create a positive ethos about disabled people and a climate where bullying of disabled children becomes less likely as a result. Investment to enable children with disabilities to participate in activities with their non-disabled peers will also help to create a positive climate for disabled children (DCSF 2007: 26).

A positive climate will be further developed by these 'Top Tips for Participation', created by disabled young people for the Council for Disabled Children:

Involve us from the start

'You can find out what's best for us by involving us'

'Don't guess what we want'

Respect us

'If you give us respect, we'll give you respect'

'Trust us – we need to trust you'

Listen to us

'Listen to me, no one else, listen to me. It's my body. Listen to me, it's my life, listen to me'

'If you don't listen to what we want, how can you give us what we want?'

Be open and honest with us

'We ask questions to help us understand our world and to grow as people!'

'Frustrating when you don't tell us stuff'

'We all make mistakes'

Make sure we get something out of it

'Give us new skills'

'Participation is a great way to help us learn how to make decisions and understand the choices we may face in the future!'

'Empower us!'

Involve all of us!

'Don't judge a book by its cover – we can all make choices'

'I may not have speech, but I have a voice – I can give my opinions, I can even argue'

Give us time

'Help us make decisions by giving your time – enough time'

'I know what I want to say – give me time'

'Give me time to get my message ready'

Prove you're listening to us

'Show us you want to listen'

'My voice is my power'

'Tell us what's changed'

Make it fun!

'We're teenagers, we're young, we want to learn'

Support us to make our own decisions

'I want more choice'

'If you listen to us you can help us get a positive outcome'

Figure 6.1 Examples from the Council for Disabled Children's 'Top Tips for Participation'

Source: Adapted from Council for Disabled Children (2009) Top Tips for Participation: What disabled young people want. London: National Children's Bureau.

Case study

The campaign Every Disabled Child Matters (EDCM) asked disabled children this question: 'If you were Prime Minister for the day, and could change one thing, what would it be?' The top three answers were as follows:

1 *Have more fun things to do:*
  'A set date or time for disabled children and their carers to access the local cinema – without being told to be quiet when we can't help it.' Kieran, 7.

2 *More respect for disabled children and young people:*
  'I would make all those involved in places like schools and colleges go on courses to give them understanding of disabilities. This would stop the lack of understanding in people . . . We are not "weird" or "retarded" and most definitely not "lazy!"' Katie-Rose, 16.

3 *Make it everyone's right to get a good education:*
  'That "average" is all a disabled child is allowed to be. We should have the same rights as the other children in schools.' Christopher, 14.

For these changes to work for children and young people, their views need to be heard: 'I want to be given the time and chance to be understood for being like I am.'
EDCM created a booklet listing the changes children and young people with disabilities would like to happen, entitled 'If I Could Change One Thing . . .'.

Enabling disabled children to be independent

One of the challenges for schools working to include disabled children is in knowing how to achieve the right balance between providing them with the help they need to be included in the day-to-day school experience and helping them learn to be independent. Schools have long considered that fostering independence in learning and everyday life is vital for children. One of the ways of achieving this with disabled children is to listen to their opinions. We need to provide opportunities for them to tell us about their experiences in school, when they need help or when they do not, and which part of a learning task presents difficulties and requires assistance.

When supporting pupils with disabilities, we should concentrate, above all, on supporting them to achieve the higher cognitive skills such as exploring ideas, questioning and challenging, problem solving and reviewing progress, rather than repetitive tasks to achieve a lower-level motor skill which may not be achieved to a fully functioning standard.

Enabling disabled children to achieve more in their learning

The Lamb Inquiry (2009) states that we have a 'hangover of a system, and a society, which does not place enough value on achieving good outcomes for disabled children and children with SEN' (Lamb 2009: 2). To challenge this, Lamb proposed 51 recommendations which, taken as a whole, aim to change the culture and practice of those who work with disabled children and children with SEN. Lamb proposes four key areas of change. The first is 'Children's outcomes at the heart of the system' (ibid.).

Efforts to narrow the achievement gap between groups of children, including those with SEN, and to ensure that all children make progress, will be documented in the proposed School Report Card from September 2011. This is a major reform to the school account-ability system, to make it 'more coherent, better co-ordinated, more streamlined and better able to recognise the full range of each school's achievements' (DCSF 2008b: 14). It will complement Ofsted inspection reports as a major source of data on schools' achievements. Another advantage is that it will lead to greater transparency, reporting each school's per-formance in a way that is clear and easily understood. The proposed school accountability system aims to:

> reward and support schools' successes in supporting their pupils' development across all five ECM outcomes . . . in helping all children at the school to achieve, particularly the most vulnerable and those at risk of not reaching their full potential, such as those from deprived backgrounds, or with special educational needs and disabilities.
>
> (DCSF 2009c: 61)

Better collaboration with the families of children with disabilities

Developing strong collaborative links between schools and families is a principle of the Children's Plan (2007) and the Every Child Matters agenda (Knowles 2009). This principle recognises that improved information sharing with parents allows parents to play a greater role in children's education. The Lamb Inquiry (2009) found that 'personal contact is a key factor for parents of children with SEN and no information system will be valued that does not make provision for face-to-face communication' (Lamb 2009: 2–3). This is also reflected in the SEN Code of Practice, which states that 'parents should be fully involved in the school-based response for their child, understand the purpose of any intervention or programme of action, and be told about the parent partnership service when SEN are identified' (DfES 2001: 17).

Case study

I was really worried that my daughter Aalia would find the move to junior school difficult. However, the school set up a 'team around the child' meeting to which we were invited, along with representatives from the infant and junior schools and the educational psychologist. My thoughts and opinions were carefully listened to and I was able to provide the school with information about strategies Aalia uses at home, such as a simplified 'now' and 'next' timetable. Her new school was able to adapt these ideas to help Aalia overcome any difficulties at school. I genuinely felt that my input had a positive impact on Aalia's school life.

These meetings have continued, allowing me to have a regular say in Aalia's development at school. When Aalia started night-wetting, the school nurse was invited to the meeting and provided some valuable advice.

My husband and I were worried that Aalia would be excluded from taking part in extra-curricular activities. However, through careful planning between us and the school, Aalia is thriving and thoroughly enjoys school.

Parents have strategies that they or their children use to manage their disabilities. This background information is vital if schools are to develop learning that has begun in the home, and should, in turn, lead to an exchange of knowledge, allowing the progress made in school to be consolidated at home. It is this expertise which should allow all those involved in education to accept parents as full partners in their children's education. However, at this point it is important to reflect on the notion of partnership. Frederickson and Cline state that 'professionals and LEAs have generally been slow to embrace partnership insofar as it requires active sharing of information and control' (2002: 18). The Lamb Report found that 'many parents felt that their concerns about their child's progress were not acknowledged, that schools did not listen' (2009: 27).

To reinforce partnership further, 'Your Child, Your Schools, Our Future' (DCSF 2009c) sets out the proposed home – school agreements and pupil and parent guarantees from September 2011. These should cover:

- What pupils and parents can expect from the school
- What pupils and parents can expect to be provided from services beyond the school to support their child's learning and development

(Lamb 2009: 27)

Activity: think about the role of parents and carers in schools you have experience of working with

Use these questions to frame your thinking:

- Are parents and carers valued in schools? How do you know?
- Do schools have a shared vision for the engagement of parents and carers in supporting the learning and development of their children? How do you know?
- How were parents able to support their children's learning? Were there any differences for parents of children with special educational needs and disabilities?
- What do schools do to encourage parents and carers to engage with the school?
- Think of a child in a school who is fully supported by his or her parents or carers. Now think of a child who does not receive that same support. What is the impact on each child?

Teaching and learning strategies for disabled children

In recent years much of the teaching and learning support provided for disabled children has been in the form of support from teaching assistants (TAs), often offering one-to-one support. Although there are many positive sides to this work and Ofsted found that 'Support by teaching assistants can be vital' (Ofsted 2004: 15), it also noted that this sometimes meant that children had too few opportunities to work independently, and that the focus was often on how children with disabilities could be kept engaged, rather than on advancing learning. However highly trained and qualified a TA, Ofsted reported that this 'was not a substitute for focused, highly skilled teaching' (ibid.: 11).

A significantly beneficial resource available in most schools which can benefit the learning of disabled children is the use of information and communication technology (ICT). ICT offers a range of tools to support individual – and personalised – learning through assistive technology (hardware) and supportive software. It also enables children with speech difficulties to communicate, allowing them to develop vital social skills.

In choosing when and how to use ICT, it is important that the views and feelings of the children are taken into account. For example, the aim of using ICT is to facilitate inclusion, but care should be taken that the technology does not isolate the child from others in the group or class. This can be overcome in some cases by children working collaboratively and by all children having access to ICT to enhance their work. It must always be remembered that the technology is to support learning, not to impede it; it should not create another obstacle to be negotiated.

Parents and those who work with the children in school should be involved in decisions relating to ICT provision. It is possible to get an ICT assessment completed, identifying software, training and support which can be accessed through the network of joined-up services.

In order for ICT equipment to be used successfully it is important that it is arranged so that pupils can use it with ease. The height of the keyboard and screen should be considered, and the use of a copy holder or angled work surface can also help. A wrist support placed in front of the keyboard and arm rests on a computer table can facilitate access. Examples of technology that can help include:

- Touch-screen computers, joysticks and trackerballs
- Easy-to-use keyboards
- Interactive whiteboards
- Text-to-speech software
- Braille-translation software
- Software that connects words with pictures or symbols

(http://www.direct.gov.uk 2009)

The use of the interactive whiteboard is ideal for hearing-impaired children because they can see what is happening. Care should be taken over seating arrangements so that children are directly facing the whiteboard and have a clear line of sight to any adults signing. For children with a visual impairment, a word processor can be used to create text using larger, **bolder** and more widely spaced fonts to help with reading. The use of a talk facility can help children with checking their work.

Developing a whole-school approach to ensuring an inclusive environment for disabled children

School leaders establish the ethos that either welcomes or sidelines disabled children and children with SEN. As part of this, they can create a culture where parents either feel like valued members of the school community or are made to feel a nuisance (Lamb 2009: 21). The Council for Disabled Children's *Extending Inclusion* notes that it is our attitudes and policies, rather than the physical environment, that can be more likely to restrict and impede learners with a disability (Stobbs 2008: 13).

Activity

Below are some examples of good practice in terms of ethos, found in schools where children with learning difficulties and disabilities made outstanding progress. Next time you are in a school, look for examples of this good practice.

- A commitment to good or better progress for all children
- Teachers who challenged themselves and scrutinised data to drive improvement
- Good relationships between staff and children

(Lamb 2009: 22)

A school's shared vision of inclusion will be apparent through day-to-day leadership at all levels. It should be clear and consistent and have, at its heart, a set of core beliefs and values that are modelled to the whole school community: 'To be successful it will need a whole-school commitment based on collective responsibility and shared account-ability' (DCSF 2009e: 8). School leaders who successfully promote an inclusive ethos for disabled children need to be effective communicators who recognise that their school community is part of a wider community and that two-way collaboration is part of a collective responsibility for children and young people with special educational needs and disabilities.

The Ofsted report 'Special Educational Needs in the Mainstream' (2003) also cites successful schools as having clear policies and procedures which have developed over time and where inclusion is seen as part of the overall improvement of the school, encouraging all children to achieve to their full potential. Those who run such schools believe that taking into account individual needs and learning styles has value for all children and is part of the drive for personalised learning. It is through this inclusive ethos that all children feel secure and able to contribute, and in this way stereotypical views are challenged and children can learn to view differences in others in a positive way. This can be emphasised by arranging for children with disabilities to work alongside non-disabled peers. Educating all children in disability issues and equality will help both the disabled and non-disabled child respect one another. This work should be seen as part of the school's programme of inclusion issues, aimed at driving out prejudice and stereotyping. It could be incorporated in either the citizenship curriculum or personal, social and health education (PSHE).

An ethos which values pupil voice is key to the success of children with disabilities; including them in decision-making opportunities is vital if the child is to have ownership, particularly regarding decisions that have a direct impact on them.

Early identification should ensure that children's needs are being met, reducing the risk of frustration that can lead to adverse behaviour and, ultimately, exclusion. National indicators currently measure the exclusion rates for children with SEN and show that they are eight times as likely to be excluded as peers who do not have special educational needs (DCSF 2009f). By 2011 there will be a national indicator showing exclusion of children with disabilities. Lamb urges that the over-representation of SEN exclusion is addressed through leaders having a thorough understanding of special educational needs and disabilities (Lamb 2009: 35).

In order to set high expectations for children with disabilities, there is a need to look beyond the diagnosis and to consider the individual needs of the child: 'The issue about the diagnosis of a syndrome is that it is a simplification . . . every child with the same medical diagnosis does not have the same educational needs' (Fox 2003: 25). It is important to consider how a child's particular needs may be met, whether in relation to accessing the curriculum, or in terms of mobility. However, Westwood emphasises that students with physical disabilities need to have the same access opportunities as are available to those without handicaps. He continues that this may 'require adaptations to be made to the environment, to the ways in which these students move (or are moved) around the environment' (Westwood 2007: 35). Indeed, this is reflected in the planning duties in Part 4 of the DDA which states that:

> schools [are required] to develop accessibility plans, to improve access to school education for disabled pupils. This includes making any necessary improvements to the physical environment of the school (such as rearranging room space, removing obstructions from walkways) and physical aids to accessing education (such as ramps, widened doorways, adapted toilets, and wayfinding systems).
>
> (DCSF 2008c: 189)

The wider social context

Mooney *et al.* (2008) identify a wide variation between local authorities (LAs) in terms of the ways that disabled children are counted and categorised. This in turn means there is a lack of consistency across the country in terms of LA provision to schools for disabled children. However, from the beginning of 2010 legislation requires LAs to have school representatives on their Children's Trust Board and to listen to what schools are saying about what is required to ensure that disabled children can be provided with an inclusive learning environment. The campaign Every Disabled Child Matters (http://www.ncb.org.uk 2009) is urging every LA to make a commitment to improve services for disabled children and their families. The campaign emphasises that these local bodies must be held to account for the services they provide.

Ofsted

Ofsted's report 'Special Educational Needs and Disability' (2004) detailed key features of effective practice in inclusion as being:

A climate of acceptance of all pupils, including those who have distinctive needs; the availability of suitable teaching and personal support; sensitive allocation to teaching groups and careful modification of the curriculum, timetables and social arrangements; assessment, recording and reporting procedures which can embrace and express adequately the progress of pupils who make only small gains in learning and personal development; widespread awareness among staff of the particular needs of pupils with significant special needs and an understanding of meeting them in the classroom and elsewhere; the availability of appropriate materials and teaching aids; and involving parents as fully as possible in decision making.

(Ofsted 2004: 19)

Conclusion

Thousands of words, hundreds of initiatives and dozens of reports have been produced by government, local authorities and schools to ensure that we do our very best for children and young people, whatever their disability. Perhaps our attitudes and actions should be summed up in just three memorable words: *Every* Child Matters. These are our watchwords for making Achievement for All a reality.

Bibliography

BBC (2009) http://news.bbc.co.uk/1/hi/england/leicestershire/8268521.stm (accessed 26/1/ 10).

Becta (2007) *Inclusive Learning: An Essential Guide.* Coventry: Becta.

Bercow, J. (2008) The Bercow Report: A Review of Services for Children and Young People (0–19) with Speech, Language and Communication Needs. London: DCSF.

CAMHS (2008) Children and Young People in Mind: The Final Report of the National CAMHS Review. London: DH.

DCSF (2007) *The Children's Plan: Building Brighter Futures.* London: TSO.

—— (2008a) *Aiming High for Disabled Children: Transforming Services for Disabled Children and their Families.* London: DCSF.

—— (2008b) 'A School Report Card: Consultation Document'. London: DCSF.

—— (2008c) *Designing for Disabled Children and Children with Special Educational Needs: Design Guidance for Mainstream and Special Schools.* London: TSO.

—— (2009a) *Achievement for All: Guidance for Schools.* London: DCSF.

—— (2009b) *Make Them Go Away.* London: DCSF.

—— (2009c) *Your Child, Your Schools, Our Future: Building a 21st Century Schools System.* London: TSO.

—— (2009d) *Your Child, Your Schools, Our Future: Timetable for Action.* London: TSO.

—— (2009e) *Achievement for All: Characteristics of Effective Inclusive Leadership – A Discussion Document.* Nottingham: NCSL.

—— (2009f) *Permanent and Fixed Period Exclusions from Schools and Exclusion Appeals in England 2007/08.* London: DCSF.

DfES (2001) *Special Educational Needs Code of Practice.* London: DfES.

—— (2004) *Removing Barriers to Achievement: The Government's Strategy for SEN.* London: DfES.

—— (2006) *Implementing the Disability Discrimination Act in Schools and Early Years Settings.* London: DfES.

Directgov (2009) www.direct.gov.uk/en/DisabledPeople/EducationAndTraining/Schools/DG _10013035 (accessed 30/12/09).

DRC (Disability Rights Commission) (2002) 'Code of Practice for Schools'. London: TSO.

—— (2005) *The Duty to Promote Disability Equality: Statutory Code of Practice: England and Wales*. London: TSO.

EDCM (Every Disabled Child Matters) (2007) *If I Could Change One Thing . . .: Children and Young People's Views*. London: EDCM.

EHRC (Equality and Human Rights Commission) (2009) *Two Years Making Changes*. London: EHRC.

Fox, M. (2003) *Including Children 3–11 with Physical Disabilities*. London: David Fulton Publishers.

Frederickson, N. and Cline, T. (2002) *Special Educational Needs, Inclusion and Diversity*. Buckingham: Open University Press.

Knowles, G. (2009) *Ensuring Every Child Matters: A Critical Approach*. London: Sage.

Lamb, B. (2009) 'Lamb Inquiry: Special Educational Needs and Parental Confidence'. London: DCSF.

Mooney, A., Owen, C. and Statham, J. (2008) *Disabled Children: Numbers, Characteristics and Local Service Provision*. London: DCSF.

National Children's Bureau http://www.ncb.org.uk/cdc/home.aspx (accessed 30/12/09).

Office for Disability Issues (2003) *Special Educational Needs in the Mainstream*. London: Ofsted.

—— (2004) *Special Educational Needs and Disability*. London: Ofsted.

—— (2006) *Inclusion: Does it matter where pupils are taught?* London: Ofsted.

—— (2009) www.odi.gov.uk/research/facts-and-figures.php (accessed 29/12/09).

—— (2010) *The Framework for School Inspection*. London: Ofsted.

Office of Public Sector Information (2009) www.opsi.gov.uk/acts/acts1995 (accessed 30/12/ 09).

RNIB (Royal National Institute of Blind People) (2006) *Where's My Book?* London: RNIB.

Rose, J. (2009) *Identifying and Teaching Children and Young People with Dyslexia and Literacy Difficulties*. London: DCSF.

Stobbs, P. (2008) *Extending Inclusion*. London: DCSF.

Teachernet (2009) http://www.teachernet.gov.uk/wholeschool/disability/defdis/tom/ (accessed 29/12/09).

Westwood, P. (2007) *Commonsense Methods for Children with Special Educational Needs*, 5th edn. London: Routledge.

Websites

http://www.altformat.org/mytextbook
http://www.bdadyslexia.org.uk/
http://www.cafamily.org.uk
http://www.childrenssociety.org.uk
http://www.cwdcouncil.org.uk
http://www.dcsf.gov.uk/everychildmatters/healthandwellbeing/ahdc/AHDC
http://www.dotheduty.org
http://edcm.org.uk/onething
http://www.equalityhumanrights.com
http://www.mencap.org.uk
http://nationalstrategies.standards.dcsf.gov.uk/sup1/afa
http://www.ncb.org.uk/cdc/home.aspx
http://www.ncb.org.uk/edcm/home.aspx
http://www.officefordisability.gov.uk
http://www.rnib.org.uk
http://www.togetherfdc.org/default.aspx

Chapter 7

Children who have suffered loss and grief, including bereavement

Gillian Goddard

There can be few life events that have a greater impact on a child's life than the death of someone close; we are passionately committed to ensuring that all children are supported in their journey through grief.

(Julie Stokes, founder of Winston's Wish, Stokes 2004: 262)

When I see my friends out with their mums and dads enjoying themselves, it hurts, it really hurts.

(Marie, 11)

Introduction

This chapter aims to identify and discuss the needs of children experiencing loss through separation, divorce, relocation or death. It will examine grief experiences in children and related underlying theory that might help school staff to respond to the needs of individual children in this situation. The impact of cognitive development on the ways in which children come to terms with loss and grief will be outlined. Ways of working in partnership with families and outside agencies will be explored, together with practical support strategies for pupils and staff.

What is the incidence of grief and loss in children and why is it the role of educators to do something about it?

In considering the likelihood of pupils experiencing loss and grief, begin with this reflection.

Activity

Recall your own childhood up to school leaving age. Did you ever experience feelings of loss or grief? Remember, that could be through changing schools, moving house and leaving friends or losing a favourite toy or pet, as well as the more obvious losses. These would include parental separation and divorce, or the death of a grandparent, sibling, parent or friend. How typical do you think your experiences are?

In reality, children live with change and loss as a normal part of their growing up. Through experience, they learn strategies for coping with this, though their understanding of what is happening to them, as will be seen later in the chapter, is often limited. Most children cope with loss successfully with the support of family, friends and school, but for some children the losses are too great, or the support structures are inadequate, to enable them to make a successful transition to their new reality. It is these children that are the focus of this chapter and to whom it is dedicated.

In terms of official statistics, it remains impossible to assess accurately the number of children experiencing loss through separation, divorce or the death of a significant other, such as a sibling, parent, grandparent, carer or friend. Government statistics record that the total child population (under 16s) for 2008 was 13.1 million (National Statistics Online 2009). The same website reports that the number of cohabiting families has risen and these obviously do not have to go through any legal process of divorce, which would mean that they are not statistically recorded except for the decennial census, last taken in 2001. This source records that 13 per cent of children live with cohabiting couples, 23 per cent of children live with lone parents, and 63 per cent of children live with married couples (National Statistics Online 2009). The trend is that fewer parents are marrying or remaining married. The Children's Society assesses that one-third of British children today live apart from their biological father (Children's Society website 2009). The number of looked after children, or children in care (CiC), between the ages of 6 and 16 is around 32,000 in England (DCSF 2009a). These children too will inevitably have experienced loss.

The data are even more challenging when trying to establish the number of children experiencing bereavement, as this is not officially recorded anywhere. However, research by Fauth et al. (2009) using a sample size of 7,500 children established that 3.5 per cent of children between the ages of 5 and 16 have been bereaved of a parent or sibling (1 in 29) and 6.3 per cent have faced the death of a close friend (1 in 16). Combined, these indicate a 10 per cent rate of bereavement experience in the child population.

What these statistics also hide is the loss experienced from the death of grandparents or other significant others, many of whom are care givers for children; thus the numbers both for separation and death must be considered as under-represented. Nonetheless, schools may need to support 10 per cent of their pupils through the experiences of bereavement and at least 30 per cent through loss as a result of separation or divorce. That represents a substantial number.

Sad but is it our job?

The simple answer to this is, yes – it is the job of educational professionals to support pupils through difficult life transitions including loss and bereavement (Children's Workforce Common Core Standards, DfES 2005a). The commitment of schools is also enshrined in the Children Act (2004), which codified the five outcomes of the Every Child Matters Agenda (DfES 2003). It is the responsibility of schools to promote the well-being of the whole child, including his or her psychological health. Even if these legal requirements were not in place, there remain two further justifications for the support of pupils experiencing such difficulties. The first is pragmatic. Achievement in SATs tests and GCSEs and standards of behaviour are almost always impacted upon adversely in pupils experiencing loss and bereavement (DCSF 2009a, Fauth et al. 2009, Statistics Online 2009,

Ribbens McCarthy and Jessop 2005). Secondly, and more humanely, it is the right of every child to receive help when he or she is going through a very difficult time (United Nations Convention on the Rights of Children 1989).

What do children experience when going through loss and grief?

Children's experiences of loss and grief are much the same as those of adults. Experiences of loss through separation, divorce or relocation have many parallels with those of bereavement (Jigsaw4u 2009).

Activity

Following on from your earlier reflection on your childhood, consider your whole life experiences of grief or loss, or those witnessed in people you know or care about. What are the types of feelings you can have when someone very close to you dies or leaves? Write these down, then consider how these feelings could impact on a child or young person in the family.

There have been many theorists who have presented psychological models for the grieving process (Freud 1915, Kübler-Ross 2005, Bowlby 1980, Murray Parkes 1995). Kübler-Ross was one of the first to theorise on the stages of grief that the bereaved experience. These theories were based on her work in the 1960s with terminally ill adults and their relatives. Bowlby and Parkes (1980) challenged her assertion that the bereaved go through a set order of stages in grief, but they identified four commonly experienced phases of grief in adults and these may resonate with your own experiences.

*   *Shock and numbness:* This is experienced mostly in the initial stages of grief when people are first given the news. The mourners have difficulty believing that the death has occurred and struggle to process or comprehend the loss. In children this can be seen as complete denial. This is a protective mechanism that shields them from the terrible pain of loss.
*   *Yearning and searching:* In this phase, survivors experience separation anxiety and still deny or are unable to accept the reality of the loss. In children, especially the young, this can take the form of physically going out and looking for the person. Dreams and nightmares trouble the griever, and sometimes they report having seen or heard the lost one during the day. Here, the mind is re-creating the person to keep at bay the terrible reality of the loss.
*   *Disorganisation and despair:* In this phase, the bereaved may have difficulty concentrating and focusing on normal activities. They forget and lose things. They often report feelings of depression and withdraw socially. They cannot see a future for themselves – certainly not one with joy or hope. Children may be listless, sad and unmotivated. They don't want to join in and seldom laugh.
*   *Reorganisation and recovery:* In this phase, the bereaved rebuild their lives, reconcile

themselves to life without the loved one and begin to experience joy, hope and positivity. Interestingly, children – especially younger children – often show this stage early on, only to revert to the earlier stages when they are psychologically strong enough to bear it, or where the psychological dam they have built to exclude such painful feelings gives way.

Whilst this model of grief experiences is very helpful, it is perhaps Worden (1996) who offers the simplest and most easily accessible account of grief processes in children. Based on empirical studies – that is, reports from those working with real children in the process of suffering psychologically from the effects of grief – he argued that there were four tasks of grieving to be completed before a child could be said to have accepted and moved on from the loss. The use of the term 'task' is significant. It challenges the perception that grief happens to an individual, who just goes through it passively. Instead he favours Freud's concept that grieving requires work or effort, and must be actively engaged with if the individual is to emerge without permanent damage (Freud 1915).

Worden's (1996) four tasks for children (and adults) are:

1   To accept the reality of the loss.
2   To live with, express and work through the pain of grief.
3   To adjust to the new world they live in where the deceased is no longer there.
4   To find and keep a special place for the deceased in their hearts, minds, through memories and/or special places (such as graves or memorial objects), yet to move on with life.

These phases do not necessarily follow this particular order; indeed, they are often experienced together or are revisited as the child reaches a point where he or she can endure the level of pain of the loss, or where new understanding of the permanence of the loss is achieved. It is whilst undertaking these tasks that children or young people (or adults) can get stuck, avoiding some tasks altogether. When this happens over a prolonged period the child is likely to show signs of psychological disturbance or behavioural difficulties, which alert those caring or working with the child to the need for additional help.

One other theory is important in helping education professionals recognise grieving processes and needs. In 1999, Stroebe and Schut proposed a new way of looking at grief experiences. Again, their work was based on years of observations from working therapeutically with adults who were experiencing difficulties with grief processing. This generated what they called the 'dual-process model of coping with loss' (Stroebe et al. 1999: 1). It argued that those experiencing loss switched back and forth between activities that focused on coming to terms with the pain and reality of the loss (grieving) and activities that concentrated on getting on with the new world and the life in which they found themselves (moving on). This jumping back and forth was normal, and both types of activity were needed for a positive outcome from the bereavement. They also argued that those experiencing loss also needed respite from grieving and struggling with new things; thus there were periods of distraction when the pain and struggle could be forgotten completely. This gave rest and was normal too. Very commonly, children, especially the young, demonstrate this jumping back and forth from grieving, to getting on with life, to shutting out both realities. These phases can change in a matter of minutes rather than weeks. Thus a child can be in deep distress and then suddenly ask what is for tea, or rush out and play. This sudden switching of mood can be very disconcerting for parents or professionals when attempting to respond to children's needs.

So what is different for children when experiencing grief and loss?

Two things stand out as distinctly different for children. The first is that they are dependent, physically, financially, psychologically and socially, on the adults around them. Built into this is real insecurity. If one parent has died, then logic dictates that the surviving parent may die also. Suddenly the world feels very unsafe to the child. Profound insecurity is often at the core of any behavioural difficulties which appear. Furthermore, when the house has to be sold and the family move, a grieving child may find themselves in a new area separated from their friends and starting at a new school, with all the stress that this involves. Silverman and Worden (1993) refer to these as secondary losses, which often have a greater impact on a child in terms of stress and well-being than the original death or loss.

In addition, if adults to whom children would normally turn to in difficulty are also grieving, the child may not feel able or willing to seek help from them. If the surviving carer is also developing depressive reactions or denial, or becoming dependent on alcohol to cope, or taking anger out on the children, then this inevitably impacts on the child's own ability to cope. Christ's (2000) study of bereaved families following terminal illness identified that the single greatest factor in children's restitution to well-being was the attitude, openness and stability of the carers and significant others about them (including teaching staff).

The second difference is that children show their grief differently and experience it differently because of the context of developmental stages. They do not have the understanding of the world, the experiences of life, the vocabulary of feelings or the cognitive wiring yet in place to fully comprehend and appreciate what is happening to them. Piaget's cognitive development stage theory (1952) goes some way to understanding the different ways of thinking in children as they grow up. There are four stages of cognitive development, according to Piaget: the sensorimotor (up to about 2 years old); the pre-operational (about 2 to 7 years old); the concrete operational (about 7 to 11 years); and the formal operational thought (about 12 years old onwards), when fully cognitive maturity is reached. In terms of rationalising the loss and death of a loved one, it is easy to see how impossible it is to comprehend the reality of such a death, and to manage the emotional state brought on by such a loss. A child in the sensorimotor or pre-operational stage, who will be unable to decentre, is likely to perceive the death of a carer or sibling as 'someone who is no longer there' or has gone away; an absence that threatens their own survival. Such a child will often feel separation anxiety and cling to objects that recall the missing person, such as clothes or shoes that carry his or her scent. The child may talk about 'mummy coming back soon' and cannot comprehend permanent loss.

The child in the pre-operational stage is often in a magical thinking stage and will often accept and draw comfort from carers' explanations of death and heaven. Sometimes, however, children at this stage believe heaven to be a place that can, like places in their earthly experience, be visited and returned from, so that if dad has gone to heaven then he will come back, like he does from work, or the child can join dad by going on the bus or train to heaven.

Children in the concrete operational stage, on the other hand, are likely to dwell cognitively in facts and in the real world. They want factual answers and logical explanations about the death, or in the case of separation or divorce, the departure. This can place mourning carers in a difficult and distressing position. The interested adult in school can help provide opportunities for unemotional and age-appropriate conversations about what has happened and provide a safe place for children to reason through events.

Cognitive development of the concept of death is significant in the child's overall processing of grief and loss. The original theoretical framework for developmental understanding of what death is was undertaken by Nagy (1948, cited in Goodwin *et al.* 1991), and remains essentially accepted by practitioners, although the age boundaries given below have been accepted now as less firm than the ones Nagy initially proposed.

To come to terms with death, children need to understand that death is:

- inevitable;
- irreversible;
- universal.

A child's understanding of this will be impacted upon by several factors. Their cognitive development as outlined above is significant. It is important to remember that children with learning difficulties where there is cognitive difficulty or developmental delay may be operating at an earlier stage than the one indicated by their age.

According to Christ (2000), children between the ages of 3 and 5 years are generally unable to understand the finality of loss, and therefore separation anxiety marks their responses and their needs. Between 6 and 8 years of age most children understand the finality of death, though they may still believe in the magical elements of afterlife. They may blame themselves for the death or departure of their carer or sibling and this will trouble them greatly. They need explanations and assurance that they are not to blame and will cope better if that happens.

From the age of about 9 years children reach full understanding of the finality, inevitability and universality of death, but it is a very lonely and stark realisation. It is really important to stay alongside a child at this time, and allow them to talk freely about how they feel.

In adolescence, some young people recapture the magical element and seek to reunite with the deceased through the occult. This often snowballs into frightening experiences, rather than comforting ones. For example, a 15-year-old girl whom I supported, whose father had died suddenly, joined a Ouija-board session run by her friends and believed that she had received the message from her dead father that she was going to die in the new year. She needed support to consider rational alternatives to the idea that this message was actually from her father.

The second factor that can impact on children's understanding of death is their stage of social and emotional development, particularly in their recognition and understanding of feelings and strategies for coping with powerful feelings in themselves and others. None of us, adults or children, can cope effortlessly with the power of grief and its pain, but children are far more likely to lack the coping strategies for something so terrible. In addition, they may lack a network of safe and strong relationships with carers, siblings and friends that will provide a cushion for the turbulence and distress of their experience. This is why children often regress in terms of emotional coping when experiencing grief and loss. They can react aggressively, hitting out arbitrarily and irrationally, or become more 'babyish'. Both reactions need sensitive management and support.

The third factor will be a child's past death experiences. If a child has seen dead animals and mortality has been explained in that context, or because a pet or distant relative has died, he or she may understand better what is happening. In a sense, this early experience has already been used to formulate a schema for death. The child can make more sense of it and know that survival is possible. This makes children resilient; such children may have already developed coping strategies for loss.

The ability to communicate feelings and ideas is another factor in coming to terms with loss and grief. As children build their vocabulary and listen to stories or conversations where feelings are explained and situations vicariously explored, they assimilate the language of emotions, facts and concepts about death and loss. A child who is encouraged to articulate feelings verbally will generally cope better than a child who has limited verbal range and therefore resorts more to physical means of expression or withdraws into silence.

Finally, the attitude and love of those around a child will be critical in helping him or her to acquire a working understanding of what is happening; a personal or family 'story' that will change through time, as new understandings emerge.

The consequences of suffering grief and loss

The Childhood Bereavement Network in conjunction with the National Children's Bureau have identified from their research (Fauth *et al.* 2009) that children who have experienced the death of a carer, brother, sister or close friend are 'more likely than their non-bereaved peers to:

- Have a serious illness which involves a stay in hospital – around 60 per cent more likely.
- Have a diagnosable mental disorder – around 55 per cent more likely.
- Have a parent who has had a serious financial crisis – around 40 per cent more likely.
- Have been excluded from school at some point – around 60 per cent more likely.

(taken from Childhood Bereavement Network leaflet 2009, unpaged)

The same study has reported that children who are bereaved are much more likely to experience subsequent stressful events in their lives. These findings dovetail with other, earlier research findings – for example, in Christ's 2000 study, and the 2005 study of mental health issues in children and young people in Great Britain by Green *et al.*

In reality, the impact of death and loss renders children and young people more vulnerable to long-term negative life consequences; though it must be said that many children come through these experiences safe, stronger and more resilient. To do this they need support, not just from family and friends, but also from any caring and informed adults around them, including teaching staff, welfare assistants, family doctors, club leaders and the parents of friends. The latter sections of this chapter will focus on the provision of that informed support.

The government's position

The emergence of official recognition for specialist provision for children and young people experiencing complicated grief has grown over the last 30 years, as child bereavement theory and research has developed (Christ 2000, Dygegrov 2008). Of similar significance is the raising of the status of children in British society from near invisibility to its present central government policy, and this has happened over a similar time scale (DCSF 2008, DfES 2005, 2003). However, the previous government's recognition of and commitment to children's well-being, according to the latest United Nations report, were still inadequate compared with other Western countries (UN Committee on the Rights of the Child 2008). British society and central government were criticised for negative attitudes to children and young people overall – as reflected, for example, in the penal system and in media coverage. This is supported by the findings of the Children's Society Good Childhood Inquiry (2007).

Activity

Take time to consider the last few sentences. As a society do we consider children and young people to be important and to possess rights? Are there elements of our present way of doing things that demonise children or youth, or dismiss them as less important than adults? Consider formulating a list of the rights children are entitled to have recognised by society. Finally consider the rights of children who are experiencing bereavement. To what are they entitled?

Winston's Wish, one of the first charities set up in the UK to support children and families struggling with the impact of grief, have produced their own charter of rights for bereaved children, modified here to focus on educational settings (Stokes 2004: 42):

- Bereaved children are entitled to receive the support they need.
- Bereaved children should feel comfortable expressing all feelings and thoughts associated with grief, such as anger, sadness, guilt and anxiety, and be helped to find appropriate ways to do this.
- Bereaved children have the right to remember the person who died for the rest of their lives if they wish to do so.
- Bereaved children are entitled to receive answers to their questions and information that explains clearly what has happened, why it has happened and what will happen next.
- Bereaved children can benefit from receiving help and understanding from their teachers and fellow students.
- Bereaved children should be asked if they wish to be involved in important decisions that have an impact on their lives (such as planning the funeral and remembering anniversaries).
- Bereaved children can benefit from the opportunity to meet other children who have had similar experiences.

- Bereaved children should be able to choose to continue previously enjoyed activities and interests.
- Bereaved children should be helped to understand that they are not responsible and not to blame for the death.
- Bereaved children have a right to tell their story in a variety of ways and for those stories to be heard, read or seen by those important to them.

These 'rights' will be investigated later in the chapter as the response of schools is discussed.

The formation of voluntary charitably funded organisations, such as the Child Bereavement Charity (CBC), the Childhood Bereavement Network (CBN), Winston's Wish and St Christopher's Candle Project, and the development of family support services in children's and adult hospices, reflects the growing recognition by professionals and the community of the need for organised and dedicated provision to support families, and particularly children and young people, experiencing difficulties because of grief. The CBN's Grief Matters for Children campaign was started in 2006 in a drive to influence government policy to make the provision of grief support for children and families, where needed, a universal and centrally funded service. It also called for official statistics to be gathered on the numbers of children experiencing bereavement of a close family member (CBN 2008). At present, provision of child grief support services is limited, geographically haphazard and small scale, principally because it is provided by small charities (Penny 2008). On the other hand, provision doubled between 2001 and 2008 (CBN 2009).

Recently, the Child and Adolescent Mental Health Services (CAMHS) Review (Davidson 2008) has acknowledged the impact of complicated grief on the mental health of children and the inadequacy of support nationally. It recommended that all local authorities provide or have access to child grief support services and expertise before the difficulties result in the onset of a recognised mental illness in the child that leads to a referral to the CAMHS. As yet the government has declined to make the provision of child grief support mandatory, almost certainly on grounds of cost. However, following a meeting between the CBN and the then DCSF Secretary of State, Ed Balls, there was evidence of increased recognition of need, if as yet no pledge for action (CBN 2009). Growing research evidence is indicating that early intervention could prevent future mental health difficulties (Christ 2000, Rutter 2000), academic underachievement (Fauth et al. 2009, Dowdney 2000, Worden 1996), negative life outcomes such as criminal involvement (Vaswani 2008) and early sexual intercourse (Sweeting et al. 1998) – and as such could save the government money in the long term.

The needs of bereaved children

Activity

Consider what you might need, as a member of staff in an education setting, if you were suddenly bereaved of a close family member. What would you need on learning of the death, around the funeral time and when you return to work? Now translate those needs to those of a child or young person, using your knowledge of their general level of emotional and cognitive development. How much is the same; how much is different?

It is sometimes surprising how similar the needs of grieving adults and children are, but also how vulnerable children are if unsupported. The role of education professionals as caring, supportive adults, unaffected personally by the loss and governed by a professional code of practice, gives schools a unique place in meeting these needs. Schools provide an environment of emotional stability, security, order and routine, sometimes in dramatic contrast to the environments in bereaved households. They also provide access to friends and distraction from painful thoughts. Schools need do very little more to help children actively in this situation. Yet it is plain from listening to accounts of children's experiences that schools can sometimes really make life very difficult for children and young people and their families in this situation (Stokes 2004).

Activity

Consider your own setting. If a pupil you support or know were suddenly bereaved of a parent, what would your school do to help? What would you do?

Winston's Wish Charter, above, gives some indication of the needs of children who are grieving (Stokes 2004). Ways that a school and its staff can respond will now be discussed.

Knowing what to do and how to respond

It really helps if a school has had the foresight to prepare a bereavement policy to take account of eventualities such as the death of a relative or friend of a pupil, or the death of a pupil, teacher or other member of staff, alongside the required critical incident policy for major accidents or trauma. Having designated people who have been trained to support the bereaved is also very helpful. Making sure that lines of communication have been worked out and letters have been drafted can save a great deal of stress at the time of the incident.

Helping children to acquire a concept of death without frightening them can also be planned as part of the personal, social and health education (PSHE) and science curricula. Showing examples of children and families coping with loss through stories and literature can also lay the foundations of coping strategies. The present secondary PSHE syllabus provides for education about death and loss, but the relevant section is often ignored because it is deemed too sensitive and distressing (DCSF 2009b, QCDA 2009). Hopefully in the future it will be implemented more consistently.

Acknowledgement of the severity of the event

All children need acknowledgement of their grief and allowances made for their state of mind in the same way that the school staff and hierarchy would respond to the needs of a bereaved colleague. In particular, it is likely – though not universal – that a child or young person may struggle to reach the academic standards previously achieved or expected. In the present personalised, target-driven education climate this can create tensions in teaching staff.

Case study: Marie

An 11-year-old girl, referred to a charity for support, was orphaned three weeks before sitting her year 6 SATs test. She was a high achiever, so in the end she sat the tests. She wanted to be with her friends and do what they had to do. After the literacy exam she wept because she had kept seeing her father's name in words in the text. Needless to say she did not achieve the level 5 grade expected, and that impacted on the school's overall achievement as it was a small school. It was to the credit of the school that the girl was never made aware of the impact her 'failure' to achieve had on the school's league table position.

Grieving pupils may also struggle to concentrate in class or choose to be less sociable than before. They may not. They may show signs of demotivation and depression, or have no apparent reaction to the death at all. Both responses fall within the normal range for children. Young children often lock down their grief and show it years after the event when they are mature enough to release the feelings, or when going through periods of transition, such as a change of key stage or school (Dyregrov 2008, Potts 2005, Brown 2000). Awareness of bereavement in the family does need to be passed on, teacher to teacher, and the issue must be considered as a potential factor in any unusual behaviour being shown.

To talk about it or not as they choose

Grieving children or young people need to be given the right to talk about how they feel with a safe, non-judgemental adult. They also need to have the right not to talk about the death, if that is what they want. Essentially children need to be in control of accessing the type of support that is given and should be given the choice of what sort of information is passed to staff, peers and friends about the death, and how this is done. Adolescents often prefer information to be extremely limited, seeing bereavement as an excluding fault that sets them apart from everyone else (Christ 2000). Despite this, they need to know that a person they trust is available to help when feelings overwhelm them.

Unfortunately bereaved children are frequently subject to peer bullying or exclusion at all ages, as a result of their bereavement; thus increased vigilance is also called for by all staff including lunchtime welfare staff (Winston's Wish website 2009, Child Bereavement Charity website 2009).

Case study: Suzie

A 7-year-old girl called Suzie (not her real name) was referred by a school for support to a grief support charity because her behaviour was poor. It turned out that her friends no longer wanted to play with her because her mother had died and she was somehow different. Once this was addressed, through circle time in the class and targeted intervention in the playground by 'buddies', the child was able to continue in that school and cope better with her loss.

Speak simply and factually of the dead and of death

Bereaved children frequently need to hear the name of the person who died and memories of that person voiced when it seems natural to do so, rather than find that the person is 'never to be mentioned' to avoid any upset. This is one of the major areas that education professionals raise when receiving training in this area. They fear saying the wrong thing and making things worse for the child and the family. Generally, keeping language simple, factual, calmly expressed but not cold, and paying attention to the responses of the child will work.

A quiet place to withdraw

Children and young people need the right to have times when they feel upset without drawing down upon themselves a fussing attention, or being urged to 'pull themselves together' and 'grow up'. The provision of a quiet place to go can be invaluable, and the right to access that even in the middle of the literacy hour or at breaks and lunchtimes. Sometimes just the option of coming in during breaks to 'do a job' for the teacher can be enough to meet their needs.

The security of sensitively applied but consistent behaviour boundaries

Children or young people may first show their grief difficulties in inappropriate behaviour that contravenes school or class rules, such as in angry outbursts. Clearly they need help to find ways of expressing anger safely. Sanctions for misbehaviour need to be given, but given calmly and without severe expressions of disapproval or anger. They also need follow-up conversations and support about the legitimacy of their feelings, as well as suggestions and strategies for expressing anger in ways that do not get them into trouble or hurt others or themselves.

Anniversaries and important dates – special memorial activities

Those staff most involved with supporting a grieving child may wish to speak privately to him or her so as to recognise an upcoming date, such as the anniversary of the death, or a birthday, or Christmas, Father's or Mother's Day. Some schools have memorial gardens where children who have lost someone they care about can plant a perennial flower as part of these events.

Re-establishing personal control

When facing sudden bereavement the world turns topsy-turvy and becomes unrecognisable. Terrible events have rendered the bereaved helpless and powerless. As a result there are often feelings of deep insecurity and disorientation. Maximising opportunities to give children control or choice, even over the smallest of decisions, can help to restore some sense of personal control and safety – for example, 'Do you want to stay in and help me this break-time or go out to play, or stay in the quiet room?' At secondary age, 'Would it be easier to do your homework in the learning mentor's room at lunch or leave it until you go home?'

Addressing fears, self-blame and insecurity

Children and young people frequently have deep worries and fears following bereavement. Many of these centre around what will happen to them or to their surviving family members – for example, a parent or younger siblings. The opportunity to talk this through with someone can be very helpful. Having been visited by the reality of death or loss, they can experience sudden terrible anxiety about whether their surviving carer has died too, and will insist on going home to check. Allowing a phone call to that carer can offer respite from that fear.

Some younger pupils will show signs of regressive behaviours as a result of their sense of insecurity.

Case study: Thomas

Thomas (name changed to preserve confidentiality), aged 4, had just started in reception and had previously lost his dad when he was 3. Despite being cognitively advanced he acted like a 3-year-old, careering about in the playground and carelessly bumping into others, not concentrating well in class, being noisy and calling out, using every free choice activity time to sit in the small tepee tent in the classroom and build the same tower over and over again. All of these behaviours were attempts to generate or call for safety and security. In this situation all that was needed was advice to the teacher on the normality of the reaction, and encouragement to accept that and offer praise when Thomas acted more in line with his stage of development. The opportunity to have some form of comfort object available was also suggested, such as a favourite soft toy.

Teachers and parents often fear that children showing signs of regression will get 'stuck' there, but in almost all cases this is a temporary but necessary state that will mutate into age-appropriate behaviour when the child feels less unsafe. They also fear giving 'special' attention or privileges to one child and see this as inherently unfair, but the principle of meeting individual need is helpful to counteract that concern.

Support and kindness shown to the family

Bereaved parents and carers may show real difficulty for many months in being organised and systematic about getting a child to school on time, with the right equipment, dinner money, clean school uniform, healthy packed lunch, homework done and appropriate signed consent form for any trips. They may struggle to get to school to pick up the child straight after school. They may have financial difficulties and be overwhelmed by their own grief and loss. An inflexible and critical approach needs to be avoided and some clever lateral thinking undertaken, such as having spare uniforms and pencil cases and PE kits around. Reassurance about their children's progress and well-being and an acknowledgement of efforts made will help to relieve their anxieties. Attention to detail in correspondence is important – for example, not sending letters addressed to Mr and Mrs when 'Mrs' has died. Parents who are supported will have more energy to support their own children. The only area where allowances may not be made is where there are indications of possible neglect or physical or emotional abuse. In these situations the school's safeguarding policy must be followed.

The uniqueness of bereavement and its absence of time limits

Finally it is important to recognise that all grief situations and responses are unique, and in most cases these responses are the right way for that individual child to grieve. It can take years to process grief. If a school and its staff can create a climate of acceptance and confidence in each bereaved child to grieve as necessary, with extra support and helpful strategies according to requirements, then children are likely to make the transition to living life to the full again. In doing so children may end up more resilient than before.

Supporting pupils one to one

Most pupils experiencing grief or loss will cope well without any one-to-one intervention from the school, provided there is open communication with the family and a sensitive and supportive environment. However, a few pupils may show signs of prolonged grief, or marked and persistent or deteriorating behavioural disturbance. Teachers, learning mentors and teaching assistants may find themselves volunteering for, or charged with, the task of supporting pupils one to one, because their difficulties with grief and loss have impacted badly on their ability to function and learn in school.

There are very helpful websites for professionals involved in this type of support, including Winston's Wish and the Child Bereavement Charity (see websites). They produce downloadable guidance and a phone line for enquiries and advice. Christ (2000) gives a very useful summary of developmentally related needs and concerns which can form the basis of one-to-one approaches. Primary-age workbooks such as Crossley's *Muddles, Puddles and Sunshine* (2000), or Collins's *It's Okay to be Sad* (2005) for younger children, can also be valuable. There are a number of fiction books that can help as well (see Winston's Wish website 2009).

In general, children experiencing difficulties will either be 'stuck' in a particular phase of mourning, unable to process what is necessary in order to move on in their grief or loss transition, or may not have the necessary support from family and friends, for a whole variety of reasons, to help them through the experience. Pupils may have difficulty in handling the intense emotions that can arise in this situation.

Support programmes and manuals tend to address several key processes:

1   Listening to the child in a non-judgemental way where the conversation is supportive, confidential and private.
2   Help in understanding what death is and what it means for the pupil in practical terms (within the developmental reach of the individual child).
3   Giving opportunities to talk about the circumstances of the death, the funeral and the family reaction, and the characteristics of the person who has died (good and bad).

4   Remembering the person in special ways, including the creation of a private and personal treasure or memory box of mementoes for use by the child through his or her future life.
5   Addressing any beliefs that a pupil might have about being to blame for a separation or death.
6   Strategies for recognising, acknowledging and managing safely or releasing the powerful emotions of grief and loss, including anger and anxiety.
7   Eventually, when the pupil is ready, assisting in a good-bye to the person, such as by releasing a balloon with a message to the deceased, written by the child, attached.
8   Being there when occasionally needed in the long term.

Pupils may not need all or any of these things; they may just need a safe adult and some creative activity to do that calms and distracts them. It is important not to force a child to talk, but instead to set up activities and let the child lead the conversation.

At secondary level pupils often prefer to talk, and don't require advice or solutions; they just need to be heard. They frequently do not want any special attention, or any action that singles them out in front of their peers as being different. This needs to be respected. Secondary pupils may also prefer to access support through chat rooms on the Winston's Wish or Cruse websites. Both have designated web pages for adolescents, with live inter-action from peers. Supporting the friends of the pupils in school can also be a very effective use of your time, as they too may have their worries and concerns.

One-to-one work also allows for contact with the carers or parents that may enable you to support them as well. Sometimes just seeing a friendly face and receiving a kind, under-standing word makes all the difference to carers who are struggling to cope.

Knowing your limits

Engaging in support for pupils with such intense emotions or desperate needs may take precious time and personal energy. It can generate anxiety and uncertainty of direction. It is important to be aware of your own personal and professional limits. If at all possible, have a mentor in school to whom you can talk and offload your feelings, within the bounds of a confidential agreement.

Advice can be sought from the bereavement charity helplines. More and more areas have access to voluntary agencies that will take referrals from schools (with parental agree-ment) for professional support of the pupil, or who will visit and talk face to face with you and offer help with resources and activities.

It is not a fault, but a safe and sensible act, to step aside when a pupil's needs outstrip your professional knowledge and skill. It doesn't mean that you no longer care or will withdraw from any type of support, but simply means that a pupil needs alternative help.

Conclusion

More children than we like to acknowledge will experience a negative life event whilst growing up (Fauth *et al.* 2009). The impact of experiencing grief or the loss of a key person will be significant, and can be damaging in both the short term and long term (CBN 2009). Pupils are entitled to be given the necessary support to move through this life transition, and schools are agents for that support by virtue of the requirements of the Every Child Matters Agenda (DfES 2003). Understanding a little about the psychological processes of grief and loss and the developmental needs of pupils can actively enhance a school's response to pupils and families suffering this way. In most situations and in most ways, a school and its dedicated, professional and caring staff, with its safe and secure routines, can really make a difference to the experiences of the grieving child. However, educational professionals are not usually trained child counsellors or bereavement specialists, and knowing when to call in professional support is the key to the successful management of this unhappy situation (Stokes 2004). As the government and local authorities become better able to recognise need, more and more children and young people will receive the helping hand they require at times of loss: 'Anyone in contact with a child has an impact on that child's mental health and psychological well-being. The challenge for all of us is to remember that and to be able to respond if things start to go wrong' (Davidson 2008: 6).

> I've really moved on. I didn't used be able to speak about my dad dying, now I can and it's okay.
>
> (Emily, 12 years old)

Bibliography

Bowlby, J. (1980) *Loss, Sadness and Depression*. New York: Basic Books.

Brown, E. (2000) *Loss, Change and Grief: An Educational Perspective*. London: Fulton.

Child Bereavement Charity website (2009) www.childbereavement.org.uk (accessed 29 December 2009).

Childhood Bereavement Network (2008) *Grief Matters for Children Bulletin*, 12 (April): 1.

Childhood Bereavement Network and National Children's Bureau (2009) *Key Findings from New CBN and NCB Research in Bereaved Children*. London: CBN/NCB.

The Children's Society Good Childhood Inquiry Report Summaries (2007) www.children society.org.uk (accessed 31 December 2009).

Christ, C. H. (2000) *Healing Children's Grief: Surviving a Parent's Death through Cancer*. Oxford: Oxford University Press.

Collins, M. (2005) *It's OK to be Sad*. London: Paul Chapman.

Crossley, D. (2000) *Muddles, Puddles and Sunshine*. Cheltenham: Winston's Wish.

Davidson, J. (2008) *Children and Young People in Mind: Child and Adolescent Mental Health Services Review*. London: DCSF.

DCSF (2008) *Targeted Mental Health in Schools – Using the Evidence to Inform your Approach: A Practical Guide for Head Teachers and Commissioners*. London: DCSF.

—— (2009) Children Looked After in England 2008. www.dcsf.gov.uk/rsgateway/DB/SFR/s00810/index.shtml (accessed 30 December 2009).

—— (2009) Primary Curriculum Review. www.dcsf.gov.uk/primarycurriculumreview (accessed 2 January 2010).

DfES (2003) *Every Child Matters Agenda*. London: DfES.

—— (2005) *Common Core of Skills and Knowledge for the Children's Workforce*. London: DfES.

Dowdney, L. (2000) 'Annotation: Childhood Bereavement Following Parental Death'. *Journal of Child Psychology and Psychiatry and Allied Disciplines*, 41: 819–30.

Dyregrov, A. (2008) *Grief in Children*, 2nd edn. London: Kingsley.

Fauth, B., Thompson, M. and Penny, A. (2009) *Associations between Childhood Bereavement and Children's Background, Experiences and Outcomes: Secondary Analysis of the Mental Health of Children and Young People in Great Britain, 2004*. London: HMSO.

Freud, S. (1957 (1915)) *Mourning and Melancholia* (Vol. 14). London: Hogarth.

Goodwin, C. and Davidson, P. (1991) 'A Child's Cognitive Perception of Death'. *Early Childhood Education Journal*, 19 (2) (December): 21–24.

Green, H., McGinnity, A., Meltzer, H., Ford, T. and Goodman, R. (2005) *Mental Health of Children and Young People in Great Britain*, 2004. London: HMSO.

Jigsaw4u website (2009) jigsaw4u.org.uk (accessed 6 January 2010).

Kübler-Ross, E. (2005) *On Grief and Grieving: Finding the Meaning of Grief Through the Five Stages of Loss*. London: Simon & Schuster Ltd.

Murray Parkes, C. (1995) *Bereavement: Studies of Grief in Adult Life*. London: Routledge.

National Statistics Online (2009) www.statistics.gov.uk/cci/nugget_print.asp?ID=2193 (accessed 30 December 2009).

Penny, A. (2009) 'Childhood Bereavement Network'. Talk to St Christopher's Hospice Post-Graduate Child Bereavement Support Course, Help the Hospices, London, January (lecture notes).

Piaget, J. (1952) *The Origins of Intelligence in Children*. New York: International Universities Press.

Potts, S. (2005) *Everylife: Death, Bereavement and Life Through the Eyes of Children, Parents and Practitioners*. Salisbury: APS Publishing.

Qualifications and Curriculum Development Agency (2009) http://curriculum.qcda.gov.uk/key-stages-3-and-4/subjects/pshe/index.aspx (accessed 29 December 2009). Personal and Social Education Syllabi for Key Stage 3 and 4.

Ribbens McCarthy, J. and Jessop, J. (2005) *Young People, Bereavement and Loss: Disruptive Transitions?* London: National Children's Bureau.

Rutter, M. (2000) 'Psychosocial Influences: Critiques, Findings and Research Needs'. *Journal of Development and Psychopathology*, 12: 375–405.

Silverman, P. and Worden, J. W. (1993) 'Children's Reaction to the Death of a Parent', in Stroebe, M., Stroebe, W. and Hansson, R. (eds) *Handbook of Bereavement: Theory, Research and Intervention*. Cambridge: Cambridge University Press: 300–16.

Stokes, J. (2004) *Then, Now and Always: Supporting Children as They Journey Through Grief: A Guide for Practitioners*. Cheltenham: Winston's Wish.

Stroebe, M. and Schut, H. (1999) 'The Dual Process Model of Coping with Bereavement: Rationale and Description'. *Death Studies*, 23: 197–224.

Sweeting, H., West, P. and Richards, M. P. M. (1998) 'Teenage Family Life, Lifestyles and Life Chances: Associations with Family Structure, Conflict with Parents and Joint Family Activity'. *Journal of Law, Policy and the Family*, 12: 15–46.

United Nations (1989) Convention on the Rights of the Child, Office of the United Nations High Commissioner for Human Rights Assembly Resolution 44/25 of 20 November 1989. www2.ohchr.org/English.law.crc.htm (accessed 5 January 2010).

United Nations Committee on the Rights of the Child (2008) Considerations of the Report Submitted by State Parties under article 44 of the Convention, Concluding Observations, United Kingdom of Great Britain and Northern Ireland, 3 October, CRC/C/GBR/CO/4.

Vaswani, N. (2008) 'Persistent Offender Profile: Focus on Bereavement', Criminal Justice Social Work Development Centre for Scotland, Paper No. 13. Glasgow: Universities of Edinburgh and Stirling.

Winston's Wish website (2009) Story Book. http://www.winstonswish.org.uk/page.asp?section=0001000100030006&pagetitle=Suggested+Reading+List (accessed 29 December 2009).

Worden, W. (1996) *Children and Grief*. New York: Guilford.

Websites

Child Bereavement Charity: www.childbereavement.org.uk.

Childhood Bereavement Network: www.childhoodbereavementnetwork.org.uk.

Cruse Youth website: www.rd4u.org.uk.

www.hospicenet.org.

Jigsaw4u: www.jigsaw4u.org.uk.

Winston's Wish: www.winstonswish.org.uk.

Chapter 8

Looked-after children

Karen Bassett

My surface may seem smooth but my surface is my mask, ever-varying and ever-concealing. Beneath lies no complacence. Beneath lies confusion, and fear, and aloneness . . .

(From the poem 'Please Hear What I'm Not Saying' by Charles C. Finn, 1966)

Introduction

Government statistics show that 60,900 children fell into the category of 'looked after' on 31 March 2009 (National Statistics, DCSF 2009); most of these are of white British origin. All schools will contain children who have been abused or neglected, and in some instances these may be children who are still living *at risk* or are *in need*, but whose level of need does not reach the requisite thresholds for action to be taken to place them into a home of safety. Most children do have caring places that they call home, with supportive, protecting, nurturing adults to interact with them, encourage them and take an interest in their development. However, for a significant number of children this level of care is either absent or inconsistent. Whatever the reasons for this, it can lead to a child and their siblings being placed in the care of others, be this a local authority children's home, foster family or adoptive family. These children are often referred to as 'looked-after' or as children in care (CiC), and they may be extremely vulnerable, fragile, distressed or disturbed; they will often present in school as pupils who are challenging to teach and may be personally and emotionally challenging to work with.

Case study

Peter, 13, has been in foster care since he was 3. His mother, an alcoholic, spent money on drink, providing little or no food for herself or her child. Daily, she would drink herself into a stupor, leaving her physically and emotionally unavailable to her son, unable to meet even his basic needs. Peter was neglected, left to fend for himself, until he came to the attention of Social Services. His experience left him emotionally damaged and in the care of a foster family, and although all his needs are met, he still struggles to show his emotions and build relationships with others. Peter has contact visits with his mother; on the surface he is accepting of his situation but beneath lies anger, disappointment and resentment which reveals itself in destructive behaviour and hurtful words towards his carers. It is then that his inner turmoil is revealed.

Whilst schools generally have more direct information about CiC, consideration should also be given to adopted children who may also have experienced trauma or loss in their lives. It should never be assumed that because children are in the safety of a new family, the impact and effect of earlier trauma or loss is no longer felt or is no longer present. Children who have experienced emotional upheaval will see the world from a different perspective to those who have not. This may have an impact on their behaviour in the classroom and sometimes their behaviour can be misunderstood (Archer and Gordon 2006).

What the law says

A court can make an order to take a child into care if there is secure evidence that there is indication that the following may be happening to a child:

- the child is suffering, or is likely to suffer, significant harm;
- the harm is caused by those the child is living with – for example, the child's parents;
- harm would be caused because of insufficient care being given to the child by the parents in the future; or
- the child is likely to suffer harm because he or she is beyond parental control.

A care order places responsibility on the child's local authority to look after the child, providing accommodation and care. The local authority is responsible for meeting all of that child's needs whilst the care order is in place. A care order can only be made for children under 17 years of age (or 16, for those who are married); it ceases if the child is adopted but otherwise lasts until the child's eighteenth birthday (www.direct.gov.uk).

Under Section 52 of the Children Act (2004), local authorities (LAs) have a statutory duty to promote the educational achievement of looked-after children. The government's Green Paper 'Care Matters' (DfES 2006a) was followed by the publication of 'Care Matters: Transforming the Lives of Children and Young People in Care' (DfES 2006b), which explores the many problems faced by looked-after children. As part of improving the lives of CiC the proposals ensure that every LA must now appoint a *virtual school head* to track the schooling of every child in care (DCSF 2009). It is the duty of these virtual heads to ensure that schools know which children are in care, and they must act to provide additional targeted provision for them.

Activity

It is good practice for schools to hold regular staff meetings for both teaching staff and support staff. Whilst information concerning CiC must be treated as confidential and shared on a need-to-know basis only, if appropriate ask a school SENCO to organise a visit from an educational psychologist or social worker who can give an overview of what it means to be a CiC, and the impact this can have on a child's educational experience and progress.

Seek permission to create a staff reference booklet that is kept in a secure area, which identifies CiC and gives helpful information about possible difficulties or triggers they may face within the educational setting. Information you could include is which key adult is assigned to them and strategies to use with the child in that person's absence. It is not necessary for everyone to know the details of the child's situation but it is helpful to know if more sensitive care and understanding is needed.

All schools have a statutory duty to ensure that all children are enabled to achieve the five outcomes of the Every Child Matters agenda (DfES 2004). In the case of looked-after children there is an even greater responsibility placed on schools, since research has shown that they are one of the most vulnerable groups in society today. Statistics (www.every childmatters.gov.uk 2009) show that in 2008 just 14 per cent of looked-after children achieved five A*–C grade GCSEs (DCSF 2009).

Social Justice is the principle at the heart of the Every Child Matters agenda. Knowles describes Social Justice as: 'ensuring all have an equal chance to attain the necessary goods and conditions they need to thrive and achieve well-being' (Knowles 2009: 5). In the case of CiC, roles that would usually be undertaken by the parents must be fulfilled by schools in partnership with the 'Team Around the Child'.

> . . . such a glance is precisely my salvation, my only hope, and I know it. That is, if it's followed by acceptance, if it's followed by love. It's the only thing that can liberate me from myself, from my own self-built prison walls, from the barriers I so painstakingly erect. It's the only thing that will assure me of what I can't assure myself, that I am really worth something . . .
>
> (Finn 1966)

The importance of education for CiC – schools and working with outside agencies

Schools supporting CiC will be better able to meet their needs if they are working in a multi-agency partnership with other bodies and professionals who have specialist skills, knowledge and understanding in working with CiC. Regular multi-agency meetings enable a child's welfare to be carefully monitored and discussed (DCSF 2009).

In most cases, CiC or those who have been adopted will have experienced a great deal of pain before being removed from their birth family; and it is likely some form of perhaps intensive therapy will be needed to help them come to terms with what has happened to them. Support of this nature must be undertaken by a trained person, but helping a child in this way is likely to be more effective if the school is aware of the help the child is receiving. It is also useful if the school can further support that help through the practice of its staff, particularly since even when in care there are still some risks involved; for example, home placements can break down as both child and adults struggle to deal with the impact of earlier trauma or loss. CiC may present with difficult or disturbed behaviour both at home and in school due to their experiences. Unless these children are understood and strategies are put in place to help them, school exclusion can occur as children struggle to cope with the changes that have taken place in their lives. Indeed, at its best, education provides opportunities for new learning experiences for the looked-after child and also promotes resilience – the inner strength, determination and flexibility we can draw on to help us through challenging times. If we are resilient we can adapt to and survive our differing life experiences (Knowles 2009).

Case study

'In homes where the baby finds no mutuality, where the parent's face does not reflect the baby's experience and where the child's spontaneous gesture is not recognised or appreciated, neither trust in others nor confidence in the self develops' (Hopkins 1990). Joseph was physically abused as an infant and has moved foster families many times. He constantly talks and interrupts in class; he likes to be the centre of things. Anxious to ensure the teacher takes sufficient interest in him, and expecting her to be available to him at all times, he pretends to struggle with work to gain attention.

Schools and supporting CiC

Inclusion

It is important that looked-after children experience inclusion; they have additional learning needs, which may or may not be immediately obvious. Winnicott (1965) stresses the importance of facilitating opportunities within school for 'second chance learning' and corrective experience. These enable children to negotiate incomplete developmental processes, and deal appropriately with any challenges. Draw alongside the child, model positive relationship through your own interactions with them and others. Use physical contact, eye contact, facial expression and body language to make them feel attended to and secure. Take time to talk to them and show interest in them and their interests, join in with whole-class activities such as circle time, or play cards or board games with them and involve others from their peer group.

Schools and differentiating learning

Differentiation is essential; tasks must be matched to developmental level. This allows children who have developed attachment difficulties following trauma greater opportunity to succeed; this is important since such children can have an extremely fragile sense of self. Learning experiences and activities must be challenging, yet achievable; they must engage children's interest and be broken into manageable chunks. Find out what children's interests are, identify the developmental stage they are at and their preferred learning style, then tailor activities to maximise these. Support the child during teacher exposition by making notes on a dry-wipe board, including key points and vocabulary. Deal with one step of the task at a time and offer children a choice of ways to present their work; for example, using ICT, drama, music or art. Keep your language simple and positive and be enthusiastic whilst speaking or directing – this will help to keep children engaged and on task.

Schools and making supportive relationships with CiC

> Please listen carefully and try to hear what I'm not saying, what I'd like to be able to say, what for survival I need to say, but what I can't say . . .
>
> (Finn 1966)

It is vital to establish trusting supportive relationships with looked-after children; this lowers anxiety, which is beneficial to global development. This, in turn, has a positive impact on how children view themselves, see others and perceive the world. Differentiating language helps children to understand the meaning of words. They may not have experienced 'kindness', or what it is to 'share': it is important to explain and give examples of what kindness and sharing mean, and at the same time to present yourself as a positive role model who can develop good relationships. Compared to others of the same chronological age, looked-after children often have a lower emotional and social developmental age; this needs consideration or their education will suffer. Trauma and loss impact upon emotional development, and this is a major factor in lack of achievement (Greenhalgh 1994: 14). Educationally disadvantaged because of their emotional disability, these children will also often display behaviours that are misunderstood.

Case study

Lucy spends most lessons fiddling with pen pots or swinging on her chair, looking out of the window. The teacher asks a question, Lucy calls out the answer and is reminded by the teacher that pupils need to raise their hands. Another child is invited to answer and does so correctly; Lucy slams a pencil on her desk. The teaching assistant moves towards her and touches her shoulder gently, saying, 'Lucy, you were very clever to know the answer to that question, just pop your hand up next time, then you won't be so disappointed.' Lucy snaps back, 'Go away and leave me alone!' Having been placed in care voluntarily by her mother, subsequent feelings of rejection resurface after her effort to participate in the lesson goes wrong; she is left feeling hurt and embarrassed. Unused to people drawing alongside, showing understanding or giving praise she resorts to the behaviour she is familiar with: rejection.

As a relationship builds with a looked-after or adopted child, the child may disclose personal information about himself or herself, as trust grows. Never promise a child that you will not tell anyone else what he or she has told you; disclosures must be passed on to the staff member responsible for child protection. Even if the child is in care, disclosures must still be passed on to the child protection officer within school. It is important that information given with regard to the child's current or previous situation or trauma is recorded; it may be of legal significance and may help outside agency experts gain greater insight into the child's psychological well-being, and even assist in the healing process (DfES 2005a).

Personal education allowance

The 'Personal Education Allowance (PEA) for Looked-After Children: Statutory Guidance for Local Education Authorities' (DfES 2008) states that looked-after children must be given one-to-one support in school and one-to-one tuition from a personal education allowance to ensure that they achieve all they are capable of. It is at the PEA meetings that need for intervention is identified; the PEA links directly to the Statutory Care Plan.

Examples of good practice that can be discussed and implemented for CiC at PEA meetings

- Combined mental and physical health planning and review meetings involving the school nurse and primary mental health care co-ordinator.
- Anger and behaviour management training for all school staff involved with CiC (DfES 2005b:19).
- Provision of 'second-chance' emotional learning through the learning mentor role to help insecure-attachment-style children adapt certain behaviours.
- Provision of additional literacy and maths sets to ensure greater differentiation for children who may be at a younger developmental stage than their peers.
- Planning formats showing clear differentiation of learning objectives, resources and outcomes that are appropriate for all developmental stages; aiding success and improving self-esteem.
- Support for other pupils who may be distressed or unable to cope as a result of witnessing angry behaviour or outbursts from CiC in the classroom.

(Caroline Alford, SENCO 2009)

Assessment of pupil progress

With 'assessment of pupil progress', which is currently being introduced into schools, personalised learning and assessment of learning is being given much greater focus. Attention must also be given to prior knowledge, talents and multiple intelligences (Gardner 1993). It is important to understand that personal, social and emotional developmental delays may lower academic achievement, but a child may well be talented in other ways or capable of displaying other intelligences. For example, a child may express himself or herself creatively through dance, needlework or gardening, rather than through a piece of writing. Celebration of alternative-style achievements and any developmental progress, however small, enables looked-after children to experience success; this helps to raise their self-esteem. Community or out-of-school learning opportunities are of immense value because they allow those children who have never been on visits before to have new experiences. Such opportunities can bring education to life and this in turn can impact positively on academic learning, helping children to discover new knowledge and understanding.

Encouragement to participate in after-school activities will also benefit CiC. Homework clubs can successfully provide support which is sometimes unavailable at home; this will aid achievement. Attendance of sports, creative or music clubs can encourage friendships to develop (Gilligan 2001: 28) and social skills to be learned outside of the classroom environment.

Families, feeling secure and attachment

Experience illustrates that families change and evolve. The notion of the nuclear family model described by Knowles (2009: 48) no longer exists as the norm (if, indeed, it ever did); care and the upbringing of children are now routinely shared among extended family members, friends, neighbours, community schemes and education. John Bowlby's (1953) work on 'maternal deprivation' suggested children are adversely affected by the absence of their mother; he suggested that they are less resilient because of it. Recent research (Bronfenbrenner 1998, cited in Knowles 2006: 34) has found that children can benefit from shared care given in the wider social context. A child given care that is 'good enough' for him or her to feel safe and be healthy will make developmental progress. Children are able to adapt, and can form attachments with significant adults other than parents – provided they are given the time and opportunity to do so.

Unfortunately, some children do not receive 'good-enough' care (Bowlby 1969, cited in Bombèr 2007: 93), either at home or in the wider social context. It is these children who find themselves in the care of the local authority, and these children who often develop insecure attachment styles (Geddes 2006). Parents may be unable to care for their child for a variety of reasons; some require support through their own difficult circumstances, whilst others treat their children as possessions to control and to do what they like with. As Knowles states, 'a child is not a possession or an object; it is a human being of itself and therefore needs to be accepted on these terms and its wants, needs and desires considered – as are those of adults' (2009: 29).

John Bowlby's attachment theory states that, depending upon the quality of interaction between a child and its parent, a child will form either a secure or insecure attachment (1951). The attachment a child forms will govern how that child values and behaves within any further relationships. We are shaped by those around us and our early experiences of care. Despite difficult earlier experiences, the mould can be re-shaped by new experiences and other significant relationships. However, in some cases this takes years, if it happens at all. Research undertaken by Lewis and Ramsay (1995) shows that babies have a predisposition to learn and that their brains have huge potential for growth and development. Insensitive care towards children causes the release of the stress hormone cortisol, which is detrimental to brain development. The earlier a child experiences stress, the greater the impact upon brain function. Excessive cortisol damages the brain preventing vital neural pathway development and leading to vulnerabilities in emotional, behavioural and cognitive ability (Gerhardt 2009: 72). Children who have suffered such stress as infants tend to have attachment difficulties and a distorted interpretation of themselves, others and the world around them.

Many looked-after or adopted children present with insecure attachment styles; as a result, their patterns of behaviour and thought may be difficult to understand. Trained experts can help foster parents, adoptive parents and teaching staff to translate these behaviours, thoughts and actions so as to improve the ways in which education is approached.

What are the attachment styles?

In *Attachment in the Classroom*, Geddes (2006) identifies the four main attachment styles. These are listed in the table below.

Table 8.1 Attachment styles

Secure	Child has had positive early experiences with parents. Good self-esteem. Manages well at school. Makes the most of learning opportunities. Does not see adults as a threat. Believes that the world is a good place to be. Is confident to go out and explore the world. Forms meaningful relationships with others.
Avoidant	May have had an abusive or depressed parent. Feels unsafe; things are out of their control. Self-sufficient, no emotional connections. Easily overlooked; makes no demands. Shuts down. Dissociates. Values achievement and accomplishment; puts tasks before relationships. High level of anxiety, eager to please and comply. Highly functional or obsessive compulsive. Feelings of sadness or isolation. Build-up of stress causes aggressive outbursts; this is surprising given the child's usual control.
Ambivalent	Inconsistent emotional and physical care, possibly from violent parents or parent with mental health difficulties. Continually 'on edge'. Latches onto significant adult, attempts to work out what the person is thinking or feeling. Addicted to seeking attention; may be chatty or interrupting. Clingy. Rejecting. Charming but superficial; makes false connections. The child is driven by anxiety to ensure that his or her basic needs will be met. Relationships are secondary to needs. Occupied with securing attention; learning becomes secondary. Blames others for hurt or upsets. Child feels unable to rely on the interest or emotional availability of anyone. Resentful, holds grudges and exhausting to work with.
Disorganised	Possibly experienced severe neglect, or chaotic or abusive environment. Adult source of security may be a source of fear, causing conflict of emotion. Expects the worst, believes no one genuinely cares or considers him or her. Tries to control everything and everyone, refuses to be dependent on anyone or reveal vulnerabilities. Loud, demanding; enjoys shocking others. Withdraws or demands to be left alone.

Disorganised	Emotionally and physically unpredictable; a health and safety risk to self and others. Hyper-vigilant, often fighting feelings of fear and panic. Struggles in relationships, desires to control or fails to connect. May struggle with learning which involves taking risks.

Children need consistency and it is important to remember that feelings and behaviours tend to intensify if there are changes to curriculum plans, or to teaching staff and arrangements. Ill health and tiredness can also have a huge impact upon their ability to cope within the school environment.

It is important to recognise and identify attachment styles where possible so strategies to support these children can be adopted. With well-planned strategies in place, these children can make progress both educationally and emotionally. It is important to also be aware that some of these behaviours are true of even the most secure children at certain times in their lives.

The effects of trauma and loss

Extreme trauma challenges an individual's coping system to the limit; temporarily overwhelmed they may dissociate from reality. The psychiatric definition of trauma includes any experience which threatens your life or your body, or any harm which is inflicted on you intentionally.

(APA 1994, cited in Gerhardt 2004: 134)

Table 8.2 The effects of trauma and loss

Trauma includes:	Trauma may present as:	The child may be suffering loss of:
Neglect	High anxiety	Birth family
Physical abuse	Hyper-vigilance	Foster family
Sexual abuse	Intrusive thoughts	Friends
Emotional abuse	Tiredness through disturbed sleep	School
Witnessing of violence or abuse towards others		Sensations of a 'secure base'
	Poor concentration	
Separation from birth mother	Daydreaming	
	Problems with short-term memory	
	Irritability	
	Outbursts of anger	
	Withdrawal	
	Passivity	

Source: Laura Dunstan, Educational Psychologist (2008)

The language of the traumatised child is 'hurt'. Undesired or unusual behaviours are a form of communication for such a child; a way to express emotions, or the danger the child has been in, or maybe still is in. It may be a desperate cry for help, and concerns should always be discussed with your child protection team or SENCO, with a log made in line with your school's policies and procedures.

Case study

You alone can break down the wall behind which I tremble, you alone can remove my mask, you alone can release me from my shadow-world of panic, from my lonely prison, if you choose to. Please choose to . . .

(Finn 1966)

Stefan's behaviour usually deteriorated around Christmas time; as other children talked excitedly of time to be spent together with their families, he would be silently worrying and wondering. He had lost count of how many arranged visits his mother had failed to attend, how many of her Christmas gifts had failed to arrive and of how often he felt on the outside looking in; included and cared for but never really truly part of the family who looked after him. Excitement usually gave way to anxiety; anxiety was followed by disappointment; disappointment led to anger, which was soon followed by guilt.

Some CiC feel overwhelmed, rejected or that they are 'different' from others. The sense of loss they have is like bereavement; they may pass through the various stages of grief as though after the death of a close family member. They may become rooted in one or more of the stages of grief and require expert help in understanding how to negotiate their progress successfully. It should be remembered that, even once the stages have been processed, the sense of loss or grief can be rekindled throughout life, particularly on birthdays, Christmas, Mother's Day, Father's Day or any other significant anniversary. As Freud (1909) stated: 'a thing which has not been understood inevitably reappears; like an unlaid ghost, it cannot rest until the mystery has been resolved and the spell broken' (Sigmund Freud, cited in Bowlby 2000: 137).

Between the ages of 7 and 9, as cognitive processes change, children move out of the 'magical thinking' stage (Piaget 1953). Some children in care may create a fantasy image in their minds about their mother or father, or their earlier life with their parents. The move from 'magical thinking' to the realisation of the truth can have a powerful impact upon them. This is the process of accepting that their mother, father, or both, relinquished care of them – or worse still, failed them in such a way that the authorities had to intervene. This may trigger 'adaptive grieving' (Brodzinsky et al. 1993), as children begin to question and understand why they are in care. Denial, anger, sadness or shame may follow as they begin to realise the reasons.

Adopted children may be curious about their birth family, wishing to re-establish a relationship with them. They can become disloyal towards their adoptive family, or, in the case of looked-after children, towards the foster family. This can be a challenging time for the families caring for them or the staff working to educate them. It is important that the grieving process is worked through, however, because this allows emotional growth. Feelings of loss and abandonment can be triggered by what many of us would consider to be normal events such as the end of term, a change of teacher or relocation of the class. Any change may provoke painful memories of earlier changes, preventing the child from being able to relax or experience joy in moving forward in the same way as other children who have not experienced trauma.

The home/school partnership

Developing a partnership between home and school is a crucial part of working with children. This is especially important for children with additional learning needs; both home and school have much information to bring about the child. Do not allow conflict or division to spoil this partnership; in sharing strategies between home and school, carers, parents and teachers can learn from one another and maintain consistency (Bombèr 2008: 252).

Additional attachment figures

Looked-after children benefit from the allocation of a key adult in school. Relationships are valuable, giving opportunity for adaptation and emotional recovery. Key adults must be chosen carefully, and it is important to involve the child in this process since they are expected to build a relationship with this adult. The key adult must not be the class teacher. The position is a challenging one; the key adult's role in the child's life must be recognised within the school community so that they are given respect and some influence in the wider decision making that surrounds the child.

Key adults must have a strong sense of self and security in who they are, since they must be able to understand what children might be feeling about themselves, or their past, and be prepared for the child to project these feelings on to them. They should be emotionally and physically available to the child, providing emotional containment through physical, verbal or affective communication, and should encourage 'relative dependency' and opportunities for 'second-chance learning'. Through support and scaffolding with commentary they can help children practise unfamiliar behaviour, such as having fun or showing kindness or affection. It is vital to communicate empathy and hope to children; they need to know that their feelings are understood and that there is a way forward for them. The key adult should advocate on behalf of the child, particularly when their behaviour has been misunderstood, and should create a support package for others so that they know how to behave should children present with challenging or unusual behaviour. In knowing children really well they can be aware of triggers and intervene actively before incidents occur. Encouraging a whole-class inclusive attitude can give children a sense of belonging, whilst building a good relationship of understanding with the class teacher means that key adults can withdraw children to work individually or within small groups should the need arise. Use of ALN resources and differentiation in an integrated manner will also support inclusion of CiC. It is strongly recommended, however, that the key adult has had some training in how best to help these children. The needs of CiC and the response to those needs by the adults around them must be managed in an appropriate way, to protect and support both children and adults.

Managing change

Looked-after children have experienced great inconsistency, so change and transition can be difficult for them. This can provide challenges to the school; for example, when children move to a new class at the beginning of a new school year, or move from one key stage to another. Again, moving to a new school altogether may seem extremely daunting for CiC.

Helpful strategies include:

- Talking enthusiastically and positively about forthcoming changes and supporting children through them. It helps to visit new settings with them, introducing them to the new teachers or key adult and giving opportunities for them to see you communicating with and trusting these adults with their continued care. Consistency and the sharing of good practice is vital; whilst handing over documentation is essential, nothing can be compared to the understanding conveyed through personal contact and discussion.
- Meeting the child on the morning of the day of change; familiar adults provide reassurance and reduce the anxiety of the unknown. Familiar objects brought from home can ease the transition from home to school (for example, a photograph on a key ring).
- Providing visual timetables and support for movement to and from lessons also helps children to negotiate a stressful and difficult time. If the change is a temporary one due to teacher absence, classroom or curricular change, support is equally necessary.
- There is a strong case for schools to use their higher-level teaching assistants to cover absence; they can offer a greater consistency of care, understanding and routine than visitors to the school are able to.
- Often children with insecure attachment styles do not understand their own behaviour and are unable to explain themselves. In verbalising behaviour and associated emotions you can help them to understand what they are feeling. Talk through the behaviour and suggest why they may be reacting as they are. For example: 'I know your teacher being away today has upset you. By throwing that book, you are showing me that you feel angry and frustrated by this change of staff. I think you are missing your teacher and feel as if they have forgotten you. Your teacher will return to school when they are better, and in the meantime they have asked me to help you do all the things that they usually help you with.'
- Often CiC, despite being placed in a secure home and school environment, will be distressed by endings and goodbyes. These can be painful reminders of past events, so it is important to be sensitive to their feelings and stagger goodbyes; in their eyes everything they know and trust is about to be taken from them once again.

Activity

To help children adjust, create two identical memory books of their time at the school to show that you will remember them. This provides a way for them to remember you too. Leave some pages blank so as to encourage them to continue with it, adding their new beginnings whilst you add your own. Arrange a temporary exchange of books so that each of you may read how your lives have moved forward. It can also help to maintain links via cards or letters, although opportunity should also be given for children to develop new relationships within the new setting.

(Wallis 2003 and Wittenberg 1999)

The importance of establishing good communication

Children who have experienced interruption in neural pathway development often have speech and communication difficulties. Only 7 per cent of communication is spoken; children can benefit from being taught to understand and use sign language, body language and facial expression. They may not have experience of certain feelings or have the vocabulary to express such feelings, and will need to be taught. Use simple language and be explicit in what you say; always check their understanding of what has been said or what is expected of them, because some children have good expressive language ability but may have poor receptive language ability.

It is important to model appropriate communication in relationship behaviours to children, particularly to those who have experienced physical or sexual abuse. Inappropriate touching should be gently and sensitively discouraged; do so in a way that does not leave the child feeling ashamed or embarrassed by their actions. Some children find it difficult to understand that it is possible to have different relationships with different people. Social skills groups and the use of social stories can help children learn to translate social situations, whilst after-school clubs can be a valuable social setting where academic pressure is removed and children can be themselves and interact on a different level with their peer group. CiC need to know where, when and with whom to share their personal stories; 'sharing' time to meet with the key adult should ideally be built into the school timetable. These children need help and guidance in knowing how to connect with others in appropriate, healthy ways.

Activity

When translating emotional states, feelings and behaviours for the child, it can be useful to wonder aloud what is happening and why it is happening. Teaching children to use mind-mapping techniques and De Bono's 'six thinking hats' helps them organise their thoughts and feelings (2000). Compose a mind map of each different emotion with them, illustrate it with personal experiences that relate to the emotion, and include new vocabulary to help develop emotional language and enable them to express themselves.

The importance of establishing permanency and constancy

Behaviour can be misunderstood; it is important to recognise that it can indicate developmental vulnerabilities. There is an order to development, and children cannot skip developmental stages; they need to negotiate each stage before progressing to the next. Piaget (1953) discovered through his studies of children that babies were unable to understand that objects and people exist even when they are outside their visual range. Babies only become able to learn object permanency by the age of about 6 or 7 months; relationship and parenting permanency develops through infants' interaction with their parents or carers as they watch them come and go in their everyday lives. Looked-after children who have been subjected to inconsistent parenting or neglect do not understand permanency in the context of relationships.

Permanency and constancy are linked: once permanency in relationship has been established it naturally leads to the parent, or carer, supporting the child to make sense of all situations and differing behaviours. A secure child understands that the parent or carer is still the parent even despite changes in emotion, words, body language, facial expression or behaviour. An insecure child is unable to build up a complete picture of the parent or carer, and will make and retain a distinction between 'loving' mummy and 'angry' mummy. This means such a child is also unable to recognise itself as being a complete person with varying emotions.

When you are working with CiC it is important to remember that their behaviour may not be representational of chronological age and they may still be working through stages of development that other children in their class have already completed. In particular, looked-after children may not have negotiated the developmental stages of permanency and constancy. It is useful for these children to play games such as hide and seek, which helps to develop permanency. You can also make connections through sensory reminders such as personal touch, eye contact and physical presence. Talk to children about what they like (and do not like), in terms of food, clothes, television programmes – whatever the child wants to talk about – sharing a book or magazine is a good way to start such a conversation. Children will also need to do this on a more personal level: what they like about themselves, what you like about them. CiC may not have had a stable caring relationship with an adult; they may not have learnt to express themselves in this way and may never have had the opportunity to 'chat' about themselves to a significant other. Talking to others – our friends and family – in this way helps us to build our identity and sense of self; without it, and without seeing ourselves reflected through others, we never know who we are.

The importance of acknowledging feelings

Looked-after children may not have experience of how to contain feelings or translate them: emotional containment is developed through significant adults acknowledging children's feelings; talking them through, explaining them, reassuring children and making them feel secure. CiC tend to be familiar with fear and anxiety and unfamiliar with phrases such as 'calm down' or 'relax'. Being excited can 'feel' the same as being scared; unless someone has explained the emotion, children can become confused about what they are feeling and what they are 'supposed' to feel, or are 'allowed' to feel. CiC may need practice in order to be able to internalise how to recognise different feelings and how they relate to context; they may also need to be taught to self-soothe. This is a strategy for coping with feelings; it might take the form of simply having a bath, or listening to music. In a sense it is about learning to 'parent' oneself – to care for oneself as though for an infant. When teaching CiC to self-soothe, you must spend time building a relationship of trust with children so that they will listen to your advice. Observe how they communicate their anxiety – do they fidget, withdraw from the room, self-harm? Show empathy and help children to identify 'triggers'; then intervene to reduce their anxiety. Use 'wondering aloud' and commentaries such as: 'I have noticed that when you make a mistake, you get angry with yourself and bang your head. I think you feel as if you have done something wrong and you are punishing yourself. You need to know that it is OK to make mistakes: we learn from mistakes, these are good learning opportunities. Instead of banging your head on the desk, let's think of some things we can do to calm down.' Identify what might have triggered the anxiety, then affirm for the child that 'it's OK' to feel like this, then provide a choice of activities – this will help to soothe the child. Choice is important; it enables children to remain in control of the situation and how they are feeling. In co-regulating children in this way, we are teaching them how to self-regulate, which will allow them to monitor their own emotions and behavioural responses. Take them to a quiet corner with comfortable cushions, bubble lamps, fish tanks or lava lamps; read a favourite book to them; play soothing music; go for a walk in the open air. Perhaps establish an agreed chair or place that they can retreat to.

The importance of establishing friendships

Children with attachment difficulties find it hard to make and keep friends; they need support with this. Allowing time for a friendship to develop between the child and yourself can help the child to progress to healthy and appropriate relationships with their peers. Provide appropriate structures for friendship to take place, perhaps by giving time to play board games towards the end of a lesson.

Breakfast clubs can provide a healthy start to the day for many children in school. They play a valuable role in the care and support of 'at-risk', 'in-need' and looked-after children, particularly in terms of developing healthy eating habits, good social skills and friendship.

Intervene actively to prevent negative labels being applied to the child; this may involve explaining clearly to other children why the child has reacted in a certain way to a certain situation or to something that was said. Discourage other children from expecting a particular type of behaviour from the child and encourage them to help the child avoid problematic behaviour. There are many excellent social skills resources available to teachers these days; make use of these to enhance social skills development. One of the most powerful methods for helping a child understand what is appropriate within friendship – and indeed other relationships – and what is not, is to model appropriate behaviours in friendship yourself. It can be very damaging and counter-productive for a looked-after child to experience the loss of a trusted and valued friendship that has taken so much more time and effort to establish than it might have taken for another, more secure child.

Resolution of conflict

CiC often find themselves in conflict with others. The 'learning mentor' role adds a new dimension to how children are supported in school, and plays an important part in helping them to understand how to deal with conflict. This adult offers emotional support to both child and teacher, giving them time to talk through any matters that are troubling them. With CiC it is important to choose one's battles, dealing only with essential issues that can make a difference to the child developmentally or academically. Providing choices allows children an element of control; remember, much of their life experience has been beyond their control.

When dealing with conflict, be explicit and empathic when asserting instructions. Use time-out and time-in cards if appropriate. When the child is calm, play games that involve taking turns or following rules, allowing you to model appropriate behaviour and resolution. When conflict is evident, remain calm, talk through the problem and discuss possible solutions before finally making a decision that is most appropriate for all. Use language wisely; these children can easily misinterpret something you have said. Children who are hurting can be astute at recognising your own insecurities and using them against you. It is important not to react to this; it is not personal, but is tied up with how the child is feeling about himself or herself. Take time to reflect and consider your own thoughts, feelings and handling of any situations. Are there lessons you can learn?

Creating a success book reminds children how far they have come and encourages them should they regress. Stay connected to children; involve only one or two adults in any conflict and advocate on behalf of the child so he or she does not feel 'psychologically' backed into a corner. Offer reparation activities immediately in order to re-establish trust and relationship. Take health and safety issues seriously; an angry child, particularly one with a disorganised attachment style, can be a danger to themselves and others. Training in restraint methods could prove to be a wise investment for the key adult's continuing professional development. Exclusion should be the last port of call for any child, and any possible measures to help prevent this should be explored.

Whilst working with CiC can be a challenging experience, the by-product of the time invested in drawing alongside them will almost certainly be professional and personal growth for yourself and developmental and academic progression for the children. In taking time to look beyond their behaviour and build a relationship of trust and understanding, you can break down any emotional walls they have built and lead them gently forward to a brighter, more secure future, where, fully supported, they may achieve all of the desired outcomes of the Every Child Matters agenda.

Acknowledgements go to my colleagues, who have informed this chapter, as part of their work with children and staff in the schools of West Sussex through their in-service training programmes. In particular: Caroline Alford (SENCO, The Orchards Middle School, Worthing); Laura Dunstan (Educational Psychologist, WSxCC); Yvette Pinnell (Primary Mental Healthcare Worker, WSxCC); and Phillipa Webb (Highly Specialised Speech and Language Therapist).

Bibliography

Archer, C. and Gordon, C. (2006) *New Families, Old Script*. London: Jessica Kingsley Publishers.
Bentham, S. and Hutchins, R. (2006) *Practical Tips for Teaching Assistants*. London: Routledge.
Bombèr, L. M. (2007) *Inside I'm Hurting*. London: Worth Publishing.
Bowlby, J. (1951) *Maternal Care and Mental Health*. Geneva: World Health Organisation.
—— (1953) *Child Care and the Growth of Love*. London: Pelican Books.
—— (1969) *Attachment & Loss*. London: Penguin.
—— (2000) *A Secure Base: Clinical Applications of Attachment Theory*. London: Routledge.

Brodzinsky, D. M., Schecter, M. D. and Marantz Henig, R. (1993) *Being Adopted – The Lifelong Search for Self.* New York: Anchor Books.

DCSF (2009) *Improving the Educational Achievement of Children in Care (Looked After Children).* London: DCSF.

De Bono, E. (2000) *Six Thinking Hats.* London: Penguin Books.

DfES (2005a) *Common Core Skills and Knowledge for the Children's Workforce.* London: DfES.

—— (2005b) *Every Child Matters: Change for Children Common Core.* London: DfES.

—— (2006a) *Care Matters: Transforming the Lives of Children and Young People in Care.* London: DfES.

—— (2006b) *Every Child Matters: Working Together to Safeguard Children.* London: DfES.

—— (2007) *Every Child Matters: Every Parent Matters.* London: DfES.

Geddes, H. (2006) *Attachment in the Classroom.* London: Worth Publishing.

Gerhardt, S. (2004) *Why Love Matters.* London: Routledge.

Gilligan, R. (2001) *Promoting Resilience: A Resource on Working with Children in the Care System.* London: BAAF.

Greenhalgh, P. (1994) *Emotional Growth and Learning.* London: Routledge.

Howe, D. (2005) *Child Abuse & Neglect: Attachment, Development and Intervention.* London: Palgrave Macmillan.

Hughes, D. (1998) *Building the Bonds: Awakening Love in Deeply Troubled Children.* Lanham, MD: Jason Aronson.

Kagan, J., Kearsley, R. B. and Zelazo, P. (1980) *Infancy: Its Place in Human Development.* Cambridge, MA: Harvard University Press.

Knowles, G. (2006) *Supporting Inclusive Practice.* London: David Fulton Publishers.

—— (2009) *Ensuring Every Child Matters.* London: Sage.

Piaget, J. (1953) *The Origins of Intelligence in Children.* London: Routledge & Kegan Paul.

Wall, Hon. Mr Justice (1997) *Rooted Sorrows – Psychoanalytical Perspectives on Child Protection Assessment, Therapy and Treatment.* Bristol: Jordan Publishing.

Winnicott, D. W. (1965) *The Maturational Process and the Facilitating Environment.* London: Karnac Books.

Wittenberg, I. S. (1998) *The Emotional Experience of Learning and Teaching.* London: Karnac Books.

Websites

http://www.baaf.org.uk.

http://www.direct.gov.uk/en/Parents/Adoptionfosteringandchildrenincare/ChildrenInCare/DG_10027535.

http://www.everychildmatters.gov.uk/caf.

http://www.everychildmatters.gov.uk/resources-and-practice/IG00060.

Chapter 9

Planning your teaching to ensure Every Child Matters

Gianna Knowles

Introduction

This book has explored the variety of intellectual, cultural, social and linguistic needs backgrounds that individual children might bring to the learning environment. The different chapters have explored a variety of factors that, if not considered and managed appropriately, may unwittingly lead those managing the learning environment to place unnecessary barriers in the way of a child's learning. In particular, the book has raised issues with regard to learning needs that must be considered in relation to: the challenges of teaching children for whom English is an additional language; those who have a special educational need; those who experience barriers to their learning because of their gender; those who have suffered loss or bereavement; those who are gifted and talented; those who are disabled; and looked-after children.

Planning learning activities and managing the learning environment is a challenge in itself. The thought of also needing to consider the range of different learning needs that individual children bring to the classroom, such as the ones discussed in this book, can seem daunting. However, while so far this book has explored the *differences* between children, this chapter looks at children's learning from the standpoint of what can unite them. For example, this may be through designing learning activities that look at working with children who share the same learning styles or *intelligences*. Or it may be through grouping children who have the same personalized learning targets or interests. Children may speak different languages; they may approach life from differing cultural or gender perspectives; they may learn at different rates; they may be coming to terms with devastating events in their home lives – but most children can be encouraged to learn if learning activities are presented in ways that meet their learning styles. That is, if a learning activity is planned with consideration given to the variety of ways that will best suit individual learners – and we can share learning styles without necessarily sharing cultures – it is more likely that learning will take place. A literacy lesson that is planned with consideration of a range of learning styles, and taught in a way that allows all children's learning styles to be triggered, will help all children to become more proficient in English, whether it is their main language or not. Similarly children who feel that their learning has meaning for them – because the subject interests them, because they have had some input into planning what they are to learn, or because they know how to assess their learning – will be more motivated to achieve. Therefore, the aim of this chapter is to explore supporting inclusive practice through consideration of learning styles and the DCSF's current priority of personalized learning.

Assuming knowledge and understanding

Before discussing how approaching teaching and learning through thinking about children's learning styles and a personalized learning approach can support developing inclusive practice, a further concept to consider is that learning takes place in a *context*; learners make sense of the new learning they are engaged in, in relation to the skills, knowledge and understanding they already have. If those who are supporting the child's learning make assumptions about these skills, knowledge and understanding, or make value judgements about what they *ought* to know, then, however carefully the lesson has been planned, children will not learn as effectively as they might. The following case study will explain this concept more fully.

Case study: the importance of monitoring and assessing a child's prior skills, knowledge and understanding

Krisjanis is in year 3. He has just joined his new school, having moved to the south coast of England from Latvia. His class is doing a history topic about the Romans in Britain. Krisjanis has studied history before and he knows that it is about researching the past. His understanding of chronology is that expected from a child in year 3. He has learnt about Latvian history and has a year 3 knowledge and understanding of Latvia's recent struggle for independence, first from the Russian empire and then from the USSR. However, he has little or no knowledge of the Romans, since although what we now call Latvia was known to the Romans, it never formed part of the Roman Empire.

The skills and understanding that are specific to the subject of history are universal; historical skills and understanding apply to whatever history is being studied, anywhere in the world. Most children who have been brought up in Britain bring to their study of history at school some knowledge and understanding of the Romans, since this historical knowledge is deeply woven into mainstream British life. It is variously portrayed through books, stories, films and other media. Therefore, many children who have been brought up in Britain, whatever their background, will recognize a picture of a Roman soldier. The child who is new to this aspect of British history begins his or her learning at a different place from the child who has some knowledge.

In this way, when Krisjanis first started learning about the Romans, those working with him thought that he was less able in history than his peer group. Even taking into account that English is an additional language for him, he still seemed unable to engage at all in the lessons. Having discussed it, the class teacher and teaching assistant began to realize that they had approached planning and teaching the work based on the assumption that all the children were already familiar with the Romans from work in key stage 1, and that most children would have some culturally acquired knowledge about the subject. Having realized that the Romans meant nothing to Krisjanis, they changed the way that tasks were presented to him and he began to demonstrate that he did indeed possess appropriate historical skills and understanding for his age range.

Good practices in teaching and learning support enable all to learn

In 2003, Ofsted published 'Yes He Can', a report that comments on the factors contributing to the success that some schools are having in enabling boys to write well (Ofsted 2003: 1). The report was written following visits to and inspections of seven primary schools and eight secondary schools. What is particularly important about the report is that the schools were chosen because the difference in performance in writing between the girls and the boys was significantly smaller than that found in other schools, and also the schools had good results overall. 'This was to avoid selecting schools where the gap was smaller than usual because of poor performance by girls' (ibid.). That is to say, the schools were selected because *all* children were writing well, although the focus of the inspectors was on those aspects of teaching and learning support that were enabling boys to write well. Therefore, in studying the main findings of 'Yes He Can', it is possible to gain some idea about what will enable all children to achieve.

Case study: factors contributing to children writing well

- There is a culture in the school and classroom where all children's intellectual, cultural and aesthetic accomplishments are valued.
- In terms of written work, value is placed on:

  1 the use of a range of writing styles and approaches – for example, report writing, recounting and instructions – and not only narrative (stories);
  2 the ability to write succinctly, as well as descriptively, is valued;
  3 the ability to write logically is valued as much as the ability to write expressively.

- Feedback is prompt and indicates clearly what has been done well and what can be improved.
- Pupils are often given a choice as to the content of their writing, even if the form or genre is prescribed.
- Writing tasks are purposeful and written for real audiences, through 'publishing' and displaying writing.
- Writing tasks are tackled in stages, with feedback or review at each stage of planning and drafting.

(Ofsted 2003: 3)

Perhaps one of the most significant aspects of the findings of this report is that it keeps coming back to the fact that children achieve best in schools where it is the children themselves and their efforts that are valued. In the case of writing, as seen above, children do well when: consideration is given to how they naturally prefer to write; there is a purpose to the writing; those who are supporting their learning help them to structure and plan their writing and give practical feedback (that is, they help the child to achieve success in the endeavour); and when the writing is finished it is celebrated by being shared with others. As the report comments, 'Many boys in particular seem to need to know that someone is watching over and caring about their efforts, to be able to see a clear purpose for their work, and to experience tangible progress in order to maintain motivation' (Ofsted 2003: 5).

Further factors that contributed to the success of the children's achievement were adults supporting and directing the learning, and teachers showing interest and enthusiasm for the tasks. In particular, boys did well in schools where there existed powerful male role models (ibid.: 7). Good teaching of basic skills was also a contributing factor to success (ibid.: 9) – that is, ensuring that children have the tools they need to achieve. In the case of writing, these tools include a good handwriting style (or access to a word processor where handwriting is difficult), knowledge and understanding of phonics and spelling rules, and knowledge and understanding of grammar rules.

Children wrote well where the schools had established a positive whole-school approach to reading, again supported by a strong home–school partnership. However, the reading culture was successful in these schools, as it was recognized that children, like adults, have a wide-ranging interest in the material they like to read. Not all children like reading fiction; some prefer to read information material, often linked to hobbies and interests (ibid.: 12). Children succeed where they are motivated by having their interests considered and those designing the learning activities are providing a 'balance . . . between support and challenge' (ibid.: 17).

Intelligence and multiple intelligences

Chapter 4 discussed the notion that, traditionally, only particular forms of behaviour have led to intelligence being recognized, and that society has only prized and rewarded these behaviours. Consequently, schools have focused their teaching and teaching methods on this notion of intelligence. In the main, the form of intelligence that has been most recognized is that which enables the child to reason in an abstract and logical way and, often, to use this ability to solve problems, sometimes producing new and innovative solutions. However, Howard Gardner's work on multiple intelligences has challenged this notion of what we might regard as intelligence and how we ought to structure learning activities for children. Gardner's work stemmed from his concern that, particularly in industrialized 'Western' societies, the notion of intelligence is based on the assumption that 'it is a single, general capacity that every human being possesses to a greater or lesser extent; and that, however defined, it can be measured by standardized verbal instruments, such as short-answer, paper-and-pencil tests' (Gardner 1993: xiii).

In Gardner's view, simply looking around at the different abilities children and adults display, particularly in the everyday tasks and functions they perform, refutes the notion that intelligence is only that which can be measured by a very particular form of test (ibid.: xiv). Gardner suggests that it is 'necessary to include a far wider and more universal set of competences than has ordinarily been considered' (ibid.). Initially, Gardner suggested there may be seven 'candidates' that might be described as intelligences: linguistic and logical-mathematical intelligences; musical intelligence; spatial intelligence; bodily-kinaesthetic intelligence; and two forms of personal intelligence, one directed towards other persons (interpersonal intelligence) and one directed at the self (intrapersonal intelligence) (ibid.). Although Gardner states that 'there will never be a master list of three, seven or three hundred intelligences which can be endorsed by investigators' (ibid.: 59), the important thing is: 'Central to my notion of intelligence is the existence of one or more basic information-processing operations or mechanisms, which can deal with specific kinds of input' (ibid.: 63). That is to say, our capacity to deal with situations that require logical reasoning or mathematical ability will be dealt with by our logical–mathematical intelligence, but our capacity to respond to a ball being thrown at us will be dealt with by our kinaesthetic intelligence.

Multiple intelligences and school-based teaching and learning

In the previous section we have seen how Gardner has identified seven forms of intelligence. This was developed by the DCSF to include nine intelligences (www.nationalstrategies.standards.dcsf.gov.uk 2010).

- Learning through *verbal–linguistic* intelligence includes activities such as: reading; using word banks or vocabulary linked to the learning activity; writing in different genres, including narrative, recount, report, instructions and poetry; debating and 'hot-seating' activities; and using humour, jokes and storytelling.
- Learning through *logical–mathematical* intelligence includes activities such as: using abstract formulae and symbols; using graphic and diagrammatic ways of presenting information; employing number sequences and calculations; encoding and decoding; exploring relationships and problem-solving; and exploring patterns and games.
- Learning through *visual–spatial* intelligence includes activities such as: visualizing images in response to ideas or stories; actively engaging the imagination; representing knowledge and understanding through the use of colour schemes; exploring ideas through patterns, designs, painting or drawing; using mind mapping to structure learning; pretending and 'making' ideas into objects.
- Learning through *body–kinaesthetic* intelligence includes activities such as: working through formal dance steps and creative, expressive dance; role playing; learning while making physical actions and gestures; drama; martial arts; physical exercise; mime; inventing games; and playing conventional sports.
- Learning through *musical–rhythmic* intelligence includes activities such as: making rhythmic patterns; making vocal sounds (singing, for example); engaging in musical composition; using percussion instruments; humming; having music as an environmental background; and showing learning through musical performance.
- Learning through *interpersonal* intelligence includes activities such as: giving feedback about learning; receiving feedback; being sensitive to others' feelings; employing co-operative learning strategies (group work, for example); learning through 'jigsawing' activities; and group projects.
- Learning through *intrapersonal* intelligence includes activities such as: being allowed time for silent reflection (as opposed to 'doing' something); engaging a range of thinking strategies and focusing and concentration strategies; being

required to use higher-order reasoning skills (analysing and philosophizing, for example); and being allowed to work independently.

- Learning through *naturalistic* intelligence includes activities such as: working with, or learning about, living things (plants, the human body and animals); learning by being outside in the naturalistic environment or focusing on global environmental issues; planting and growing things; exploring wider social issues, psychology, and human motivations.

While each of the intelligences listed above has its own body of skills, knowledge and understanding, each can be used as a means to gain knowledge in other areas (ibid.). Following the 'triggers' in the list above, we might, for example, use music to learn spellings and mathematical times tables; use body movement to bring to life and explore different periods of history; and the skills of comparing and contrasting to analyse characters in a story (ibid.). And, if children are taught about multiple intelligences and their own multiple intelligences, 'how to access them, how to strengthen them, and how to actively use them in learning and in everyday life' (ibid.), then it is likely that they will be more motivated to learn and will achieve more.

Activity: planning learning activities that include a range of learning styles

- While working with children over the next few days, keep with you a checklist of the different intelligences you see being displayed.
- Keep a record of the learning styles, or intelligences, that lesson activities trigger.
- Do some intelligences and learning styles dominate the way that activities are planned?
- Are there any intelligences and learning styles that are never used?
- At your next planning meeting see if there is an opportunity to explore introducing a wider range of ways in which learning can be accessed.

Activity: how are literacy and numeracy taught in your school?

While working with children who are undertaking literacy and numeracy activities, ask yourself the following questions:

- Which learning styles and intelligences are being focused on?
- Are all children able to access the learning intended?
- Could the activities be made more accessible to more children if other learning styles were used?
- Do I have the opportunity to discuss this with colleagues, or influence the planning of activities, thereby removing the barriers to learning being experienced by some children?

Meeting diverse learning needs through visual, auditory and kinaesthetic learning styles

Many schools now use the visual, auditory and kinaesthetic, or VAK, approach to learning.

The VAK approach

This approach encourages schools to plan varied activities in response to a range of learning factors. It is suggested that schools use ideas about learning styles to consider how:

- lessons can be varied and interesting to engage children in using visual, auditory and kinaesthetic modes;
- different subject disciplines can promote and develop particular ways of learning – for example, art and design could support and develop visual perception, and PE could support and develop kinaesthetic learning;
- mixing different types of materials, elements and explanations can aid children's attention and help them learn more effectively.

(DfES 2004: 53)

- *Visual* learning takes place through the use of pictures, charts, diagrams, video and ICT images, and may also include the written word. A learning activity that incorporates visual learning would:

  - ask children to collect information from carefully selected visual sources that support the intended learning;
  - follow up their initial hypothesis with further research, conducted independently, or through carefully selected support material; and
  - explore their new knowledge and understanding by representing it in a visual way.

  (ibid.)

- *Auditory* learning takes place through:

  - listening to explanations;
  - taking part in discussions;
  - giving oral presentations.

  (ibid.: 54)

- *Kinaesthetic* learning takes place when learners are physically engaged in a task:

  - through role play; and
  - practical tasks.

  (ibid.)

Case study: a history lesson taught through VAK

The children are learning about Victorian schools. They are working in groups.

Visual learning:

Each group is given a picture of a Victorian classroom. Different groups given a specific focus to research:

*   How is the classroom organized? How are the children and teacher seated?
*   What do they seem to be learning and how do you know?

Having agreed the answer to their question, the group must then use other sources available to research two other facts about Victorian schools and make a poster showing what they have learnt. Each group then presents the poster to the rest of the class using role play, either as a Victorian pupil or teacher. Depending on the age of the children, provide a timer for each group and ask them to ensure their presentation does not last more than the time allotted.

The learning activity may take place across a number of lessons. If you are supporting the learning help the class and individual groups structure the completion of the task by providing specific instructions in manageable 'chunks' and by conducting 'mini-plenaries' throughout the teaching sessions to re-focus on what learning is taking place, allow groups to share interim ideas with each other, highlight good practice and ensure that learning is progressing at an appropriate pace.

Auditory learning:

Auditory learning happens through the children being given the opportunity to discuss the pictures and their ideas. When they have completed their posters, they present them to the rest of the class, explaining what they have found out and what their posters show.

Kinaesthetic learning:

This learning style is used as the task is a practical activity, involving moving around to collect resources and make a poster. Rehearsing the presentation of the poster through role play and the final presentation also reinforce kinaesthetic learning.

As has already been discussed in this chapter, if information is presented to children in a variety of ways, and they are allowed to record their learning in ways other than writing, it is more likely that they will engage in their learning and be motivated to complete tasks. This is not to say that using a recording method other than writing is somehow 'easier', but that it can provide a recording medium that is more in tune with a child's own learning style, and therefore better enables such a child to take on board the intended learning for any given activity. Therefore, in planning any lesson activity it is necessary to think through how the learning can be presented and recorded – visually, aurally and kinaesthetically.

Think wacky

Smith and Call suggest that where key facts need to be learnt, 'think of slightly absurd ways of teaching them and installing them in memory' (1999: 66). This gives the children's memory a 'key' or 'handle' to attach the new information to. An example they give is of a teacher who used a foam hand, the sort sold at concerts and sports events, to help embed subject-specific vocabulary in a science lesson. For example, when she held it as a 'thumbs up' sign the class stood up and chanted 'up with evaporation'. When it was held in the 'thumbs down' position the children sat down and chanted 'down with condensation' (ibid.).

Plan for brain breaks

Brain breaks are based on the notion that human beings are naturally active creatures. Children's attention will wander, and this may affect behaviour if children are expected to remain still and silent over a period of time. Indeed, planning brain breaks into lesson activities usually has the effect of preventing any unwanted behaviour from occurring. Brain breaks help to keep the children in the most receptive state for learning, since a brain break involves physical activity, and this, in turn, increases oxygen supply to the brain and releases neurotrophins, which are natural neural growth promoters. Movement also promises some relief from stress (ibid.: 153). Knowing when to have a brain break is a matter of professional judgement. It will depend on the physical attentiveness and energy levels of the pupils, which you will come to know through experience. The best approach is to have a number of brain-break activities in mind and use them as seems appropriate (ibid.: 155).

What does a brain break look like?

*   *Cross crawl:* In turn, children lift their left knee and touch it with their right hand, then lift their right knee and touch it with their left hand, and repeat the process a number of times.
*   *Rub-a-dubs:* Children circle their stomach with their right hand while their left hand pats their head. Then they change and reverse the circling.
*   *Chop-chop:* In pairs, children take it in turns to massage a partner's back and shoulders and conclude with the sides of the hands, chopping with a gentle, firm movement (ibid.: 152).

Personalized learning

In *Personalised Learning: A Practical Guide*, the DCSF defined personalized learning as being about schools working with children and parents 'as partners in learning' in responding to a child's learning needs, to enable all children to 'achieve and participate' in their learning (DCSF 2008: 5). With regard to inclusion and achieving well-being, as defined by the Every Child Matters outcomes, personalized learning seeks to ensure that 'a child's chances of success are not limited by their socio-economic background, gender, ethnicity or any disability' (DCSF 2008: 6). The DCSF acknowledged that children from disadvantaged groups, including all those groups this book has discussed, 'are the least likely to achieve well' (ibid.). For these reasons, personalized learning is put forward as a strategy that will 'narrow attainment gaps and raise achievement for all' (ibid.).

A pedagogy – the nine features of personalized learning

These features are not to be regarded as mutually exclusive; it is accepted that the features are interwoven and cross over with each other. However, they are seen as a framework for planning for personalized learning.

High-quality teaching and learning is about ensuring that all children can participate in and progress in terms of their learning, in all activities. This involves planning learning activities to ensure that tasks are differentiated so that all children can access the task and progress in their learning. Sometimes this will be through having a learning task that all children can access, but on the basis that they will achieve at different levels of attainment according to their needs as they complete the activity – differentiation by outcome. Or it may be about having a learning activity that is specifically differentiated for a particular need – differentiation by task.

For example, in working on a theme about the seashore, children can choose to pursue an aspect that interests them and follow this through at their own level and in relation to their own needs. What must be remembered about differentiating by outcome is that children still need to be making progress in their learning, and although they may be working on different aspects of the theme, their learning still needs to be supported. Alternatively, you may want all the children to know particular facts about Britain's coastline, but you may differentiate the task to enable the different groups of children in your class to access the learning – differentiation by task.

For high-quality teaching and learning to happen in the way just outlined, *target setting and tracking* of individuals' progress is essential. For learning to be properly personalized to their needs, children's learning should be monitored and clear targets set for the next stages. Effective target setting and tracking is underpinned by *focused assessment*. Assessment enables those working with children to be confident that the children are making progress in their learning and that new learning activities build on the foundations of a child's prior learning achievement. For assessment and target setting to be worthwhile in promoting learning, children need to be involved in the process. Since personalized learning is about individual children, they need to 'understand how they are doing, including what they are doing well, and what they need to do to make progress' (DCSF 2008: 20). It is necessary to work with children to explore worthwhile assessment processes, using 'assessment for learning' (AfL) and 'assessing pupil's progress' (APP).

The features of personalized learning we have already explored are seen as being the basic aspects of '"quality first", class-based, teaching', or what the DCSF referred to as wave one of the personalized learning approach (DCSF 2008: 26). However, it is also recognized that not all children will achieve all they are capable of through the wave one approach. For these children, additional small-group or one-to-one *interventions* might be needed so as to enable them to make progress in their learning – wave two of a personalized learning approach. However, wave two interventions should be as 'fully compatible with mainstream practice' as possible (ibid.). For children who are still struggling to achieve through wave two interventions, schools need to consider wave three support, which may include one-to-one tuition, particularly where a child might benefit from having an intensive focused input to help with a particular skill or new concept he or she is struggling with. However, 'individual tuition supplements existing learning – it can never replace it. This approach also builds in the necessary adjustments for disabled pupils and pupils with SEN' (ibid.).

Case study

Charlie and Jaylin are 7. They are very interested in the seashore theme and both want to find out more about crabs. Charlie's prior assessment from previous work on 'people who help us' showed that he had not made the progress expected in terms of finding information from sources such as books and the Internet. Jaylin has arrived recently from Poland and English is an additional language for him. He can read and write Polish to the level that would be expected for a child of 7, but is still building up his confidence to 'have a go' in English. In discussion about how targets would help support Charlie's and Jaylin's progress in this aspect of their learning, the TA and class teacher decide that both boys would benefit from some wave two (small–group) support.

The TA talks to Charlie and Jaylin about success criteria for their work on crabs. She has some pictures of different species and has labelled them with their English and Polish names. The boys choose two crabs each to find out about and they set their success criteria:

Charlie's and Jaylin's crab book

Charlie: hairy crab and velvet swimming crab.
Jaylin: shore crab (*brzeg krab*) and edible crab (*jadalny krab*).

• Four sentences about each crab.
• Use two books to help (*książkowy* (2)).
• Use Internet to help (computer).

The boys worked with the TA, who helped them find books and websites and worked with them so that they understood how to focus on relevant information and to use only the information they needed. The boys became so interested in their research that they included pages on why crabs move sideways and what they eat. Jaylin also wrote two further pages in Polish. When Jaylin's mother picked him up from school, the TA and teacher were very keen to show her his work and to know what he had written. Jaylin's mum laughed when she read his work and said he had written about how crabs use their pincers, she said '*pazur*' and made a 'nipping' action with her hand, to catch their prey.

At the end of the theme the class presented their work to each other and put their individual contributions on display for each other to look at.

Using different ways of *pupil grouping*, depending on children's learning needs and the learning activity, is also a feature of personalized learning. Children might be grouped by 'age, ability, friendship groups or gender' (DCSF 2008: 31). Research shows that children working together to learn co-operatively in different groupings can add to a sense of belonging to a class or community, helping children from diverse backgrounds work together (ibid.). Deciding how to group children for different learning activities is also about successful management of the *learning environment*. Ensuring that the learning environment supports a personalized learning approach means thinking about how best to organize the environment to suit the learning activity – for example, thinking about access to resources, be they traditional resources such as books, or technologies such as PCs and laptops. Thought also needs to be given to using resources such as 'outdoor classrooms' and other suitable learning areas that may be located in the 'school grounds and immediate locality' (DCSF 2008: 35).

All successful personalized learning in primary schools needs to be underpinned by sound *curriculum organization*. In most instances, this means planning based on the National Curriculum. One of the strengths of having a National Curriculum is that it ensures that all children have equal access to the same range of skills, knowledge and understanding. However, while the National Curriculum prescribes a core range of 'knowledge, skills and understanding, organised by subject' (DCSF 2008: 39), the DCSF stated 'that schools have freedom to personalise the curriculum which they offer' (ibid.). This essentially means that while schools need to ensure that the learning outlined in the National Curriculum is provided for children, they have a free hand to decide how to present the learning in terms of learning activities. Equality, in terms of learning, is not only about presenting the same things to be learnt by all children; it is also about ensuring that all children can access the learning, and this will require different approaches for different children, depending on their needs. So in the case study above, for example, while all children were learning about the seashore, Charlie and Jaylin accessed that learning through activities designed to meet their specific needs.

A central principle of personalized learning is 'helping children and young people to discover or develop new interests and talents' (DCSF 2008: 44). Those schools already offering extended provision as designated extended schools are in a strong position to support learning in this way, since they can offer an *extended curriculum*, over and above the requirements of the National Curriculum, and can provide a wider range of learning support and opportunities for children and their families – again, to suit the needs of the children. The DCSF saw extended schools as being well placed to support personalized learning as they 'work with a range of local providers, agencies and other schools to provide a "core offer"' (DCSF 2008: 44) of extended services. An extended school's 'core offer' will include: a variety of additional support activities for study (homework clubs, for example); PE, sport and many of the traditional 'after-school' clubs, such as drama, dance, environmental or 'green' clubs, etc. Extended schools also offer childcare from 8 a.m. to 6 p.m., 48 weeks a year; parenting and family support; and 'swift and easy access to specialist services such as speech and language therapy' and 'community use of facilities including adult and family learning and ICT' (ibid.).

The primary concern of this book has been to explore the wider needs that children bring with them to school, and how schools can develop inclusive practices to ensure that children's needs do not become barriers to their learning. The ninth feature of the DCSF's principles for personalized learning is about *supporting children's wider needs*. The DCSF recognized that 'children of all abilities and backgrounds can experience difficulties which impact on their learning, their attendance, their self-esteem or general attitude towards learning more generally' (DCSF 2008: 48). We have explored how personalizing learning through considering what happens in the classroom can enable barriers to learning to be overcome. However, the principle of the extended curriculum and supporting children's wider needs acknowledges that in order to thrive some children need support that goes beyond traditional school hours and follows them from school into their community and homes. Schools have always known that what happens in the community and at home can make an impact on a child's achievement in school. To ensure that they are supporting children's wider needs, schools need to develop practice that ensures there is 'close communication with parents and carers' and multi-agency links to support vulnerable children (DCSF 2008: 52).

Case study

Waterfall primary school is situated in a deprived rural area. Many of the children begin school with levels of attainment below those expected for children of their age. In considering how to support the wider needs of these children, the school decided to look at how it might build stronger partnerships with other agencies that would help to provide more targeted support for particularly vulnerable children and families. These agencies included: the police, particularly community support officers; health workers and social services; child protection; and the local children's centre. It was also suggested that the school develop a partnership with CAMHS – the Children and Adolescent Mental Health Service.

One member of staff, a teaching assistant with a background in health, was designated as having responsibility for liaising with these support agencies and for setting up meetings when necessary, where representatives from a range of agencies could get together, usually with the children and families themselves, to find ways to meet the wider needs of vulnerable children and their families. The school quickly found that links with these agencies in the wider community meant that all agencies could share care for the children and families, and that support could be ongoing. For example, support offered by the children's centre could 'follow' children and their families when they transferred to other schools. The new school did not have to 'start from scratch' in terms of determining need and support for the child or family. Families, too, became more trusting of the school, knowing that it would be there to support them through unexpected events.

Assessment for learning (AfL)

In our exploration of the DCSF's nine features for personalized learning, we briefly explored the place of assessment. Indeed, for teaching to be effective, assessing what has been learnt is central to progressing learning appropriately. As a strategy, the DCSF saw the practice of assessment for learning (AfL) as being good practice in this area. While teachers and TAs have long been engaged in the process of assessing children's learning, one of the significantly different aspects of assessment through AfL is that the 'children themselves will be involved in monitoring their own achievement by being involved in the assessment process' (Knowles 2009: 104). Not only this, but AfL also recognizes that assessment strategies which support learning include the use of both summative and formative assessment. Summative assessment is when judgements are made periodically about overall performance or achievement; for example, looking at a range of writing by a particular child across a half-term period and making an assessment about the overall level that child is writing at. Formative assessment is more ongoing, it is composed of the day-to-day judgements we make about how children are responding to the learning activities they are engaged in and how we might modify or change what we ask children to do in response to our assessment of what is happening.

> While assessment is central to successful learning, where it is most successful is where outcomes from assessments are used to plan the next stages in a child's learning and where feedback that results from an assessment being made can be acted on by the learner – or the teacher, to inform the next step in the learning process.
>
> (ibid.)

Similarly, assessment can sometimes be about teachers and TAs being more concerned with marking and grading work, 'rather than with helping the child with what precisely is to be learnt' (ibid.). In the same way, feedback to children as a result of marking their work can often focus on what they have not done, or are still unclear about, rather than where they have been successful in their learning and what the next steps are for them. The AfL process has been developed from the work of Black and Wiliam, most notably from their publication *Inside the Black Box: Raising Standards through Classroom Assessment* (Black and Wiliam 2003). Their work explores the notion that for learning to be effective, children need to be part of the whole process. They need to know what the learning intentions are for the activity and what the success or assessment criteria are. They need to be able to receive feedback throughout the learning process, to help them know if they are achieving the success criteria. This feedback may come from the adults working with them, or from each other. Learning in this way involves the recognition that it is a dynamic, ongoing process, in which the learner is an active participant. Teaching is not something that is 'done to' the learner.

The DCSF took some of the principles of Black and Wiliam's work and devised its own approach to AfL, which it saw as going hand in hand with the successful use of personalized learning. In explaining the DCSF's approach to AfL, the Qualifications and Curriculum Development Agency (QCDA) described AfL as being 'based on the idea that pupils will improve most if they understand the aim of their learning, where they are in relation to this aim and how they can achieve the aim' (www.qcda.gov.uk).

Activity

The characteristics of AfL are listed below. If you have the opportunity to be in a classroom that uses AfL, look to see if these characteristics of good AfL practice are in place.

- Learning goals or outcomes are shared with the children at the beginning of a learning activity.
- Children are given – or help devise – success criteria so that they know and recognize what they are aiming to achieve.

- Feedback about how the child is achieving in the learning activity – in line with the success criteria – forms an ongoing part of the learning process. Feedback may be from adults in the classroom or other children.
- AfL is a means by which every child can progress in his or her learning in the light of individual previous achievement.
- Both the teachers and the TA work with the child to review and enable him or her to reflect on individual progress.
- Children who are new to the idea of AfL will need to be taught how it works and to be shown how it can be a worthwhile tool in helping them to achieve.
- Where AfL is used effectively and is an embedded part of effective personalized learning and teaching, it can boost both a child's motivation and self-esteem with regard to learning.

Case study

Bluebell primary school has been using AfL for about a year now. The teacher who had responsibility for setting it up began by trialling it in her own classroom and then introducing it to the rest of the school. She says, 'the children were used to having what I am learning today (WALT) statements for learning activities so they saw also having success criteria as being a natural follow-on from that. To begin with, I would give the success criteria in the form of an "I can" statement. So, for example, if the learning for the literacy activity that day was "to use adjectives to make story-writing more interesting", then the success criteria might be "I can use adjectives to describe nouns; I can use adverbs to describe verbs".

'To begin with, the TA, the children and I would look at "anonymous" pieces of work and discuss how we could feed back to the writer about how they were meeting the success criteria. This helped the children to test out with each other that they knew what nouns, adjectives, verbs and adverbs were. They could also rehearse the best way of giving feedback to each other by thinking about how the descriptive language being used was improving the writing. For example, was the writer simply using any adjective or adverb, or really thinking about using words which would help to create atmosphere and meaning. Using AfL in this way has improved children's engagement with their work, as they are now part of the whole process; it's not just me saying "do this", then marking their work. It has raised self-esteem and the children do automatically ask each other for feedback, or offer it to each other.'

Conclusion: providing children with the opportunity to demonstrate what they can do

The overriding theme of this book has been about understanding where individual children are 'coming from' in terms of the skills, knowledge, understanding and attitudes they bring to school. It has discussed how understanding the needs of individuals can enable those who are planning and devising learning activities to provide better teaching and learning support. The focus of this chapter has been on the learning styles that all children share, whatever individual cultural and gender attitudes they come to school with, or whatever their learning ability may be. If learning is planned to meet how the child learns, it is more likely that the child will have a positive experience of learning and achieve the standards that he or she is capable of. Children need to be engaged in learning that develops and stretches them and excites their imagination.

Below is a final activity you might like to try. If you have attempted to understand better the potential barriers to learning for just a few of the children you are working with, and have sought to support them to feel more included in school life, then record your achievement on a 'feeling good about ourselves' display, as described below.

Activity: a 'feeling good about ourselves' display

Decide on the theme for your display – a plant with lots of leaves and petals; a tree with apples; a line of cars or trucks; a train with lots of carriages; etc.

- Each member of the class – children and adults – has a leaf, or a petal, an apple, a car, etc., and writes on it something that has happened recently which makes them feel good about themselves. Help the children who struggle with writing; allow the children to write in whatever language they wish (you might want to write an English translation as well); the emphasis of the activity is on helping children recognize the good things that are happening for them.
- Help the children to think about what they want recorded by giving examples from your own life and writing your own leaf.
- The 'feel-good' notes will say things like: 'My mum said she loved me'; 'Aziz played football with me at play'.
- Assemble the leaves into a display.
- Repeat the exercise frequently. Add to the display and let it 'grow' around the room.
- The activity can also be done verbally, particularly if you want to focus children when they are excited or very lively after some particular activity.

(Developed from an idea in Wetton and Cansell 2001: 13)

Bibliography

Alfrey, C. (2003) *Understanding Children's Learning*. London: David Fulton Publishers.

Black, P. and Wiliam, D. (2003) *Inside the Black Box: Raising Standards through Classroom Assessment*. Maidenhead: Nfer.

DCSF (2008) *Personalised Learning: A Practical Guide*. London: DCSF

DfES (2004) *Primary National Strategy Excellence and Enjoyment: Learning and Teaching in the Primary Years: Section 3 – Diverse Learning Needs*. London: DfES.

Gardner, H. (1993) *Frames of Mind*, 2nd edn. London: Fontana Press.

Knowles, G. (2009) *Ensuring Every Child Matters*. London: Sage.
Ofsted (2003) 'Yes He Can: Schools where Boys Write Well' (HMI 505). London: Ofsted.
Smith, A. and Call, N. (1999) *The ALPS Approach*. Stafford: Network Educational Press.
Wetton, N. and Cansell, P. (2001) *Feeling Good – Raising Self-esteem in the Primary School Classroom*, 2nd edn. London: Forbes.

Websites

www.nationalstrategies.standards.dcsf.gov.uk/node/83386 (accessed 18 February 2010).
www.qcda.gov.uk/4334.aspx (accessed 18 February 2010).

Index